STUDY GODS

Study Gods

HOW THE NEW CHINESE ELITE PREPARE FOR GLOBAL COMPETITION

YI-LIN CHIANG

PRINCETON UNIVERSITY PRESS

PRINCETON & OXFORD

Published by Princeton University Press
41 William Street, Princeton, New Jersey 08540
6 Oxford Street, Woodstock, Oxfordshire OX20 1TR

press.princeton.edu

All Rights Reserved

Library of Congress Cataloging-in-Publication Data:

Names: Chiang, Yi-Lin, 1984– author.
Title: Study gods : how the new Chinese elite prepare for global competition / Yi-Lin Chiang.
Description: Princeton, New Jersey : Princeton University Press, [2022] | Includes bibliographical references and index.
Identifiers: LCCN 2021059955 (print) | LCCN 2021059956 (ebook) | ISBN 9780691210483 (paperback) | ISBN 9780691210490 (hardback) | ISBN 9780691237190 (ebook)
Subjects: LCSH: Adolescence—China. | Elite (Social sciences)—Education—China. | Social status—China.
Classification: LCC HQ799.C55 C447 2022 (print) | LCC HQ799.C55 (ebook) | DDC 05.2350951—dc23/eng/20220211
LC record available at https://lccn.loc.gov/2021059955
LC ebook record available at https://lccn.loc.gov/2021059956

British Library Cataloging-in-Publication Data is available

Editorial: Meagan Levinson and Jacqueline Delaney
Production Editorial: Jaden Young and Ellen Foos
Jacket/Cover Design: Lauren Smith
Production: Lauren Reese
Publicity: Kate Hensley and Charlotte Coyne
Copyeditor: Joseph Dahm

Jacket/Cover Credit: Cover images (left): metamorworks/iStock, (right) Fabio Formaggio/Alamy

This book has been composed in Arno.

10 9 8 7 6 5 4 3 2 1

For my parents, with love and gratitude

CONTENTS

Illustrations

Tables

ACKNOWLEDGMENTS

THIS BOOK began as my dissertation project at Penn. I am deeply indebted to the many people who have supported me throughout this journey. My greatest thanks go to Annette Lareau, my advisor and academic parent, for her mentorship and undying support. Her invaluable feedback and encouragement have sustained me from the beginning of fieldwork to the completion of this book. Annette taught me how to collect and analyze ethnographic data, how to frame a question, and how to navigate academia. Her persistence in inquiring about the conceptual contributions of my work was especially illuminating. This book would not exist without her guidance. I am also extremely grateful to Randall Collins, who taught and led me through the theoretical concepts critical to my research. His encouragement fueled my motivation to complete this study, and his suggestions greatly shaped this book. Emily Hannum introduced me to the field of Chinese education and continued to play an important role throughout the project. As the only committee member who could visit me in Beijing during fieldwork, she was a source of invaluable insights. Special thanks to Hyunjoon Park for his intellectual and emotional support. My committee and their genuine interests in this project have kept me afloat through the struggles of academic writing. I extend my deepest appreciation to Jere Behrman, Irma Elo, and Guobin Yang for their support and encouragement throughout graduate school. Yeonjin Lee, Li-Chung Hu, Sarah Spell, Hyejeong Jo, Aliya Rao, Natalie Young, Sangsoo Lee, Phoebe Ho, Chris Reece, Doga Kerestecioglu, and Duy Do made my life in McNeil Building brighter.

At Beijing, I was lucky to meet friends who shared similar interests at the Chicago Center and in Taiyueyuan. Chen Chen, Denelle Raynolds, Chenjia Xu, Stephanie Balkwill, Mary McElhinny, and Nathan Attrill turned fieldwork into a fun and exciting experience. Genuine thanks to my "uncles and aunts" in Beijing: Dong Zhao, Deng Zhengrong, Yan Shijian, Liu Xiufang, and Liu Yong. They took me under their wings in the city, helping me with everything I needed from apartment hunting to introducing me to school personnel. I could not have carried out this study without their relentless support.

I returned to Taipei after living in the States for twelve years. My colleagues in the Sociology Department at National Chengchi University gave me time to readjust and space to develop. Other Taipei-based faculty supported me by expressing their constant excitement about this manuscript. Hsuan-Wei Lee, Jack Neubauer, and Kevin Tseng are wonderful colleagues and stimulating interlocutors. Friends outside Taipei also provided unwavering support and assistance. Thanks especially to Alice Yeh, whose advice and support I can always count on. Junhow Wei, Ran Liu, Cole Carnesecca, and Jaap Nieuwenhuis are friends in need and friends indeed.

Fieldwork is economically costly, especially longitudinal work conducted overseas. During the course of research, I received generous financial support from Penn and in Taiwan. I was able to carry out fieldwork in Beijing through the Otto and Gertrude K. Pollak Summer Research Fellowship, the Judith Rodin Fellowship, the President Gutmann Leadership Award, and the Provost Fellowship Award for Interdisciplinary Innovation offered by the University of Pennsylvania. The book writing grant approved by the Ministry of Science and Technology (108–2410-H-004–194-MY2) financed my follow-up visits with students around the world.

I wish to thank Meagan Levinson at Princeton University Press, who brilliantly suggested that I turn my initial yearlong study into a longitudinal one. She was incredibly patient as I spent years gathering follow-up data, undertaking new analysis, and completely rewriting the manuscript. Many thanks to Jaqueline Delaney and Jaden Young for their assistance throughout the production process. Ideas from this book were presented at Princeton University, the University of Wisconsin–Madison, the Pennsylvania State University, Peking University, National Tsinghua University, and Academia Sinica. I appreciate the comments and insights I received there, as well as those of the anonymous reviewers who read an earlier draft of the manuscript. Peter Harvey, Sherelle Ferguson, Blair Sackett, Soo-yong Byun, Jonathan Mijs, and Ben Ross read and commented on chapters of the manuscript. The ideas presented here have also benefited from the feedback of anonymous reviews and suggestions by Murray Milner, Yu Xie, and Shamus Khan.

I had the privilege of enduring support from my family, who has been integral in supporting me throughout my research endeavors. My parents instilled in me the habit to focus on research and led by example. They are not only my source of entry into fieldwork but also the earliest onset of this study. Their decision to send my brother and me to a private middle school in Taipei introduced me to a foreign world of the elite. Unbeknownst to them as they consoled a then-traumatized teenage girl, the differences between middle class and affluence would a decade later spark her interest in studying elites.

Last but certainly not least, I am indebted to the participants in this study. I would like to thank the parents and teachers at Capital and Pinnacle schools, especially those who accepted me into their classrooms and their homes. This book would not exist without the generosity and openness of the students who shared eight years of their lives with me. My argument sometimes requires that I portray them in unflattering ways. Even so, these young men and women who were born to rich and educated parents are sensitive to social injustice and see themselves as empowered to contribute to social equality. They cared deeply about issues such as rural poverty, refugee displacement, the wildlife trade, and environmental pollution. I found them to be kind, companionate, and occasionally awkward. I remain exceedingly fond of them and loyal to them, and I am ever grateful for their trust, friendship, and generosity. It has been a pleasure and honor to witness the transformation of these quirky teenagers into accomplished young adults.

Introduction

BEFORE GRADUATING from Cambridge, Ashley Fang received multiple job offers.[1] Two of them seemed especially attractive. She could move to Switzerland and embark on a career at one of the largest commodity-producing firms in the world, or she could go to the top-ranked business school in Europe. Either option put her expected income at about $100,000 upon entering the labor force. After thinking long and hard about which option would most quickly lead her to her imagined ideal life, Ashley decided to take the offer in Switzerland. One year later, feeling fed up with living in Zurich, which she called "a tiny European town," she joined a Japanese company and moved to its branch office in Singapore. Ashley was earning significantly more than in her previous job. She also paid lower taxes in Singapore, and the company offered better benefits compared to her colleagues working at the headquarters in Japan. When asked about her future plans, Ashley paused and brushed her shoulder-length hair aside. She then crossed her arms and said that she could stay at her current company and move her way up or transfer to another company for higher income. "Alternatively," she added with a confident smile, "an MBA in the U.S., Harvard or Wharton, is also possible."

The same year Ashley completed her studies at Cambridge, Xiangzu Liu graduated from a top-ranked department at Nanjing University, halfway across the world. During his senior year, Xiangzu debated his options after graduation. He received a few offers from companies (thanks to the tight connection between his department and the industry) and was admitted to two top-ranked PhD programs in China. After some consideration, Xiangzu decided to pursue a graduate degree in hopes of starting his own company in the future. He decided to go to graduate school in Beijing for networking purposes and immediately became an important member in his advisor's client-sponsored projects. After setting up his LinkedIn account, he was soon offered a consulting position and began working for an American company that invested billions of U.S. dollars in China. Xiangzu is tall, dark, and sturdy, carries himself with an air of confidence, and speaks in a sophisticated, firm tone that distinguishes him from most young adults. At the age of twenty-four, although officially a PhD student, he earns within the top 10 percent of incomes in urban China, is frequently involved in business meetings and conversations involving trade secrets, and drives a new black Audi to school. Eager to learn more about the international market, he plans to apply for a one-year exchange program in the United States before graduation.

Ashley and Xiangzu belong to a new generation of global elites. Like many of their similarly elite peers,[2] they graduated from top universities around the world, work at large international corporations, and often aspire to build their own financial empires. This group of young adults grew up wealthy, received a world-class education, live comfortably, and are expected to lead luxurious lifestyles. Elite youth who were born and raised in China in particular have attracted much attention as the country has established itself as the largest economy in the world. Depictions of these elite youth dazzled Western audiences in movies such as *Crazy Rich Asians* (2018) and TV shows like *Ultra Rich Asian Girls* (2014–15). Their arrival on U.S. campuses boosted luxury car sales, and the tuition they pay sustained private schools in Europe.[3] The growing interest in the new generation of elite Chinese reflects the phenomenon that global wealth is shifting to China. The country has become one of the largest holders of U.S. debt and home to the second largest number of billionaires in the world.[4] Four of the ten richest self-made billionaires under the age of forty are Chinese, while only three are American.[5] Mainland Chinese buyers are purchasing businesses in the United States and Europe, including GE Appliances and Volvo.[6] These consumers, armed with cash, are also widely considered to have driven up real estate prices despite sluggish economies around the world.[7] A growing body of literature discusses China's eminent rise to power, and books such as *When China Rules the World* have become global best sellers.[8] Furthermore, news headlines such as "The Giant Chinese Companies Shaping the World's Industries" and "China's Campaign to Dominate the Global Economy" hint that China and the country's elites will direct the global economy in the near future.

Simultaneously, China is using its newfound wealth to exert influence in areas such as media, technology, and education. While news outlets in the West are experiencing budget cuts, China's state-run media continue to raise their game by offering competitive salaries in global locations such as London and New York.[9] China's rapid technological advancements have allowed the country to catch up and compete with the United States for dominance in artificial intelligence.[10] Higher education is booming in China, whereas the number of tenure-track faculty in the United States declined after the economic crash of 2008.[11] Chinese universities now compete with their American counterparts for faculty, the former often advertising their state-of-the-art facilities and offering salaries higher than U.S. averages.[12] Additionally, Chinese universities are winning the international ranking competition: according to the 2021 *Times Higher Education* rankings, Tsinghua University (one of the two top universities in China) is not only the top-ranked university in Asia but also in the top twenty in the world.

Theory goes that the new generation of elite youth in China often are the unintended agents who help with the country's plot to conquer the world.[13] While these speculations are unproven, Chinese adolescent elites are establishing themselves as among the best and brightest in the world. Chinese students outperform other students in international competitions such as the Programme for International Student Assessment (PISA) in science and math.[14] According to the PISA report, even disadvantaged students in China perform better than the comparably underprivileged students in other OECD countries. In anecdotal discussions among faculty, Chinese students are applying for American graduate programs at ever higher numbers and with GRE scores higher than those of native English-speaking applicants. These generally high-performing Chinese students are going global at an unprecedented rate. Chinese students are the largest group of internationals and account for about one-third of foreign students at American, Canadian, and Australian campuses. U.K. government statistics show that the number of Chinese students is greater than the sum of those from the next top five sending countries combined.[15] Some receiving countries, such as the United States, have tightened immigration policies and steadily decreased the number of student visas issued.[16] Yet, when they were asked, the drop in visa quotas was not a concern to many Chinese students, who reported having unhindered plans to study and later work in the United States.[17]

There are ample indicators suggesting that China's elite youth are en route to dominating the global economy. How exactly are they doing that? How do affluent, privileged students, like Ashley and Xiangzu, acquire elite status not just within their country but internationally? This book identifies the largely hidden but important process through which elite adolescents reproduce elite status in the face of global competition. Specifically, the examples of elite youth from China highlight the need to examine status reproduction from an international perspective. The elite are typically perceived as a small group who are influential in their home country.[18] However, as societies become increasingly interconnected, resources and people flow much more frequently across borders. In a globalized era, elites travel between continents, reside in different countries, and accumulate social and financial resources wherever they go. Despite their different nationalities, elites build relationships with each other as they share the same campuses, take the same internships, and work with one another. Considering these intertwined pathways, the new elites are no longer a small group influential within the borders of their own country. Instead, they have become an association of diverse nationals who pursue similar lifestyles, careers, and goals largely unhindered by political or national boundaries. How elite Chinese youth join the new generation of global elites thus sheds light on status reproduction more generally.

Data for this book come from long-term ethnography and interviews with socioeconomically elite students in Beijing, along with their parents and teachers. I followed twenty-eight elite students for over seven years (2012–19), beginning when they were in eleventh and twelfth grades. I document their trajectories as they go through important transitions in life—graduating high school and college and entering graduate school or the labor force in China, the United States, Europe, and elsewhere.

I propose that elite Chinese youth are systematically successful in the competition for global elite status by becoming "study gods" (*xueshen*), a term they use to describe exceptionally high-performing students. Studying, however, is not the identifying behavior that characterizes study gods. Study gods are "godlike" in that they effortlessly and hence supernaturally excel in school, while other students, "studyholics" (*xueba*) included, study nonstop. Being a study god does not mean being the most popular kid on campus, nor does it highlight one's wealthy family background. It is related to neither physical attractiveness nor athletic talents.[19] Instead, it means that the student has elevated status in school and is believed by peers to be innately superior. When interacting with peers, study gods occupy the center of attention; when interacting with adults, they enjoy teachers' pampering and parents' indulgence. Importantly, the making of study gods is fundamentally an elite status reproduction process. Because study gods are defined by (effortless) academic achievement, qualification is contingent on top academic performance. The threat of downward mobility is thus imminent, as a study god can fall short of glory at any time by "underperforming" on exams. In this respect, parental assistance that helps raise children's test scores comes to play an important role in the creation and sustainment of study gods.

In the chapters ahead, I report the findings for the young adults whom I followed. I show that by the end of high school these young men and women have learned an assortment of skills that compose a recognizable repertoire of behaviors expedient to the reproduction of elite status in global society. They have come to appreciate and navigate the status hierarchy, expect differential treatment by peers and superiors according to status differences, and draw on external parental assistance when they encounter obstacles that potentially harm their status reproduction goals. These experiences in school and at home during high school shape the young elites' long-term trajectory in meaningful ways. The students carry over these understandings and polish these skills in American (and European) campuses. They apply the lessons they learned in high school as they enter graduate school or the labor force. Those who had an intimate understanding of the school status system are able to develop strategies that allow them to stay at the top or at the very least avoid falling to the bottom. The skills used for daily interactions with peers and teachers are later applied to navigate workplace relationships with colleagues and authority figures. Family members also play a key role at critical moments. When in school, parents help their children overcome bumps on the road, oftentimes by offering backup plans with global insight that adolescents cannot foresee. After graduation, their elite parents continue to provide safety nets in case the child's career ambitions are unfruitful.

Like their counterparts from other countries, the elite Chinese students in this study are a global-oriented bunch. All must deal extensively with other global elites through attending college or graduate school abroad, participating in exchange programs, or working at international corporations. Not all of them obtain equally lucrative positions upon graduation. Many choose to embark on careers in the financial world, while a few express passions in fields such as environmental protection, technology, or academia. However, even the futures envisioned by those who are less successful are considered enviable by average students in China and elsewhere. Although what students do in high school does not necessarily determine their future outcomes, as I will show, the students who became study gods were able to polish the skills relevant to elite status reproduction and therefore perform better than peers who had not been as academically successful. The skills that the study gods acquired in high school thus appear to be valuable and privileged in occupational settings across societies.

The elite of the twenty-first century are internationally oriented and well-off by Western standards. The Chinese elite youth in this study are both a cause and product of increased inequality in China, where the gap between the rich and the poor is among the widest in the world.[20] Such a context means that the stakes are greater, as those who experience downward mobility are less likely to regain elite status. Considering China's global influence, becoming elite in China implies becoming elite on a global scale. Increased inequality at the national and international levels also suggests heightened levels of status anxiety, prompting elite parents to heavily invest in children's education as a way to safeguard their future.[21] Keeping in mind these broader social trends, this book is not simply about the elite Chinese youth who are "good at" the "game" of life but about a group of young adults who are trying to establish themselves as the new global elite.[22]

Elite Education and the Game of Status Reproduction

Teenagers have many goals and dreams to keep alive. Some have specific ambitions such as becoming musicians, lawyers, doctors, actors, or undercover agents. Others may have a vague idea for a career or simply want to have a good life. The futures that they envision, however, are not fantasies but encompass career aspirations that take root in daily life and are constantly negotiated or compromised. For example, a child may decide what she wants to do by observing the lifestyles in her family and community. Children might also change or reevaluate their goals through daily interactions with peers and teachers, whose opinions of and expectations for them shape their self-expectations and career aspirations. In brief, ideas about what to expect in adulthood are critically related to one's socioeconomic background.[23] Because children's family backgrounds, personal and demographic characteristics, and the people they meet will critically shape their outcomes, and because these influences take place and carry meaning throughout adolescence, status transmission across generations is largely successful.[24] Status reproduction is often easily observed in many societies. This phenomenon is partially reflected in the age-old saying "like father, like son." The Chinese saying "dragons beget dragons, phoenixes beget phoenixes, and the children of mice make holes" also directly refers to the same phenomenon. In many societies, including in China, children of the elite become the future elite, children of the middle class stay middle class, and working-class children stay working class.

According to Pierre Bourdieu, status reproduction is like a card game in which the players are families who compete for the grand prize of high status.[25] Each player is dealt a hand of cards, and each must strategize to maximize the chances of winning. However, from the get-go, the players do not stand on equal ground. They likely have vastly different cards, with a few players dealt winning hands and many stuck with losing cards. They also differ in their skills, as some deploy more strategies than others, whereas a few might have no strategy at all. Finally, despite sitting at the same table, the players are not equally knowledgeable of the rules. Some are familiar with the myriad special rules and wild cards, but others might be oblivious.

The elites are like a group of privileged players in the game of status reproduction. They are dealt exceptionally good cards, which is the amount of economic, social, and cultural resources at their disposal. The elites are typically strategic players. For instance, elite and affluent parents practice intensive child rearing that increases their children's chances of success. These parenting practices include "concerted cultivation," which involves a high degree of time management and interaction with agents in powerful positions, usually teachers and school personnel.[26] These parents adopt a "by-any-means approach" to problem solving to deal with troubles that arise in their children's schooling, and they inevitably resolve the issues by negotiating with teachers and school administrators.[27] And while some elite parents do not insert themselves into their children's daily schedules, they nonetheless practice strategies that their less-resourceful competitors cannot when they perceive their children to be in trouble.[28] Most importantly, the elites are familiar with the rules. In fact, they are the group that sets up the rules and runs the game.[29] After all, among the many cultural repertoires, the elites decide on the benefits that a particular taste ascribes to its beholder. Unsurprisingly, they assign higher value to the ones they themselves already have.[30]

The futures that children and adolescents envision require educational degrees and certificates. Elites competing for status reproduction often use education as a key means to transmit privilege, and they develop the necessary skills to succeed while in school. Literature on stratification considers education an important predictor of future outcomes.[31] As societies increasingly value credentials, educational attainment itself often becomes a prerequisite or signal of status.[32] The schooling process trains elite youth to compete for global status. During high school, elite adolescents must cultivate class-based cultural taste, develop the ability to skillfully utilize knowledge, exhibit a relaxed attitude when interacting with superiors and inferiors, and dissociate from markers of nonelite status.[33] After entering college, these elite youth continue to refine the marks of elitism and form networks with similarly elite alumni.[34] Upon college graduation, these youth enjoy higher chances of finding employment with influential corporations and more access to power.[35] Considering its importance and the degree to which it shapes individual outcomes, education is arguably the most important means by which elite adolescents achieve future socioeconomically elite status. In other words, the decades of schooling form a valuable time in which elite students familiarize themselves with the rules of the game of status reproduction.

Having exceptional familiarity with the underlying rules of status reproduction is one reason why elites are so successful in pursuing status reproduction. Yet the scope of status competition through education is changing: historically, these elites were competing just domestically, whereas foreign degree holders have now joined the competition. The numbers of actors and institutions involved also seem to be increasing. This change in the setting and participants suggests that while education remains critically important, the specific rules of elite status competition at a global level may be somewhat vague. After all, elites from different countries do not share an identical understanding of the rules that govern such competition. For example, selection takes place as early as fourth grade in Germany and as late as twelfth grade in the United States. In other words, elite German youth are groomed for elite pathways earlier than their American counterparts.[36] Elites in each country also emphasize and reward different types of individual talent. In countries that teach only one foreign language, elites may consider multilingual ability an important asset for global competition. By comparison, multilingualism may have a different meaning for elites in Luxembourg, where schools train students to be fluent in at least three languages. The outcomes of success in each education system have also become difficult to compare. It is unclear whether an elite American boarding school, a British public school, or a Chinese international school offers students more status advantage. Similarly, it is difficult to determine which school, be it an Ivy League college, Oxbridge, one of the *grandes écoles*, or *Qingbei*, offers better employment prospects for its graduates.[37]

When the process, timing, and criteria that determine educational success vary by country, the guidelines that govern status competition at a global scale are often unclear even for elites.[38] However, upholding a common set of rules is a prerequisite for players who desire to participate in any game. What, then, are the rules that the global elites set up when competing for status reproduction? What must they learn to compete for elite status against their opponents across the world? In this study, choosing and getting into the ideal college, whether in China, the United States, or the United Kingdom, was a major life event for the elite students. The families in China saw college as the first step that determined whether or not a child would become a future elite. Students in school openly predicted that study gods such as Ashley would not only go to a top university but also be successful in any future endeavor. Teachers even routinely encouraged them to think of themselves as the possible future prime minister of China. The elite students learned that internationally recognized educational success was the kind of success that bestowed the top rewards. Ashley received college admission offers from Cambridge and Carnegie Mellon. While the two universities were equally selective, her decision to attend the former was a calculated choice based on the perception that Cambridge had greater international prestige than Carnegie Mellon. Xiangzu's decision to pursue a PhD despite receiving a full-time consultant position at a multimillion-dollar American company was a deliberate plan made with an eye on future international entrepreneurial ambitions.

As scholars have pointed out, students of privilege choose prestigious institutions to effectively compete against other comparatively privileged students or to attain an even higher level of education in order to compete.[39] In the cases of Ashley, Xiangzu, and many others, their educational decisions were deliberate and made in light of the rules governing elite status reproduction. By immersing themselves in the playing field and winning the education competition against peers around the world, the children of elites learn to develop the skills that will facilitate their pursuit of global elite status. In due course, the rules governing an education-based status reproduction competition emerge.

The Adolescent Elites from China

Elite Chinese adolescents seem to be successfully engaging in the global competition for status as they attain educational success. These affluent, high-performing students then embark on careers that put them in high income brackets. They appear to be able to carry out their career plans regardless of the impact of international policies. In 2018, President Donald Trump revised the STEM visa program to shorten the time Chinese students are allowed to stay in the United States after graduating. However, many Chinese students remained confident and reported unaltered plans for their future.[40] With their achievements in international competitions, predicted future success, and high level of confidence, the adolescent elites from China are formidable global competitors, so much so that teenagers from developing countries often cannot compete. These Chinese students know the rules for status competition and are determined to carry through their education strategies with the resources at their disposal. Most important of all, they intend to reproduce their parents' elite status not (or not only) in China but worldwide.

Considering that these socioeconomically elite teenagers from China are highly competitive and largely successful in their endeavors, surprisingly little is known about the process through which they achieve global elite status. The elite youth from China have only recently come into the limelight. China's economic reforms in the 1980s led to the rise of a group of new socioeconomic elites who achieved high status through educational success.[41] Like in many other countries, in China education plays a crucial role in determining elite status in the postreform era. One's level of education has become a strong predictor of entry into the political and economic elite.[42] With parents who achieved upward mobility through educational success and who expect that their children's admission to top colleges will be their first step toward future elite status, the students in this study are among the first generation to have grown up in a stable, revolution-free communist China. They are the first generation of Chinese in recent history who are pursuing educational success not merely for the goal of upward mobility but also to reproduce their parents' status and to carry on the privilege they have enjoyed since their youth. Additionally, the participants in this study represent the educational experiences of the upper end of the social spectrum in an increasingly unequal Chinese society, where the gap between the top earners and the rest has grown considerably and where academic competition is among the fiercest in the world.[43]

Elite parents in China attained their status through academic competition and continue to engage in this competition as they support their children's journey to success. This process creates successive generations of elites who are familiar with deploying education as a vehicle for achieving high status, who have experience, and who are skilled at playing the game.

Using intense academic competition as the primary means of obtaining socioeconomic domination has had its benefits and unintended consequences. On the one hand, the Chinese teenagers in this study were born in the 1990s under the one-child policy, which was enacted with the hope of constructing a new generation that would become the vanguards of China's modernization.[44] In a sense, these teenagers are carrying out the government's plans. They have obtained tertiary education at top institutions around the world and have paychecks that put them at the top 20 percent of earners in the developed countries in which they work. On the other hand, as I show in this book, some of them are entitled and expect differential treatment by peers and authorities. At the same time, and not surprisingly, they are under very high levels of pressure. Even though their parents are able to "buy them the sky," as the title of Xinran Xue's book suggests,[45] these adolescents often have higher levels of fear and anxiety in general than their peers in Western countries.[46] The most common cause of suicide in high school and college is perceived academic underperformance.[47] In this book, I show in vivid detail how the next generation of elites from China is equipped with the tools to engage in international competition. I see the micro-interactions between students and adults as intertwined dynamics that come together in the process of elite status formation. Through up-close analysis, I suggest that the new generation of global elites skillfully employ their tangible and intangible resources to compete for status against others in an era of increased globalization.

This Study

Elite students do a lot of work to realize their dreams, often with high levels of parental support and resources from others around them.[48] When I embarked on this study, I was interested in understanding this process. By choosing to focus on student experiences instead of the perspectives of schools or parents, I hoped to capture the students' own understanding of status competition in global society. My approach meant moving beyond national borders to examine how highly privileged students struggle for dominance against competitors from a myriad of countries.

Studies of elites are rare. To my knowledge, this project is the first that follows socioeconomically elite students over time. This book is based on observation and interviews with elite Chinese students over seven years, from 2012 to 2019. (The methodological appendix details how the study was conducted.) I interviewed twenty-eight students who attended five high schools ranked in the top ten (out of almost three hundred high schools) in Beijing. To better understand the influence and expectations of adults, I also interviewed the students' teachers and parents. Two of the five schools agreed to classroom observations and allowed me to freely talk to students. The two schools that became the primary sites of fieldwork are Pinnacle, a historically prestigious high school established in the Qing dynasty, and Capital, a new school that rose to prominence in the twenty-first century. I conducted intensive participant observation with eight Pinnacle and Capital students. I followed each student ten to fifteen hours a day for five days. When on campus I sat through classes, studied, and shared meals with them. Outside the classroom, the students and I hung out in the city, at movies, or in theme parks. I also waited for them or accompanied them to test sites on National College Examination days. Through these activities, I became acquainted with many of their classmates and schoolmates.

Although visiting the homes of the elite is difficult, I was able to carry out home observations with four of the eight key informants I shadowed. I visited three boys' families, each between one to three times, three to seven hours per visit. I stayed with a girl's family for four days. I wanted the parents and children to ignore me and carry out their daily activities during these visits. While my presence was acknowledged, I was able to somewhat slip into the background when the parents and students were focused on chores or studies. I sat on the living room floor when observing family life and rode in the back of the car when accompanying them to test sites and restaurants. As I discuss in the methodological appendix, students' and families' acceptance of me increased my confidence that the interactions I observed were routine.

It has been seven years since I began my fieldwork. In 2012, these students were in the eleventh and twelfth grades, at the high point of exam pressure and knee-deep in college applications. By 2019, they had graduated college and become young adults who were in the workforce or in graduate school. I kept in touch with all twenty-eight students through online messages and texts on WeChat, Renren, and Facebook. I visited each student twice on average after they graduated from high school and met up with those who happened to be living closer to me, in Philadelphia, almost annually. The students reported that participation in this research was enjoyable. They were visibly delighted to see me and were happy to keep in touch after they completed high school. Seven years after high school, the girls still hugged me and took selfies and locked arms with me when we walked together. The boys greeted me with smiles and often carried my backpack or took me on walking tours. Some of them offered to let me stay at their apartments for future visits. All of them still called me "big sister" (*jiejie*) as they used to do in high school. These interactions assured me that the young adults I once accompanied to class—now members of the global elite—continued to accept my presence and were willing to share with me a glimpse of their world.

Organization of the Book

In order to answer whether and how the new generation of elites from China might dominate the global economy, one must first understand whom these people are. Chapter 1 provides an overview of the new generation of elite Chinese. I examine the experiences of these youth within the context of rising social inequality. I situate this study against the backdrop of a growing number of international students from China studying in Western countries. Chinese students' craze for going abroad for tertiary (and secondary) education reflects their common perception that receiving a top, global education is a secure pathway to success. This phenomenon suggests that they believe that they must acquire the necessary skills in top schools in order to guarantee their future high status and to be deservingly elite at a global level. Consequently, the schooling process becomes a critical period during which the next generation of elites in China learn about the rules of global status competition and train for status warfare.

The following chapters examine the ways in which elite Chinese students are equipped to pursue status reproduction. In school, these students develop an intricate knowledge of the status system and how to skillfully navigate the social hierarchy. They understand that building positive relationships with peers and teachers heavily depends on their positions in the status system. Furthermore, the importance of obtaining high status is driven home to the adolescents by parental involvement in their education, especially at times of educational crisis. Borrowing the card game metaphor to portray status reproduction, chapter 2 describes the rules of the game and elite students' familiarity with them. The students possessed an intricate knowledge of the qualifications that bestow status in school. Specifically, they used test scores and perceived diligence to set up a clear status system with four groups: study gods, studyholics, underachievers, and losers.[49] Drawing on ethnographic data from Pinnacle and Capital, I show that students in different status positions navigated the status system in different ways. Students who later went to Western universities found their understanding of the status system unchallenged throughout college. Consequently, they continued to uphold a status system determined by test scores (or GPAs) and considered themselves as having top status in American universities. Students who went to Chinese universities soon realized that they were lower performing than their nonelite classmates, who came from populous and hence more competitive provinces and "study all day long." After a few test defeats, the elite students quickly changed the rules by setting up a new status system, such as one that values knowing how to "have fun" over test sores, in which they had top status.

Chapters 3 through 5 examine how the new generation of elites learn the sets of status-based behaviors through interpersonal relationships. Chapter 3 focuses on peer interactions. The elites often must maintain relationships with competitors who are equally, less, or more elite. The students in this study seem to have perfected the skills in cultivating peer relationships during high school. Through daily interactions and close friendship ties with low-status peers, high-status students maintained their distinction while neutralizing status inequality. Simultaneously, the low-status students learned to rationalize and sustain the hierarchy after consistently losing to their high-status peers. The result was genuine admiration of the dominant by the subordinate and mutual support of the status system regardless of one's status. In other words, by interacting with classmates of different abilities, the elite Chinese students prepared themselves for future interactions with colleagues and collaborators who have varying levels of abilities and positions in a company.[50]

Another important relationship that elites must cultivate is with authority figures. Chapter 4 turns to student interactions with teachers. Patterns of student-teacher interaction systematically differed by student performance in high school. While teachers often demanded respect (especially in a Confucian culture), the study gods could disregard, ignore, and actively defy teachers because they knew that teachers had vested interests in producing high performers. In comparison, the low performers who understood that teachers did not reap rewards from their performance became quiet and obedient. Follow-up visits with students after college showed that student descriptions of their relationships with company supervisors sometimes paralleled the relationships they had had with teachers in high school. Consequently, just as the elite students expected differential treatment from teachers in school based on their academic performance, they anticipated that employers would favor those with high employee performance.

Chapter 5 explores the process through which parents groom their children in the pursuit of global elite status. I show that parents drive home the importance of status to their children. Parents became external supporters of the student status system in school by forming patterns of parent-child interaction that reflected the child's status in school. Parents of study gods gave unconditional support and granted considerable freedom to their children. By contrast, the low-performing children were subject to heightened levels of parental supervision that led to a sense of constraint. While all parents cared for their only child, the divergent displays of parental support and interaction patterns contributed to a growing sense of freedom or constraint depending on the child's status in school. Consequently, the top-performing elite students who were study gods expected maximum family support and were highly assertive, while the others did not and were not.

Chapter 6 focuses on the importance of crisis management as part of elite status reproduction. While parents were able to intervene in their children's college applications and exam preparation, they typically took a back seat and let their children lead. However, the overall lack of involvement did not mean they were completely hands-off. In chapter 6, I present evidence that parents were heavily involved as soon as they sensed that their child's college outcome was at risk. Parents were not involved in their children's job hunt but they would be if the children had trouble navigating the job market. In due course, the parents led by example and drove home to their children the necessity of having backup plans. While no students made use of their parents' backup plans when transitioning to the job market, they reported that their parents were more than ready to step forward when needed. Importantly, many students made backup plans for themselves and implemented those strategies when necessary.

In the concluding chapter I revisit the general question of how the new generation of elite Chinese might come to dominate global society. I point out differences in elite education between China and the United States as well as the important ways that their schooling process did *not* prepare them for elite status in the future. For example, they are likely limited by their overall lack of engagement in extracurricular activities, anti-Asian sentiments, and the bamboo ceiling. Overall, I identify crucial skills that elite Chinese youth acquire as they try to become study gods and the rewards these skills reap as they compete for global elitism.

Combined with two appendices, the chapters further existing understanding of elites in an era of increased globalization. Chinese students are arriving at the United States and other Western countries in larger numbers and at earlier ages. These elite students often stay for jobs on Wall Street, with major consulting firms, and for companies such as Amazon, Google, and Facebook. In fact, the students in this study who are working in the United States have starting salaries that put them at the top 5 to 20 percent of earners in the United States, the United Kingdom, Singapore, and Hong Kong. These youth are not trained within their national borders. Western universities, corporations, and countries all contribute to the rise of the global elite from China. This book broadens prevailing conversations about how the Chinese prepare their younger generations for an increasingly competitive world and offers a cautionary tale for other countries that are also struggling for global dominance.

1

The New Elites from China

I met Na, a tall girl with short hair, at the principal's office at Central. A few sentences into our conversation, I casually commented that she seemed to care a lot about test scores. Na frowned at my cavalier attitude and responded solemnly, "Let's say the cutoff score for Peking University was 660, but you only got 600. From this very moment, your life would be different. It's as if you graduated from Harvard. Could you say it's the same as graduating from any other university in the U.S.? Could you? No. They're not the same. You'd get different internships, work at different companies, and have different careers. Right? Just saying 'I'm from Peking University' would give you a [head] start."

GOING TO COLLEGE means different things to different students. Some see college as a dream, others as a ticket to future financial security. For elite students in China, higher education itself is not a possible stage of life but a certainty. In our interview, I asked Na about her college plans. She patiently explained that going to college was never a question. Instead, whether she could get into a top university was the issue. Students focusing on the tier of the university, instead of simply going, is understandable in countries with very high college attendance rates. In societies that have undergone significant educational expansion, the quality and prestige of the institution matter a great deal for status outcomes.[1] After all, when everyone goes to college, *which* college one enrolls in is key to claiming individual superiority. However, in countries like China, where higher education is available to fewer than half of all students, entering college is generally regarded as an achievement.[2] In fact, most students in China are not as confident about college attainment and would be relieved if they were as certain about it as Na and her schoolmates.

Na was clearly not an ordinary student from China. Her emphasis on college choice, as opposed to college itself, showed that she belonged to a unique group—the socioeconomically elite youth who marked distinction and sought to establish themselves above others. Furthermore, Na mapped out her career trajectory based on university admission outcomes. This suggested that she saw something far greater at stake as she fought for her dream school. It was not college placement that Na and others like her devoted themselves to, but future status, for which college was a "starting point" that directly shaped each person's outcome.

Like Na, every student in this study believed that university placement determined their future. They embraced greater educational competition and were highly skilled therein. However, higher education was not always strongly associated with elite status in China. During the Cultural Revolution, political affiliation had the strongest impact on status outcome.[3] At the end of the Cultural Revolution, the government reinstated the national entrance exam (*gaokao*), established economic reforms in the 1980s, and carried out a series of educational reforms in subsequent decades.[4] Simultaneously, a group of socioeconomic elites who achieved their status through educational success emerged in Chinese society.[5] Higher education rapidly expanded after 1998,[6] but college attainment continued to yield significant income returns and remained a prerequisite for economic and political elite status.[7] Alongside rapid social change, social inequality in China significantly increased, and there is evidence of social polarization: the income gap between the top 10 percent and others has grown considerably, and the percentage of family income spent on education is fifty times greater for the poor than for the rich.[8] Intergenerational transmission of income, the degree to which parental income determines children's income, is greater in China than in other countries.[9] Given the rapid social change, increased levels of inequality, and high intergenerational elasticity, potential downward mobility has become a serious concern because children who descend the status ladder are unlikely to climb back up.

In such a context, education as a primary vehicle for status reproduction takes on particular significance. In China, as in many other countries, top university attainment is key to obtaining elite status.[10] Graduates from Peking and Tsinghua, the two top universities in the country,[11] enjoy benefits that alumni from other universities do not. These include 95 percent employment rates upon college graduation (when policy makers are concerned about the country's overall low college employment rates),[12] starting salaries that are 50 percent higher than the national average for college graduates,[13] and powerful alumni networks in politics, academia, and economics.[14] Given that these benefits carry long-term consequences, elites understandably see obtaining top education credentials as the optimal pathway to passing on their socioeconomic positions.

Gaining entry to top universities, however, is easier said than done. Educational competition in China is arguably the most intense in the world. Chinese higher education selects students through the National College Entrance

Exam (*gaokao*), a nationwide two-day standardized examination held annually on June 7 and 8.[15] The exam consists of six subjects: Chinese, math, English, and either the humanities (geography, history, and politics) or sciences (biology, chemistry, and physics). High school graduates who take the gaokao are ranked by their exam scores and receive only one admission offer based on their rankings.[16] While about 40 percent of the test takers are admitted to college each year, only 0.08 percent of them enroll in Peking or Tsinghua.[17] This rate is lower than the admission rates to the *grandes écoles* in France (less than 5 percent) and comparable to the Ivy League acceptance rate if all U.S. high school seniors applied (about 0.1 percent).[18]

The overall minimal chances of success prompt the elites to draw on other resources to navigate the educational system. One is the *hukou* system. In China, benefits and social security are tied to one's hukou, which is one's residential location. Educational resources are no exception, and urbanites enjoy significantly more educational opportunities and greater quality of schools than rural residents. Admission rates also depend on hukou. Universities designate admission quotas to each province, favoring students in the same area.[19] Peking and Tsinghua are located in Beijing, thus the relatively few Beijingers enjoy more quota than students in more populous provinces. In the past decade, Peking and Tsinghua have admitted about 1 percent of Beijing students annually. By comparison, for admission Shandong students needed to land in the top 0.1 percent in the province, Guangdong students the top 0.03 percent.[20]

In addition to obtaining an advantageous hukou, elites also send children to the "right" high schools, which offer expert training for the gaokao. Studies find that top high school attendance is so important that family background no longer significantly influences college outcomes when top high school attendance is controlled for.[21] In Beijing, schools ranked in the top ten (out of 291) are clearly distinct from others. Compared to the Beijing average of 1 percent acceptance rate, these ten high schools send about 15 to 25 percent of their students to Peking and Tsinghua annually. In top high schools with ability sorting, half of the students in the top classrooms matriculate to the two universities. With the schools' success rate, elite youth flock to top high schools, which accept only a few hundred students per cohort. Enrollment in top high schools primarily depends on test scores, and students must score in the top 10 percent of the High School Entrance Exam to be admitted. Family background also helps, as those who score narrowly below the admission cutoff can pay a hefty school sponsorship fee to make up a two- to three-point difference (out of 580). The fact that this practice is legal and widely utilized suggests that elite families, being the group who can afford the fees, perceive top high school attainment as an important step toward elite status reproduction.

There is no doubt that elites in China hope to pass down their socioeconomic status to their children. However, staying elite in China is not the end
goal for these families. Instead, they pursue elite status at a global scale. Many
elite parents in this study supported their children's educational competition
with an eye on global competition. In doing so, some elite families had an in-
ternal timeline of sending children abroad after graduating from Peking or
Tsinghua. Another common pathway was to send children to the West for
college.[22] Claire's mother, a physician with a PhD, belonged to the latter group.
In our interview, she directly and clearly stated the family's ambition:
"[Claire's] father came from a very small village in inner Mongolia. He got into
college and came to Beijing. [Claire's] goal was to carry on her father's legacy."
She looked me in the eye and said firmly, "She will follow her father's footsteps
and go from Beijing to the world." Claire's family was wealthy, highly educated,
and well connected in China. Yet they were not content with staying at the top
in Chinese society. They expected children to pursue elite status worldwide.

Elites are not the only ones who send their children abroad. The number of
international students from China studying in Western countries has grown
considerably,[23] and families from a range of socioeconomic backgrounds
choose between higher education systems domestically and abroad. Working-
class parents try to send their children abroad when they see little hope of upward mobility in China; and middle-class ones see Western education as a "new
education gospel."[24] While the long-term payoff for Western higher education
in general is debatable,[25] most families believe that foreign college degrees yield
favorable career and income returns upon graduation in the country of destina-
tion and in China.[26] Despite uncertain returns on college education in aggregate patterns, top university graduates are indeed high-skilled employees
sought by national and provincial governments as well as enterprises. Among
those who return to China, 93 percent find employment within six months of
arrival; over a quarter enjoy starting salaries that are about three times the national average. They are expected to lead successful business ventures should
they start their own companies.[27] Thus, like the elite youth who stay in China,
those who go abroad for college contemplate not going to college but *which*
college. Also like their domestic-bound peers, these foreign-bound students
have an exceedingly narrow definition of top universities. The students in this
study considered only Ivy League universities, Stanford, MIT, private universities ranked in the top thirty in the *U.S. News* rankings, and Oxford and Cambridge as top universities. They knew about other universities and liberal arts
colleges but simply did not hold those institutions as equally prestigious.

It is difficult for Chinese nationals to enroll in top universities in the United
States.[28] Not only do they accept very few Chinese students each year, but
students also must navigate the different higher educational selection systems.

In this sense, elite parents heavily invest in children's education from an early age and prioritize children's educational success over other family events.[29] These parents hire application agents that connect high school students to professors at American universities for personalized training, with faculty compensation up to $2,000 per hour.[30] Top high schools also play an important role in preparing elite children for college abroad, such as hiring American college admission officers as academic counselors and organizing curricula that mimic those of American high schools. Students from top high schools are highly competitive. Using SAT scores as an example, in 2013 the median SAT score for Chinese students in Beijing was 1,455 out of 2,400 (1,050 out of 1,600 in the new scoring system).[31] By comparison, the lowest SAT score in the top high schools I visited was 1,800 (1,300 in the new scoring system), which was in the top 20 percent by U.S. standards.[32]

In short, high school is a critical period during which elite youths acquire the necessary skills in top schools to secure for themselves an elite future at a global level. The elite youths from China are a group of teenagers who grew up with affluence, high educational achievement, and pragmatism about status competition. In our conversation, Na frankly and correctly assessed the long-term status advantages associated with top university attainment without reading the scholastic reports and statistical evidence that I cited. Surprised, I asked where the seventeen-year-old girl arrived at this understanding. Na tilted her head and thought for a split moment, but then shrugged. "I don't know. It came naturally, like, parents, classmates, friends." Na's natural response showed that she and her elite peers were groomed for educational success, regardless of in which country they went to college. To the extent that educational competition is a key step that unlocks future elite status, these students anticipate competing for global status. Most importantly, they have been well prepared.

Training Grounds for the Future Elite: Top High Schools in Beijing

The Qing dynasty abolished the imperial examinations in 1905 and established modern, Western educational institutions. Student selection into these schools was determined by factors such as family background up to three generations, physical appearance, and a recommendation letter from a government official who came from the same area. Although students from ordinary backgrounds were not officially excluded, these selection criteria resulted in a student body consisting only of elite boys.[33] In fact, schools' catering to the elite was unsurprising, given that these schools were established to train elite children into knowledgeable servants who could help the emperor govern the empire. Fifty years later, in the early years of communist China, these top high schools continued to educate the children of elites. There was even division in the type of high-ranking cadres' children that each school admitted. Some educated the children of government officials; others taught those from the military. Students in top high schools were also politically involved, as they later became active in the Cultural Revolution and battled against teachers.[34]

Fast-forwarding to the twenty-first century, the same high schools that had been at the center of elite reproduction and political struggles shed these reputations. Instead, they became widely known throughout the nation for academic excellence. These schools adjusted to elites' diversifying demand for educational trajectories in China versus abroad. Elite families decided whether to send their children abroad for college no later than tenth grade, which is the first year of high school.[35] To best prepare students for top universities around the world, elite high schools have established separate but equally professional systems to prepare students depending on their targeted countries. Upon enrollment, students must choose between attending the domestic department, which prepares students for excelling in the gaokao in China, or the international department, which specializes in sending students to top universities in the United States and elsewhere.[36]

While selection to both domestic and international departments is strictly based on exam scores, students in top high schools remain considerably homogenous in terms of family background.[37] Simply put, most are elite. Omega, where expensive-looking black limousines surround the school gate at the end of class every day, is known to groom the children of high-ranking government officials in Beijing. Central and Highland, which have consecutively produced the top performers in the city for years, work closely with the modern-day literati of China. Pinnacle was established on imperial grounds. Capital specifically educated the children of high-ranking military cadres. Teachers in these schools estimate that the median family income of their students is about 1.5 times higher than the top 10 percent in urban China.[38] Additionally, they emphasize that a considerable proportion of students come from families with access to power, mostly through the military or government. Such homogeneity in pupils' socioeconomic backgrounds across two centuries suggests that changes in student selection methods have had little impact on the admission outcomes and that top high schools continue to serve the elite.

Pinnacle and Capital High Schools

Top high schools are no doubt the training grounds for the future elite. Pinnacle and Capital, the main sites of fieldwork in this study, are two examples. Pinnacle has been a traditional top-performing high school since its establishment in the early twentieth century. It is so academically stellar that the media have referred to it as "the god-like high school." Capital was at first an up-and-coming school established in Maoist China. Since drastically improving its ranking, it has become one of the "super high schools" in the nation. Capital and Pinnacle offer domestic and international departments to prepare students for college in China and the United States. Students in the two schools share an identical curriculum, have the same schedules, are highly competitive in the gaokao, and are successful in American university applications. Both schools have retained their association with the military, giving the schools a certain degree of independence from the government.[39]

Congruent with their task of training the elite, the campuses deliver different but equally elite vibes. Pinnacle has about fifteen hundred students on its fifteen-acre campus in the heart of Beijing. Despite being located on a bustling street, the campus felt like a secret garden. Pinnacle had the school's name carved in calligraphy on the stone walls by the gates and in the lobby of the main building, respectively half blocked by parked bicycles and a grand piano. Students in both the domestic and international departments took courses in a white concrete building beside the school gate.[40] Inside the building, their hexagon-shaped classrooms were warmly and minimally decorated. The upper half of the classroom walls were painted white, the lower half light blue. The sun shined gently through the soft orange curtains. Each room had four sets of windows, two facing outside and two facing the hallway. At the front was a blackboard and small screen; at the back was a bulletin board that publicized student test scores and achievements. Pinnacle used ability sorting to distinguish top performers from the rest. During my visit, by the end of twelfth grade students in top-performing classrooms had so many achievements that the announcements, printed on A4-sized paper, coated the entire wall. In other classrooms, class leaders nailed handwritten highlights of each subject to caution classmates against common mistakes. Teachers who put thought into decorating their classrooms abided by the minimalist guideline. A math teacher celebrated Christmas by setting up a small plastic Christmas tree at the corner beside the blackboard; the tree stayed there until the end of school year in June. A Chinese language teacher put a bookshelf of classic Chinese novels under the bulletin board, which read "silence" in a huge font. Pinnacle students were indeed quiet in class and during breaks. Few chatted in the hallway, and those who did spoke in low voices.

Pinnacle's campus resembled a museum. The campus was an exhibition of traditional Chinese architecture and artwork. While the main building, in white concrete, appeared modern, other buildings were constructed at the turn of the twentieth century. Red courtyard houses (*siheyuan*) converted to administration offices stood beside a stone bridge on a tiny artificial pond that led toward a pavilion surrounded by bamboo. A few steps away, goldfish swam circles in another, larger pond. Further inside, students often sat and read in a corridor under lush green trees during nice weather. The corridor connected two general activity buildings. One had a set of *bianzhong* and a grand piano in the lobby,[41] while the other held a ten-foot-wide replica of an armillary sphere with four black stone-carved dragons supporting the hollow globes that majestically sat at the center. Pinnacle had artwork scattered around campus. Two dozen works of calligraphy hung on three sides of the lobby in the main building. Classroom hallways were filled with slogans written in elegant calligraphy, all of them encouraging students to focus on college preparations. One in the hallway on the second floor read, "Create excellence in all aspects, achieve [your] goal in the gaokao, serve [your] country, repay [your] parents, and fulfill [your] occupational dream." A six-foot-tall metal monument showing teenagers playing tug of war overlooked the track field under the sun. Other monuments were scattered about the lawns, greeting students, teachers, and visitors as they roamed around campus.

About an hour to the southwest of Pinnacle is Capital, where some four thousand students (about half in middle school) share a forty-acre campus. Located on the edge of the city, Capital dominates the area, distinguishing itself from its surroundings with extravagance and a strong sense of internationalism. I was greeted by a fifteen-foot-tall red public artwork that resembled the school's motto at the front of the school gate. After passing the armed security at the front gate, I immediately saw the international department, housed in a newly renovated white building. At the entrance of the department was a large flat-screen TV with slideshows of students' admission outcomes. After being impressed by the success of the department, I passed by the academic counselors' office, home to foreign counselors, before arriving at the lobby, whose walls were decorated with dozens of international flags. At the center was a globe, its width the size of two adults' outstretched arms. The only non-international component on the first floor was the lush green plants that stretched tall on shiny white tiles that reflected the sunlight. At the time of my visit, student classrooms were located on the second to fourth floors and filled with elements that encouraged them to aim high in educational competition. These included printed slogans in the hallways and a huge world map on the wall at the center of the second floor. The map showed sixteen universities in North America and Europe—where students should aim. The five U.S. schools included MIT, Stanford, Harvard, Princeton, and Yale, with Harvard's name bolded and in a larger font. Across the Atlantic, Cambridge was also in a larger font (but not bolded), along with Oxford and the London School of Economics and Political Science. A few others in other Western countries also made the list.

After exiting the international department, I had to walk through the track field, a park-size lawn with a stone pavilion, a school auditorium, and a gym, to arrive at the domestic department, Capital's iconic setting. The department consisted of three five-story red brick buildings overlooking a courtyard of trees, specifically modeled after Harvard's campus. Every building had a student study lounge, with squeaky redwood floors and dozens of five-foot-tall bluish-gray velvety sofa chairs back-to-back. Classrooms in both departments were identical. Each square-shaped classroom contained about thirty or forty white metal desks neatly aligned in rows on the polished beige tiles that reflected the light from the ceiling. Each room contained a wall-length blackboard at the front of the room, with flat screens above it, a long bookshelf at the right, and two teacher's desks at the front and back corners of the room. Like Pinnacle teachers, those at Capital decorated each classroom according to their field of expertise. The school offered minimal guidance on overall taste, thus the classroom decorations ranged from extravagant to austere. A biology teacher changed his classroom into a greenhouse by growing a row of plants on the windowsill as well as inside the room and hung a human blood circulation diagram on the opposite wall. A Chinese language teacher filled the wall with world maps, lists of historical events, and student test scores and rankings until there was no space left. An English teacher filled a bookshelf with English novels and dictionaries, turning the classroom into a mini library. On the other hand, a math teacher simply put his measuring tools on top of the bookshelf and allowed students to fill the rest with their books and test papers.

At the very end of campus was the school cafeteria, resembling an American food court. Students lined up in front of vendors in dozens of booths for various daily specials. Yet despite the apparent diversity of choices, many students disliked the food and complained about the repetitive cuisine. The campus was silent during class. But during break, student chatter filled the hallways as they loudly greeted friends from other classrooms. The students were so energetic that teachers often needed to shout to stop them from running in the hallways.

In short, Pinnacle demonstrated elitism with architectural elegance, high culture, and historical artifacts on campus. It was a place where students studied in serenity and learned to carry themselves with poise. Capital demonstrated elitism with its geographic grandeur and cosmopolitanism. It was a place where elite students freely roamed in open spaces as they traveled between brightly colored, internationally themed buildings. While different, both schools were distinguished from their neighborhoods. It was on these campus grounds that the future elites from China were trained for global competition, starting with successful competition for top universities in the country and abroad.

Preparing for the Gaokao

Exactly twelve days before the gaokao, the twelfth grade students in Capital lined up on the sports field at seven o'clock in the morning. A girl with short hair and a sharp voice boarded the podium. She stood in front of the microphone and said loudly, "In twelve days, we will race toward the battlefield of the gaokao. The encouragements of our teachers and parents are the shields in our hands. Our effort and diligence are our swords." She talked for about five minutes, comparing the exam to a final battle and promised that the cohort would "fight for the highest honor for the school." After the girl finished, Mr. Liu, a twelfth grade teacher, boarded the podium and gave a similar speech. He started with, "In just twelve days, you will march toward the battlefield of the gaokao" and ended by saying, "Twelve days later, you will bring honor to [our] school. Ten years later, you will become important people in your occupational fields. Twenty years later, you will become the pillar of society, of our country, of our nation."

The gaokao is serious business, and it would be a mistake to think that it is nothing more than a high-stakes exam. Like the girl and the teacher in this example, many compare gaokao to a battle in which students are the soldiers fighting for not just their lives and futures, but also their schools and their nation. This analogy shows that the gaokao had become more than an exam that screens students for higher education. Instead, elite students perceived its results to be a matter of collective survival and group prosperity. With this additional meaning, gaokao scores naturally became students' primary focus. The seriousness of gaokao outcomes practically guaranteed that no other criterion would have comparable significance throughout high school.

Collective Focus on Test Scores

Nothing captures the attention of the public across the nation like the gaokao does. Netizens draw public attention to the exam by tweeting gaokao memes every summer; consider, for example, a 2017 poster of an imaginary film titled *Gaokao* with gruesome-looking teenagers in the background (see Figure 1.1). The media glorify the top-scoring students by writing extensively about the teenagers' life histories up to high school graduation, granting them instant national fame. Local governments implement policies to assist families with exam-taking children on test days. On the days leading to gaokao, *Beijing Daily* (the official Beijing municipal newspaper) spends about five pages (out of forty) publishing government support for families participating in the gaokao. This includes allowing them to park in police parking spots on exam days and ordering the police to clear traffic for students' families should they run late to

FIGURE 1.1. Meme for the National College Entrance Exam.
Translation: (Top) The large-scale production war epic film.
(Middle) College Entrance Exam, hitting theaters on June 7 at
9 AM. (Lower) One pen, one life. Is it fate, or the human mind?
(Bottom) Produced by the Ministry of Education of China.
Starring all exam takers and parents in the nation.

the test sites. Scattered throughout the pages is information about how to best take care of the exam-taking child, such as experts suggesting eating breakfast sixty to ninety minutes beforehand. On exam days, each test site is equipped with an ambulance and armed security at the gates. The exam takers are allowed to enter upon showing their exam permits, while their anxious parents and worried teachers are barred. The neighborhoods surrounding test sites have their roads blocked and experience an annual influx of visitors on those two days. But despite the recurrent hassle, locals do not seem bothered in the slightest, as they set up large signs reminding each other to be quiet so as not to disturb the test takers.

If even bystanders—netizens, the media, local governments, and people in the neighborhood—express great interest in the exam results, students, their teachers, and their parents, all of whom have vested interests in the outcomes, are understandably devoted to it. In the high schools I visited, students intensely competed among their peers on a day-to-day basis. Test scores were generally public information. Many teachers posted lists with students' names, test scores, class rankings, and previous rankings on classroom walls or bulletin boards. Schools flaunted students' detailed test scores with the "honors list" on pink paper with very large fonts in the hallways. When gaokao results were available, schools would list the names of students admitted to Peking and Tsinghua on the school website and print posters for display at the school gates. Some schools such as Capital moved toward withholding information on individual test scores. But these policies were no hindrance to students obtaining such information. Students figured out each other's scores by asking directly and through teachers, who shared detailed results when asked. They even utilized their family networks. Parents compared their children's test scores via social media, as information traveled at light speed. Yehua, a boy at Pinnacle, once picked up his test papers and slowly made his way to the door. Within thirty seconds, before he had stepped outside, his classmate shouted out across the classroom, "Yehua! You got 140?" He added, "My mom said your mom told her" to signal credibility. At top high schools, asking for someone's test scores was a normal conversation starter, and talking about each other's test scores was like discussing the weather.

Students competed over test scores intensely. Classrooms of students, prompted by teachers, challenged other classrooms to produce the highest average or have the top performer. Interschool competition was common, given the public nature of test scores. Teachers did everything in their power to boost the school's average gaokao scores. They persuaded Olympiad winners, who were usually high performers, to take the gaokao even though they had already received guaranteed admission. The competition-focused mindset also led teachers to make borderline paranoid comments about students at other schools. One of the clearest examples took place in Mrs. Li's physics class at Capital, during which the middle-aged teacher warned a classroom of twelfth graders, "At the test site . . . students in other schools will come and stab you because you're from Capital. Do not listen to them, do not help them. Whatever they say or offer, they're trying to hurt you."

Mrs. Li was not alone in describing exam takers from other schools as enemies who would do anything to harm her students. Many teachers were wary of students from other schools, likely because they took full responsibility in preparing students for the gaokao. In China, parents (including the elite) took the default route and deferred to the teachers about gaokao preparations. Parent-teacher meetings took place in auditoriums, where about five hundred parents listened quietly to teachers lecturing onstage. Individual meetings were rare and discouraged by teachers. Many teachers expressed that parental visits were "completely unnecessary" and "a waste of time," and they tried to "end conversation within a few sentences."[42] One summer, Pinnacle asked all homeroom teachers to visit students' homes. Teachers acknowledged the good intentions of this policy but nonetheless complained bitterly about it. Met with extreme reluctance and pushback, Pinnacle's administration halted this policy.

Parents treated teachers as experts who held knowledge that was otherwise unavailable to them. Most accepted teachers' plans without question by default. Even when parents did not understand teachers' plans or announcements, they kept their questions to themselves and did not ask for clarification.[43] Although parents adopted a hands-off approach, they were not negligent. The elite parents in this study supported their children by providing an optimal exam-focused environment. For example, they paid overpriced rent for apartments close to schools to minimize children's commutes. Units that once housed a top-performing student garnered especially high rents, as landlords often doubled or tripled prices for future residents. In addition to paying for housing when they owned assets in the city, parents made personal sacrifices to increase their children's gaokao scores.[44] A documentary called *Senior Year* showed parents in Fujian obediently nodding as the teacher exhorted them to refrain from getting divorced that academic year and that acing the gaokao was more important than winning the lottery.[45] News about parents concealing grandparental illnesses so as not to distract their children from exam preparations was reported annually. Occasionally, parents of high performers went so far as to hide the other parent's sudden death for the same reason. Considering that the adults and others in the surrounding environments collectively focused on the gaokao, it was no wonder that elite students elevated the test's importance to the point where nothing challenged its centrality to student life.

Contingencies in Beijing

High-stakes exams around the world, including the gaokao, are usually straightforward and easy to navigate: in these admission systems, exam scores alone determine college placements. Yet the structure of the gaokao in Beijing entails a whole set of contingencies that affect student outcome and must be carefully handled. At the time of my fieldwork (2013–14), one of the most

TABLE 1.1. Extra Points Available for Beijing Students

Type	Extra points in 2013	Extra points in 2014
1. Top tier in the National High School Olympiad[a]	Guaranteed	10
2. Pass the university-specific additional test	Up to 60	Up to 60
3. Exemplary behavior[b]	20	10
4. Athletic achievement[c]	20	20
5. Ethnic minority	10	5
6. Principal's recommendation[d]	60	60
7. Peking and Tsinghua universities' winter camps	Up to 60	Up to 60

Note: Each student can receive only one type of extra points.

a. In addition to giving 10 extra points, Peking and Tsinghua universities significantly lowered the admission cutoff scores for these students in 2014. The extra points were abolished in 2015, but the lowered cutoff remained in place.

b. This is the "Three-good Student" (*sanhao xuesheng*), which was abolished in 2015.

c. The government steadily reduced the types of sports that qualified.

d. Peking and Tsinghua universities allocate one or two quotas to selected top high schools in Beijing each year.

potentially rewarding (or damaging) contingencies was the extra points system. Students could obtain extra points that counted toward their exam score. While there were multiple sources of extra points, students could keep only one set. Table 1.1 provides a list of extra points available in 2013 and 2014. With the exception of minority status, obtaining extra points was time-consuming. Students spent as little as six months to prepare for the university-administered additional tests and as long as two years to compete in the High School Olympiad. Furthermore, as shown in Table 1.1, the sources and expected gains from the extra points changed frequently and with short notice. In 2014, two months before the Olympiad, the government announced that gold medalists in the National High School Olympiad would no longer receive guaranteed admission. This devastated Yulang, a girl who had devoted two years to Olympiad preparations at the expense of studying for the gaokao. The same year Lili, a student at Capital, almost wept when she told me that her dream school had suddenly canceled the additional test a few months before it commenced.

Another Beijing-specific hurdle was the college choice system. Students received only one college placement after handing in their list of choices. In most of China, college choices were intuitive decisions based on students' gaokao scores. However, students in Beijing submitted up to five selections in May, before taking the gaokao in June. The risk of making choices before seeing one's exam scores was articulately reflected in the official name of this system: "submission through guessing."[46] Student placements were further complicated by a student-school matching process, in which students needed to factor in university-specific restrictions. For example, top universities admitted only students who listed them as their top choice. Some universities accepted being second when the first was a top university, while others simply refused to be listed beyond the second choice. Many universities allowed students to bump them down the list but raised the cutoff score (imposing an increasing number of deduction points) for every additional rank lower on the list. Finally, these criteria changed at universities' discretion, and admission processing time varied. In a parent-teacher meeting, the vice principal at Capital repeatedly warned parents of the importance of choosing the top choice: "By the time a university has sent a [rejected] student's exam score to the next, the [latter] may have already given all of its offers and cannot admit the student," despite the candidate passing the admission cutoff score.[47] A girl at Omega summarized how elite students approached the system: "Only the first choice you put down counts. The second is already a backup; it's not nearly as good. Basically, nobody wants to go to their second choice."

These potential risks introduced complications into an originally straightforward selection system. Elite students who prepared for the gaokao needed to stay informed about these contingencies and watch for changes that could happen at any time. Students and their families thus had to extend considerable effort into competing for extra points and substantial time into making the safest college selections.

Daily Life in the Domestic Department

Having a singular focus and with high levels of uncertainty, elite students spent their three years of high school preparing for the gaokao. In fact, many considered themselves to have been preparing for the gaokao for "over a decade," "since young," or "ever since I could remember." Early during the fieldwork, I asked Xiangzu and his three friends at Omega how long they studied each day and what they did for extracurriculars, upon which they looked at me as if I was crazy. "You might as well say twenty-four hours," one answered while rolling his eyes. Another responded sarcastically, "What do you mean by 'extracurricular activities'?"[48] In another interview, Na, a student at Central, eloquently described the Chinese education process as "making a gong: the last swing of the hammer decides the sound." In other words, the gaokao being the last swing determined student outcomes and gave meaning to "over a decade" of hard work. Echoing Na and the other students, a teacher told me, "Preparing for the gaokao is a full-time job." I soon realized that this was a literal description of students' devotion to the gaokao. For elite students in top high schools and all others who aimed at Peking and Tsinghua, an hour awake was an hour of exam preparation.

In top high schools, teachers fit three years of exam material into two years of coursework to hone student's test-taking skills. All activities in the third and last year of high school were thus exam preparation activities. A typical day in twelfth grade, the last year of high school and the height of exam preparation, would unfold like this. Students arrived at school by seven thirty for the first test of the day. An exception was Capital, where Monday mornings were reserved for flag-raising ceremonies on the sports field—when selected students boarded the command post to be publicly awarded for their achievements. Teachers expected students to focus on the ceremonies. But most students secretly studied exam preparation notes hidden in their pockets or sleeves and mechanically applauded those who, according to one student, "must have done something good."

Class periods started promptly at eight o'clock. While tenth and eleventh grade students took a few courses unrelated to the exam, such as philosophy, twelfth grade students took only exam subject courses and physical education.[49] Classroom activates were a routine of students working on a test and teachers reviewing test questions. I learned quickly that if students took a test in one class, the next would be a review session, the one after that another test, then another review session, and so on. Students were tested all the time in twelfth grade. They took daily quizzes over multiple subjects, weekly tests, midterm exams, districtwide mock exams, and finals. Even physical education served the purpose of boosting exam results: the subject was on the high school graduation exam, and student health was necessary to maintain student schedules. Students went through eight (or nine) periods with ten-minute breaks between classes and a one-hour lunch break.[50] Teachers frequently used up most of the break to review one or two more questions. In what was left, students lined up for the restroom, took naps, discussed test questions, or studied at their desks.

Classes ended at five thirty, when students were dismissed for dinner. Almost all twelfth graders returned within an hour for night study, with teachers patrolling the hallways. Schools take night study periods seriously. Teachers claimed that night study situations were directly related to gaokao outcomes and reported about them in parent-teacher meetings. While students could choose how late they stayed, almost all left between nine thirty and ten thirty. By the end of the day, students wearily dragged their feet toward the front gates, through which they had walked fifteen hours before. Students continued to study after arriving home and reported going to bed between eleven and two o'clock in the morning (Table 1.2 presents a weekday schedule of the domestic department). Weekends meant more studying. Many of the twelfth graders pressured by the gaokao put on their uniforms and studied in school all day on the weekends, typically arriving by nine in the morning and leaving

TABLE 1.2. School Schedules at Capital and Pinnacle

	Domestic and international departments (fall semester, 12th grade)	International department (spring semester, 12th grade)	
		Capital	Pinnacle
7:00–7:20	Arrive at school		
7:20–8:00	School starts[a]		Arrive at school
8:00–12:25	Periods 1–5	Arrive at school	Class periods
12:25–1:35	Lunch break	Lunch break	Lunch break
1:35–4:00	Periods 6–8	Class periods	Class periods
4:00–5:30	Self-study		
5:30–6:30	Dinner break		
6:30–9:30/10:30	Night study[b]		

a. Activities include working on tests, self-studying, and attending the flag-raising ceremony.

b. Night study usually takes place in 12th grade.

around nine at night. Weekend study sessions were similar to night ones, with teachers patrolling the campus, students studying quietly, and school bells sounding as if it were a weekday. Spending between twelve and fifteen hours per day in school, students had little or no time for outside tutoring, cram schooling, or shadow education.[51]

Applying to Universities in the United States

A few twelfth graders at Capital invited me to their math class presentation in May. They were given the task of examining the statistical relationship between two variables. Two girls, Liz and Tina, decided to check out the relationship between SAT scores and college admission outcomes using data from "the CUUS 2016 cohort," which contained a sample size of a few hundred. I sat in the back of the classroom and listened to their presentation. The two girls pulled up a PowerPoint slide that showed, in large print, "SAT Scores and University Admissions." Liz, a cheerful girl with short hair and pimples, walked to the front of the room, smiled at her classmates, and introduced their project. She effortlessly attracted her classmates' attention by announcing the title of their presentation. The students who had been dozing off or secretly texting under the table immediately raised their heads, sat up straight, and attentively looked at the screen in front of the room.

Liz pointed to the screen, scanned the room, and said straightforwardly, "This should be what all of us care about the most. I mean, what all of us *cared* about the most." (This cohort had already taken the SAT and had received their college admission results.) After Liz's warmup, Tina, who was quiet and shy, presented the findings. She first showed a scatterplot with a clearly positive association. "The higher the SAT, the higher ranked the school, this is pretty obvious." Sounding a little nervous, she spoke at an accelerated pace, fixing her eyes on the screen. "All the dots are around the line. So, we can see there is truly a relationship between the two. We did hypothesis testing to prove that they really are associated." The students looked attentively at the slides as Tina concluded, "Our conclusion is, although we very much want to tell ourselves that getting a low SAT score doesn't mean we'll end up at a low [ranked] university, the data show that the SAT in fact determines what university we get into." The audience nodded in agreement, signaling that they found the conclusion persuasive.

Students in the international department knew how to apply for American universities. They built portfolios, wrote essays, solicited letters, and fought for grades during high school. Yet these efforts aside, they strongly believed that SAT scores predicted application results. The fact that Liz and Tina decided to investigate the association between SAT scores and application outcomes, out of infinite other topics, signaled their very strong interest in the SAT even after they had taken the test. The word "SAT" instantly capturing the interest of students (looking up and attentively gazing at the screen) showed that Liz and Tina were not alone: most if not all the students in the classroom shared their interest. Although it was less than a month before graduation, these elite students had not put their applications behind them. Instead, SAT test scores remained what they "cared about the most."

All Eyes on the SAT

Students are not the only ones who focus on the SAT. The media, netizens, and local businesses do so as well when it comes to applying to American universities. Media commonly refer to the SAT (and ACT) as "the American Gaokao."[52] Reporters write extensively about students who receive perfect scores on the SAT and those who obtain multiple acceptances from top American universities each year. These stories detail how these students prepare for the SAT and which university each chooses to attend, turning them into models for other aspiring students and their families. Netizens join in by tweeting the stories and adding congratulatory remarks. College students in the receiving country or institutions also share these news reports in their social media circles and express eagerness to meet the incoming freshmen. Much like the students who received top scores in the gaokao, SAT top performers experience immediate fame in their city, province, and country, even across continents. SAT preparation is a thriving industry, as cram schools (or "shadow education") specializing in SAT training sprout up in school districts.

Bookstores near schools cater to local clientele by offering racks of SAT guide-books, vocabulary manuals, and mock SAT questions at the front of the store. Some of these bookstores do so to a degree that students complain about the limited selection of other literature.

American-bound students and families know that U.S. universities use a selection system that evaluates each applicant holistically, but they focus on SAT scores and compete over them. In a sense, students approach the SAT as if it were the gaokao. I was surprised by students' obsession with test scores since my first encounter with the international-bound students. Mr. Long, a math teacher and key informant at Capital, invited me to substitute teach a physics class by introducing students to American college life. After my brief presentation, the students immediately followed up by asking questions such as, "Will I get in to Bryn Mawr if my SAT score isn't that high?" "Is it true that Chinese students need higher SAT scores to get into the same universities as American students?" and "Should we prepare for the GRE and SAT simulta-neously?" It turned out that all the questions I took were about test prepara-tion and SAT scores. Students focused their attention on the SAT to such a degree that no other topic commanded comparable student interest. The stu-dents would forget to bring their textbooks but never their SAT vocabulary sheets. Their lecture notes were in unrecognizable handwriting and peppered with scribbles, scattered on their desks, in book bags, or between books. By comparison, their SAT notes were neatly written and kept in clear folders, ready to be pulled out at any time.

Students compared SAT scores during breaks, during meals, and after school. The students were so attentive to each other's scores that they even secretly discussed them during class.[53] Although the test was taken individu-ally, SAT scores were public information. Students compared SATs with peers in their classrooms and across cohorts and schools. Believing that American universities reviewed all Chinese applicants in one pool, they engaged in com-petition with rivals outside of Beijing. Students utilized information from cram schools, personal networks, and online chat rooms to gain information about each other's SAT scores. Hannah, a Capital student accepted to Johns Hopkins, told me that her freshmen cohort's SAT scores ranged from perfect scores to two hundred points lower. While this could have suggested that American universities accepted Chinese students with a range of SAT scores and that SAT scores were not as crucial as the students thought,[54] students ignored this possibility and remained fixated on the test.

Comparing SAT scores was a standard greeting among the international-bound students. They answered honestly and expected each other to provide the same courtesy. Many did not enjoy these SAT-filled greetings but nonethe-less participated. Selena, a Capital student who mostly hung out with students from another top high school, was particularly upset about this norm: "Chinese students. The minute you meet them, they're like, 'How much was your SAT?' [Then] they'd say, 'Oh I got lower than you did,' [or] 'I got higher than you did.' Like that." Students were also emotional about other students' test scores. They despised low achievers with expressions such as someone "only got" a certain (low) score on the SAT or "ended up going" to a (low-ranked) university. They respected high achievers, describing the latter group as "great" or "so good." Students remembered each other's SAT scores for years, even if they had lost touch with each other. The common focus on SAT scores, the attachment of emotions to SAT outcomes, and the fact that SAT scores were part of their long-term memory all suggested that for elite students the SAT took on meaning beyond a simple test.

Parents devoted themselves to helping their children prepare for the SAT. Elite parents, with their affluence, often spent a considerable amount on their children's preparations. Itemized expenses each year included approximately $15,000 for international department tuition,[55] $3,000 for cram schools, and $100 per session for private tutors.[56] Outside of the school year, parents sent their children to summer camps in the United States to enhance their English ability, typically with budgets up to $50,000. On top of these costs, students made up to five trips to Hong Kong or Singapore to take the test, and parents willingly footed the bill for flights, hotel rooms, and registration fees. Parents also gave unquantifiable support. Many reported spending nights researching American universities, waking up early to make a fresh loaf of bread for the child every day, or searching for qualified tutors to boost their SAT scores. Parental efforts revolving around the SAT indicated that it was of central importance to them.

Students' and parents' focus on the SAT, however, was a source of discontent to the school counselors. While families saw the SAT as the basis for college choice, counselors saw SAT scores as a cutoff that students simply needed to pass and emphasized finding the best "fit" between university strength and student interests. However, because parents had more control over students' application lists than the counselors did, school counselors sometimes felt a sense of powerlessness in their profession. Tom, an American counselor at Capital, complained with a frown behind his antipollution mask that many parents simply "took out the rankings on *U.S. News*" and told their children to "apply to the schools ranked in the top ten or the top thirty." Even when Chinese national counselors, such as John, tried to dissuade parents from making decisions exclusively based on SAT scores, parents immediately silenced them with accusations such as "You're being so inconsiderate!" The different understandings between parents and counselors over the SAT led to counselors' frustration and the implicit allegation that parents prevented them from doing their job. Chris, an American counselor at Capital, summarized counselors' feelings of powerlessness with a sigh, "In the end, it's the parents' and students' list."

Although counselors thought parents' focus on the SAT was evidence of them being uninformed, the elite parents in this study argued that doing so was a rational response to uncertainties in the American college application system. Parents acknowledged that the higher education selection system in the United States was significantly different from the exam system in China. They understood college admission outcomes did not depend on test scores and were anxious about children's college portfolios. Yet, the problem, as Tracy's father explained, was that they "didn't understand . . . why extracurricular activities were important, what purpose they served, and what could be demonstrated in these activities." They wanted to know the relative importance of each criterion, but no such information was provided. Consequently, without this crucial piece of information, parents felt compelled to focus on something with a clear standard—SAT scores; the higher, the better.

Sensing that children did not receive adequate support in SAT preparations from the counselors, who dissuaded them from focusing on the only criterion they felt was controllable, parents sent children to cram schools and private tutors that specialized in SAT preparation. International departments in this study had a similar policy of discouraging students from hiring private counselors, but the policies were rarely implemented. Central had a zero-tolerance policy, which led to families secretly seeking external advice. Pinnacle and Capital discouraged this practice by emphasizing counselor credentials in parent-teacher meetings, but all except one of the international-bound students in this study utilized private tutoring or counseling services. Some schools collaborated with specific agencies, while others could not care less, as Omega students were known to have exceptionally large budgets for hiring private counselors and tutors.[57]

The discrepancy between counselors and parents was exacerbated by the lack of contact between the two parties. Counselors often noted that they welcomed parents and believed it was important to have smooth communication with the parents. However, most parents did not meet with children's counselors. Foreign counselors attributed the lack of communication to language barriers. While language might have been an important factor, John, the Chinese counselor rumored to have the most parent visits in Capital, reported that only "about a quarter of the parents" contact him in any format over the academic year. Even the exceptions proved the rule. Brandon's father was the only parent in this study who fully trusted and worked closely with their American school counselor, William. The father praised William for being "exceptionally [experienced], honest, and familiar with many universities in the U.S." Yet, even so, he rarely communicated with the counselor and did not provide any specific example of how William assisted Brandon. In other words, like their counterparts in the domestic departments, elite parents in international departments generally did not contact counselors.

Daily Life in the International Department

Despite applying for the same universities, the international-bound students in China did not have a high school life similar to that of American high school students. Instead, their schedules were largely identical with those in the domestic department until the application deadline. Students arrived at school by seven thirty, went through five class periods with ten-minute breaks in between, had lunch, sat through three more class periods, had dinner, and studied at school until nine thirty or ten thirty at night (Table 1.2 presents typical student schedules in the international department). Of course, there were minor differences between the two departments. One was the timing of application pressure. The height of college application activities in the international department took place in eleventh grade, during which students often claimed that their levels of anxiety surpassed those of their domestic-bound peers. Tony, a dark-skinned high performer at Capital, expressed anguish about eleventh grade: "I felt like I was dragged behind a car my entire eleventh grade. [I] was striving like hell to catch up." He acknowledged the need to please teachers, preview and review course materials, and complete homework after classes. However, he "didn't have time to do that." Instead, he had his hands full "studying for the SAT, preparing for the AP tests, and taking the ECE."[58] Tony's recollection showed that he, like his classmates, prioritized test preparation over all other admission requirements and felt the competing demands were overwhelming.

Since schools did not offer SAT preparation, which was key to students and families, students went to cram schools or private tutoring sessions on weekends. Seeing that students intuitively spent their entire eleventh grade and first semester of twelfth grade on test preparations, top high schools worried that students would neglect other admission requirements, which would in turn negatively affect the school's admission outcomes. With their prestige on the line, top high schools took action to enforce student involvement in activities that American colleges appreciated. Capital designated at least one class period for on-campus activities that counted toward extracurricular participation every afternoon. While the students only grudgingly attended these activities, these experiences later became examples of demonstrated leadership in their application essays. Capital's effort was minimal compared to other schools, some of which organized overseas student volunteer activities for the same reason.[59]

Student schedules in the international department were changed completely once the students received their admission outcomes in the spring semester of twelfth grade. They no longer stayed late, nor did they study at school on the weekends. International departments did not share a standardized curriculum, and thus student schedules were flexible and depended on their course loads. Capital students often arrived at school around noon for classes in the afternoons; Pinnacle students reported going for class in the morning and leaving school after lunch. Students were free to choose electives of their interest, provided that they were offered. Capital had a course on AP microeconomics for a few years because they hired a teacher who held advanced degrees in the field. Another top school in the city had plans to offer a course called "Writing in the Social Sciences," which no school in this study offered. Having flexible school schedules and being free to arrive or leave school during the day, these twelfth graders could pursue their interests outside of school. For example, Alex found himself thoroughly enjoying a martial arts class; Joe focused on finishing his volunteer work before the summer. Many of the students traveled to East or Southeast Asia; a few decided to binge-watch Korean dramas.

Summary

To the elite youths, transitioning to college was not just an educational milestone. It was a critical step that determined whether they could compete for future elite status. With such an understanding, the gaokao was more than an exam that determined students' college placement in China; the SAT had meaning beyond U.S. college applications. Instead, students strongly believed that high scores on these tests, which led to top university placement, were tickets to engaging in global elite status competition. Connecting top university attainment with long-term status benefits, elite students focused on competing against their peers for top university admissions and willingly buried themselves in textbooks and mock exams throughout high school. They competed against each other daily, aided by the publicization of their own and peers' test scores.

Elite parents, who gained their status through educational success, shared their children's mindset and were dedicated to their educational competition. A key step to grooming the future elites was to send them to top high schools whenever possible. These top high schools were aesthetically elitist and academically high achieving. They boasted successful track records of cultivating elite adolescents since their establishments as early as the Qing dynasty. Teachers in the schools took training students for top universities as their personal responsibilities. By preparing for college, elite students who enrolled in these schools immersed themselves in status competition within China and internationally. It is in these environments that the future elites in China were given the tools to successfully compete for elite status around the world.

2

Taking One's Place

"Yo, have you ever heard of study gods?" This was Xiaolong's opening line for our first conversation. It was almost dinnertime. I had been watching students pack up their books and walk out of the classroom, asking myself whether I should go home before it snowed. Xiaolong, who sat beside me, was also shoveling textbooks into the black backpack that hung on the back of his chair. I hesitantly responded, "No, I haven't." Surprised by my answer, he turned toward me and looked me in the eye. "What about studyholics? Not even underachievers or losers?" Those terms sounded Martian to me. With his right arm on the back of his chair, left elbow on his knee, Xiaolong smiled and slowly said, "Well then, let me tell you all about them."

WHEN I ENTERED the schools, I initially looked for signals of popularity or exclusion, which were the usual markers of elite status.[1] While there were certainly popular students and those in leadership positions, these traits did not seem to be as significant to the students as to myself. The popular students were at times sneered at by their peers; the attractive individuals did not enjoy special privileges. Even the classroom leaders, a position obtained through voting or assigned by teachers, could not exercise their power and were often ignored by their classmates. A few showed off their collection of luxury goods on social media, but they received few "likes" and failed to garner much attention. The athletes had trouble finding people to join them on the sports field, and the artistic students' talents were virtually invisible to others. Clearly, if status reproduction in the Chinese high schools was a card game, I had yet to learn how to play.[2] What, then, were the rules of the game? What were the characteristics that bestowed status among these elite, top-performing Chinese students?

As the students, including Xiaolong, explained later, the status system in their world is established on a single rule: test scores determine status. This guideline determines status across schools and is followed by students in both domestic and international departments. Believing that test scores determine college outcomes, students see test scores as the determinant of status and use them interchangeably with rankings and college placements.

In elite adolescent society, where the average is top performance by world standards, the gap between high and low test scores is understandably narrow. In the domestic departments, the high-status groups consist of students whose test scores are around the cutoff score for Peking and Tsinghua universities, or ranking within the top 3 percent in Beijing.[3] In the international departments, the cutoff is about 2200 on the SATs (1510 in the new system, or the 98th percentile in the United States), a magical number that students argue is necessary for admission into an Ivy League school. Low-status groups include all who regularly score below the school average. The precise average varies, but this information is easily calculated through the schools' practice of publicizing test scores. SAT scores are not publicized, but students make them de facto public information by sharing their results after each test. The average SAT scores are usually between 2100 and 2150 (1470–1490 in the new system, or 96th–97th percentile in the United States).[4]

While the rules of the status system are simple and straightforward, students nonetheless encounter a few hurdles. One is that their test scores often fluctuate. Paying close attention to peers' performance, students often told me that "nobody consistently gets low test scores," and even top performers "might slip [do poorly] on one or two tests." Considering the frequency of tests, changes in test scores pose a threat to the status system by introducing variations. The student-reported solution is to "ignore occasional changes" in individual performance and "focus on [one's] average." In other words, the issue of test score fluctuation arises from student observations through monitoring each other's performance. Ironically, they resolve this problem by following each other's test scores even more closely.

Another issue of using test scores to determine status is that students in top high schools often achieve comparably high test scores. Each year, half of the students in the top-performing classrooms at Pinnacle enter Peking University (PKU) or Tsinghua University (THU). Capital annually celebrates a list of students admitted to the Ivy League or other comparable institutions. Highland does not bother with the PKU and THU acceptance rates but instead concentrates on producing the top performer in the gaokao. Since it is impractical to have as many as half the students in one classroom occupying top status at the school,[5] the students adopt "ease" as a second criterion to subdivide the high- and low-status groups. The students define ease as the opposite of diligence, hard work, or effort. Student demonstrations of ease consist of whether and how much one participates in activities unrelated to college preparation, such as online gaming, playing sports, eating, and sleeping. In their minds, ease is a quantified measure of an individual's time use.[6] Among those with comparable test scores, the few with ease have higher status than those without. Yet despite rewarding status for ease, the students remain focused on test scores in their daily conversations. In this status system, ease is important only when many students receive comparable test scores.

The Chinese-Style Adolescent Status System
Study Gods (Xueshen)

Based on the rules that determined status positions, the elite students use test scores and ease to establish a fourfold typology in both the domestic and international departments (see Figure 2.1).[7] At the top of the hierarchy are the "study gods," *xueshen* in Mandarin. Students define study gods as "those who don't work too hard but whose test scores are very high." Study gods are rare and unevenly distributed across schools, cohorts, and departments. There are typically fewer than four or five study gods in any department cohort, and some even have none. Omega is known for having more study gods than other schools. Robert nicely summarized this impression: "Omega definitely has an assembly of study gods. You can tell by their incoming cohorts. They take the best and brightest in Beijing."

An example of a study god was Kaifeng, a soft-spoken boy of average height at Highland. Kaifeng was clearly a top performer and one of the few students whom teachers selected for the High School Olympiad. Kaifeng declined the invitation at first, thinking that the competition was not worth the effort. However, he had a change of heart in eleventh grade, a year after the others had begun to prepare for the competition. As he explained in our interview, "I realized that the Olympiad was a one-day competition, but the gaokao took two days. If I can be done in a day, I'll just go for the one-day option." In other words, he took the Olympiad route to minimize his effort in exam preparation. With just one year of preparation, Kaifeng landed in the top tier of the Olympiad and received guaranteed admission to PKU at the beginning of twelfth grade.

After Kaifeng signed the enrollment agreement with PKU, Highland teachers persuaded him to also take the gaokao to boost the school's average score. While Kaifeng was compelled to agree, he thought that the goal set by his teachers (above the school average) was too easy. Instead, he set for himself a more "appropriate" goal, which was to become the top performer in the subject of his expertise in Beijing. Kaifeng reported being motivated enough to work hard even after he had received the admission contract with PKU. He voluntarily stayed in school until ten thirty every night and studied alongside his classmates. However, his efforts seem to have stopped there. When other students studied in the classroom, Kaifeng played with a Rubik's cube or

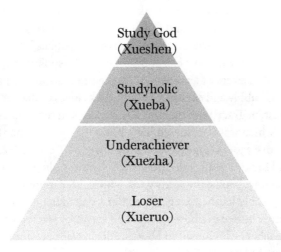

FIGURE 2.1. Status System in Top Chinese High Schools. The number
of students in each status group is not represented in this figure.
Generally, study gods and losers are the two smallest groups. There
are more studyholics than study gods and losers combined, and
underachievers are the largest among the four groups.

solved math problems that were beyond the scope of the exam, just for fun. In
our interview, Kaifeng admitted to watching "two or three episodes of anime"
or playing online games for "a little while" before going to bed around midnight. He also regularly discussed the anime and reported on his gaming to
classmates. A top performer but demonstrating minimal effort, Kaifeng qualified as a study god and the ideal representative of Highland for the school to
introduce to a foreign researcher.

Studyholics (Xueba)

The second group is the "studyholics" (*xueba*), a term meaning "study tyrant."
Studyholics are students who "work very hard and have high test scores."
Studyholics are more common than study gods, yet they nonetheless consti-
tute a small percentage of the student body. They often achieve test scores
comparable with those of the study gods but are excluded from the top status
group primarily for their lack of ease. Despite being placed below the study
gods, the studyholics have high status in school by virtue of their excellent test
scores. Studyholics are the driving force behind many top high schools' average exam scores and college admission outcomes. Tony, for example, argued
that Capital dramatically boosted their test scores and were comparable with

Omega in admission outcomes thanks to the hardworking studyholics: "Omega has more study gods, and Pinnacle has both study gods and studyholics. [But] Capital produces an abundance of studyholics."

Tracy, a skinny girl with short hair and large eyes who spoke at an accelerated pace, had all the markers of a studyholic in the international department at Capital. She was bubbly and energetic, but the dark circles under her eyes made her look exhausted. Tracy took the SAT a few times and received a combined score of 2200, which was considered high, but not as high as the study gods, who scored above 2300. Despite the slightly lower SAT score, Tracy later attended Johns Hopkins alongside friends who were study gods, a result she deemed satisfactory. Unlike the study gods, who exerted minimal effort studying, Tracy was visibly hardworking. Whenever I visited her classroom, she always had her nose buried in a book, worked on essays, or was memorizing SAT vocabulary. Teachers who hoped to boost student interest in course materials sometimes initiated casual discussion with students during class. However, Tracy rarely responded and instead pulled out other assignments in such instances. Tracy's classmates and teachers rarely saw her rest or take breaks. In our conversations, they often jokingly commented that she was a workaholic.

Toward the end of high school, the graduating cohort in the international departments had all received their placements. The students took things easy, and most no longer stayed up late to study. That is, most except for Tracy, who continued to study diligently. In the last two months of twelfth grade, Tracy often hid herself in vacant classrooms because her classmates were "too noisy" and distracted her from studying. After catching her studying alone a few times, I approached her in a vacant room and asked what she was working on. Tracy explained in a serious tone, "I'm taking AP courses. They take time and I need to do well so [Johns Hopkins] will still take me in. I'm also taking placement tests." I nodded. Tracy gestured for me to sit beside her and showed me a single-spaced, multiple-page essay on her laptop screen. "This is my dorm application. I wanted to stay in the most popular dorm on campus, so this application needs to be nearly perfect. I've been working on this for a few days already." She then signaled that I should leave her alone by fixing her eyes on her laptop. Having very high test scores and putting every minute into studying, to the point of spending days on something like a dorm application, Tracy was a solid studyholic.

Underachievers (Xuezha)

The third category is the "underachievers" (*xuezha*), literally meaning "study dregs." Underachievers are students "who don't work hard and don't have high test scores." Because the benchmark for low test scores is peers' average performance, a sizable proportion of the student body potentially count as having low status in school.[8] To subdivide these students, the underachievers are a group that places special emphasis on the notion of ease. Importantly, the underachievers demonstrate lighthearted mannerisms to stay afloat above the bottom category.

One of the underachievers in the international department was Robert, a tall, dark-skinned, charming boy at Capital. When I first met him in eleventh grade, Robert reported aiming to score "at least above 2100 no matter what" on the SAT. However, after taking the test five times in eleventh and twelfth grades, his combined score was only 2050, below average at Capital.[9] He later attended George Washington University along with two other classmates, the three of whom all scored below average in the international department. Robert also had unsatisfactory academic performance. In fact, his test scores in school were so low that, when I asked his teacher, Mrs. Hua, about his school performance, she responded with a frown. Robert also demonstrated his laissez-faire attitude toward studying in his economics assignment, which was to analyze the costs and benefits of an activity. Robert chose to assess "playing computer games." He reasoned that the cost of playing computer games was that "it took time away from studying." But because playing games "made me feel good," he concluded that the benefits outweighed the costs and "it was necessary to keep playing computer games" at the expense of college preparations.

Robert demonstrated a clear lack of effort in studying. I shadowed him in the spring of twelfth grade. Classes ended in the afternoon in spring semester, when all of them had received their college placements. After the bell sounded, quite a few students worked on assignments at their desks and showed no intention to leave. However, Robert packed up his books and dashed out the door almost immediately. I once called out and asked where he was going. Already in the hallway, he reluctantly came back and said hastily, "I'm going to Gongzhufen." He spoke so fast that I could not understand him. I asked again, "Huh?" He sighed and said again, "I'm going to Gongzhufen. Bye." He was already out of sight when I heard the last word. Some students who overheard looked toward the door with dismay. I was at a loss about what he meant. Seeing my confusion, a girl sitting near me explained, "He's going to do online gaming at an internet café in Gongzhufen." The others then outed Robert for his online gaming behavior. A boy loudly shouted across the room, "We even saw him walk out of an internet café on the weekend last semester!" Another quickly joined in by adding, "We were going to tutoring for the SAT, while he was doing online gaming!" Having below average performance, Robert did not have high status in school. Yet compared to his peers who had tutoring sessions after school or on the weekends, Robert was at ease. His lack of effort enabled him to remain an underachiever and cushioned him from falling to the absolute bottom of the hierarchy—the "losers."

Losers (Xueruo)

"Losers" (*xueruo*), or the "study weaklings," form the absolute bottom of the hierarchy in top high schools in China. Losers are students who "study very hard but still get low test scores." Like the underachievers, losers in the domestic department often attend prestigious universities in China (usually outside Beijing).[10] Those in the international department later go to public universities in the United States and Canada or private universities that are not in the Ivy League or other institutions with comparable levels of prestige. While many students claim to be underachievers, very few self-identify as losers, and most refrain from outing peers as losers. Despite the lack of self-identification, students frequently commented that "there are losers in every school." Students in the same schools also share a consensus of whom the losers are. To the untrained eye, losers are the hidden figures because they are usually loners. Yet they become instantly recognizable when one observes student interactions: losers often have one-sided conversations with peers, and students' laughter dies down in their presence.

Pan, a tall, slender girl with short hair in Pinnacle, was a rare individual who self-identified as a loser. I interviewed Pan at a local coffee shop a few days after the gaokao. At first, she nervously claimed that she "might have" been an underachiever. After I asked her to define the status groups, she immediately retracted that statement and instead identified as a loser. She moved to the edge of her chair and hunched over, leaning in close to explain in a low voice, "I counted as a loser. I was the type who never did well on tests. Sometimes I did, but mostly I didn't. . . . In twelfth grade, [I] spent a lot of time studying, all day and night." She then gave her schedule in detail, explaining that, "I got up at six o'clock; I went to bed at ten or eleven o'clock. Except for three meals a day, I was always studying in between." It later turned out that this was her schedule for weekends. On weekdays, she stayed for the entire night study period, which ended as late as ten o'clock, and went to bed around midnight. With these activities, Pan was visibly hardworking compared to her classmates.

Despite her diligence, Pan consistently performed below average on her test scores in the classroom. Pan later enrolled in a prestigious university outside of Beijing and majored in arts, which was one of the school's stronger concentrations. However, I noticed that she did not seem as thrilled as the others about her placement when I congratulated her in the summer. Her homeroom teacher later provided an explanation: although she technically attended her "top choice," her dream school was the arts program at THU, which had a cutoff score that was "out of her reach." As a result, she had to cave in and aim for a lower-ranked university. Even after choosing a university with lower cutoff scores, Pan still had a bumpy ride in the college process. She tried to go for the "exemplary student" award but failed. She also failed the university-administered additional tests, leaving her as one of the few students in the classroom with no gaokao bonus points. To be clear, Pan was not low-performing by national standards. With a gaokao score of 665, putting her in the top 5 percent in the city, she could have been a studyholic elsewhere. Yet being in a classroom where half the students were expected to enter PKU or THU, Pan was decidedly low-performing by comparison. Demonstrating high levels of effort but without high test scores, she became an example of a loser and had very low status at school.

Overall, the students share a consensus over the definitions and meaning of status groups. The fact that all students uphold the status system and its sorting criteria indicates that the system is considerably powerful. Furthermore, the terms are so common that they have become slang. When drawing attention to study gods' exceptionally high academic achievement, the students often said, "come worship the god(s)." Alternatively, "being a studyholic" indicates that one is studying. Students also said they were "underachieving" when they wanted to take a break from their test preparations. In instances where students decided to give up on something, they would jokingly shout out, "loser explosion (*ruobao*)!" followed by bursts of laughter.[11]

Navigating the High School Status System

The students have a clear understanding of the status system in school. Status is conferred upon the individual based on a combination of test scores and demonstrations of ease. They also understand that the rewards of test scores or ease differ by whether one possess the other, as well as the situations in which each trait is rewarded. However, winning in status competitions involves more than knowing and agreeing with the rules. The players must be actively involved and must strategize to win, which is to obtain high status, or to avoid losing, which is falling into low status. Armed with intricate knowledge of the rules, the elite students formulate strategies according to their positions in the hierarchy and choose tactics that best fit their interest in maximizing status school.

Study Gods and the Strategy of Priorities: Ashley "Just Had to Choose" Cambridge

Having both good test scores and high levels of ease, the study gods uphold the system by making decisions based on the highest rewarded characteristic. These students understand the significance of test scores and the rankings they generate. On top of that, they know that ease additionally grants top status on the condition that they achieve high test scores and are highly ranked. Based on the rules and their positions at the top, the study gods employ a strategy of priorities by first focusing on obtaining high rankings. They then demonstrate ease. The study gods subscribe to this strategy in many decisions, from test preparations to college applications.

An example of a study god who used the prioritizing strategy is Ashley Fong, a student at Pinnacle. Ashley was a bright-eyed girl with a mature demeanor that gave her the nickname "Auntie Fong." I met Ashley at the beginning of twelfth grade. With an SAT score of 2230 that placed her securely among the top in her cohort, Ashley applied for top-ranked institutions in the United States. However, being uncertain about her application outcomes, she later decided to apply to more schools. For most students, submitting additional applications means applying for lower-ranked institutions in the same country. However, this could not be further from what study gods have in mind.[12] In fact, Ashley's additional applications consisted of top British universities that required similarly high SAT scores and were comparably ranked with the American ones she had applied to.

I visited Ashley in the spring, a few days before the college decision deadline. As soon as Ashley saw me in the hallway, she quickly led me to a vacant meeting room to privately update me. To begin with, while most of the students received one or two offers, study god Ashley had received four: Cambridge, Carnegie Mellon, Northwestern, and Brandeis. She immediately turned down Brandeis, which was ranked lowest among the four. Nor was she fond of Northwestern. However, Ashley had trouble choosing between Cambridge and Carnegie Mellon. She described the excitement when she received the offer from Cambridge, but had been losing sleep after the offer from Carnegie Mellon arrived in her inbox the next week.

During the impromptu counseling session, the usually calm, reserved "Auntie Fong" looked nervous as she compared the two options. She sighed heavily, "I just don't know which to pick. I really, really like Cambridge, but I don't want to give up Carnegie Mellon." There were good reasons to attend either school. She explained, "Carnegie Mellon's computer science program fits my interest the most. Their alumni get good placements straight after graduation, and in the exact field that I want to go into!" She sighed again, "But Cambridge is my dream school. I've been in love with the campus ever since I visited a few years back." I congratulated her and suggested that she could discuss these offers with her parents and compare the pros and cons of each school. Ashley nodded and sighed again. She turned quiet, seemingly lost in thought.

In late spring, Ashley and I went on a half-day tour of Beijing together. As soon as we met near the subway station, Ashley told me that she had decided on Cambridge, where she would study economics. With a smile, she described the family discussion process and scoring system that they had created to compare the two universities. "I chose Cambridge because it's more prestigious, it's ranked higher than Carnegie Mellon. Cambridge will have more opportunities for me just by being there. My heart hurt for giving up Carnegie Mellon; I was sad for a few days. But I just had to choose Cambridge." She paused and said, "Judging by the application essays, Cambridge preferred students who had specialized, solid expertise in designated subjects more than American universities." She added confidently, "My high test scores would be an advantage [there]."

The importance of rankings became increasingly clear as Ashley's college application process unfolded. Armed with their high SAT scores, study gods such as Ashley considered applying only to top-ranked universities that required students to have very high SAT scores. Although a few of the study gods felt uncertain about their admission outcomes, none applied for lower-ranked universities that accepted students with lower SAT scores. Ashley's refusal to apply to universities ranked below Brandeis showed that, as a study god, she excluded herself from possibly moving down the status hierarchy and sought to maintain her high status by submitting additional applications only to universities that were of similar positions in global rankings. Ashley followed the same guideline and focused on maintaining her high status when deciding which offers to turn down. Using the same rules of the status system, she turned down Brandeis and the program at Northwestern because either the school or the program was insufficiently ranked. Additionally, her being torn between Carnegie Mellon and Cambridge was due to comparable institutional rankings. As she was interested in computer science, Carnegie Mellon's top-ranked computer science program enticed her to accept their offer. However, Cambridge ranked above Carnegie Mellon and was within the top five in the world. The decision between the two schools in fact reflected choosing between a top-ranked program in her field of interest versus a top-ranked university.

Ashley's final decision to choose Cambridge was partly due to considerations of status ("more prestigious," "higher ranked"). However, she also explained her decision by evoking notions of ease. Ashley offered two main reasons for Carnegie Mellon: fit of interest and the opportunity to realize her ambition to become a computer scientist upon graduation. Neither was related to ease, and the latter even entailed hard work. By comparison, she could not specify the "opportunities" that Cambridge offered and was ambivalent about economics, the program that accepted her. Yet her two reasons for Cambridge were its "beautiful campus" and perceived advantage over other students ("high test scores"). Both reasons pointed to having ease in college. Ashley is an example of a study god staying on top of the status system by strategically choosing her battles: she first fought for the highest-ranked institution and then chose the competitions in which she could demonstrate ease. In this example as in others, the combination of institutional rankings and personal ease outweighed personal interests and occupational fulfillment.

The story of Ashley's college decision did not end there. As part of having study god status, Ashley's college choice was public information at Pinnacle. News about her college decision traveled to the domestic department. A week after my excursion with Ashley, Fei, a study god in the domestic department, expressed approval of her choosing Cambridge over Carnegie Mellon. I had been chatting with Fei about his Tsinghua acceptance at his parents' apartment when he criticized the extreme significance of test scores in society. To my surprise, he suddenly brought up the example of Ashley.

Fei slouched in his wooden chair beside the desk. Frowning, he said, "I want to change the way society evaluates a person. Sometimes I think that getting low scores doesn't mean you can't do anything. I've been thinking about this. Test scores don't determine a person's quality. Like, Ashley, you know?" Fei paused to make sure that I knew Ashley. I nodded. Fei continued, "I personally think Ashley is outstanding. But if she didn't get into a top, world-class university and weren't amongst the top achievers, she'd be a nobody. Thank goodness she got into Cambridge. It's a matter of status. That Carnegie Mellon? It sure isn't well known. In China, Cambridge is much more persuasive [in signaling] your ability. Heck, why do we evaluate things like this?" He paused after criticizing himself, then quickly shook his head and concluded, "But I personally think doing economics in Cambridge is much better than computer science in Carnegie Mellon."

The epilogue of Fei's comment showed that other study gods in different departments shared the same concerns. Although Fei disliked the rules of the status system, he nonetheless upheld them. In Fei's analysis of Ashley's situation, he had not thought about taking into consideration individual interest or fit with a program but simply focused on rankings. Other study gods approved of Ashley's decision to prioritize university rankings and were content that she, like them, had played by the rules.

Studyholics and the Strategy of Studying: Dehong Stopped Taking Breaks

Being a high-status group in school, studyholics are primarily concerned with preventing downward mobility. Studyholics are not enthusiastic about claiming study god status, and most do not try to move up the status ladder. One reason is that students see the distinction between study gods and all other groups as an impassable gulf. More important, pursuing study god status means demonstrating ease. Yet decreasing studying time increases the chances of having lower test scores, which puts them at risk of falling into the under-achiever group. A studyholic becoming an underachiever is more than simply taking a step down the hierarchy. Rather, it means dropping from high to low status. Furthermore, studyholics face heightening levels of status threats because the average amount of effort among the student body gradually increases as college application deadlines and the gaokao draw near.

The studyholics respond to threats of downward mobility with what they habitually do best—studying. Taken in this light, studyholics' lack of ease is not simply a group characteristic but also a strategy that they employ to stay on top. The strategy of studying, however, unintentionally makes the study-holics vulnerable to crashing into loser status if their test scores drop. Study-holics who put in more effort face an increased possibility of becoming losers, which in turn would lead to even more studying. Stuck in the vicious cycle between effort and vulnerability, the studyholics often have an utter lack of ease toward the end of high school.

Dehong offers a typical example of the studyholics' studying strategy to maintain high status. Dehong was a sturdy boy at Capital who decided to go for studyholic status in eleventh grade. In his own words, his decision to work hard was "a gamble" because he could have become a loser if his test scores never improved. Luckily they did, and Dehong became a studyholic in school around the beginning of twelfth grade. Dehong steadily increased his study-ing. In tenth grade, he read manga during break time to relax. Reading manga, however, was unhelpful for the gaokao. In eleventh grade, Dehong studied over breaks and limited his relaxation time to thirty minutes after dinner. Instead of reading manga, he watched thirty minutes of Hollywood movies, which helped him prepare for the listening section of the English subject in the gaokao.[13] By the second semester of twelfth grade, Dehong studied to the point that he barely took any breaks at all. When he wanted to take a break from studying, he would do a few minutes of pushups at the end of the hall-way with an open textbook in front of him. In his words, doing pushups served the purpose "to increase my physical strength for the gaokao." But because "everyone else is studying in the classroom, I've got no time to spare." He had to study at the same time so the few minutes of pushup breaks were not "wasted."

Dehong's effort did not stop there. As the gaokao approached, he stopped doing pushups altogether. He walked at a rushed pace in school and barely had time to talk to anyone. Two weeks before the gaokao, I sat in a classroom with a few students, waiting for night studies to start. Dehong rushed in to pick up a notebook from a friend. Seeing me inside, he gestured to me with a nod and turned away. Before he exited the room, I shouted his name and loudly asked if he was getting better test scores given his intense schedule.

"No, heck no!" Dehong quickly walked back toward me, shaking his head with widened eyes. He then inhaled and explained in a low voice, "I know where I'm at. There are about three hundred people in Beijing between me and the PKU admission cutoff. There's no way I can outcompete three hundred more people. I really cannot. Other people are picking things up, and I don't want to lose out. I'm doing my best; there's seriously no way that I can do better. I'd be lucky if I stayed where I'm at right now and not move down." He then quickly walked out.

The studyholics like Dehong are status anxious. Feeling threatened by increased competition toward the end of high school ("people are picking things up"), the studyholics study as hard as they can and as much as they can ("I'm doing my best"). The strategy of increased studying seems counterintuitive. The studyholics could have attempted to move into study god status by studying in secret. Dehong could have gone somewhere secluded to do pushups, but he did so in the hallway and under the public gaze. This is because he perceived few chances of moving to the top of the status system ("I really cannot"). Instead of aiming for top status in school, the studyholics are primarily concerned about potential downward mobility ("lucky to stay where I'm at and not move down"). They are unconcerned about being separated from the study gods who are always at ease, and instead focus on being distinguished from the underachievers or losers.

Dehong was not the only studyholic caught in a spiral of increased study time and increased risk of losing status. Many other studyholics share the same worry and often take even more drastic measures. For example, Ziyi, a studyholic girl at Capital who later went to Tsinghua University, pulled two or three all-nighters before each mock exam in twelfth grade. Tracy, another studyholic in the international department, studied all day long until peers considered her a workaholic and later had an anxiety attack before the college application deadline. Together, these examples show that the studyholics' strategy of studying carries consequences, including physical and emotional tolls. However, they willingly deny themselves breaks, suffer from a lack of sleep, and endure anxiety attacks for the sake of sustaining their high status and gaining admission to a top university. When competing for status in high school, the studyholics play by the rules and seek to stay on the winning side at all costs.

Underachievers and the Swan Strategy: Jiaqi's Daily Show

The underachievers are like a bevy of swans. They gracefully glide together on campus but furiously paddle under the water. The underachievers often see the swan strategy as necessary to maintain their positions in school. Like the studyholics, the underachievers do not try to obtain the top status in school.

In fact, they mostly do not even try to have high status but are primarily concerned with not falling into the bottom category. Being only one step above the losers, the underachievers are aware of the possible downward mobility and strategize with the goal to prevent themselves from utterly losing in status competitions. This is done carefully by consistently demonstrating the key characteristic that distinguishes them from the losers—ease.

The underachievers are some of the most strategy-conscious players. One among them is Jiaqi, a sturdy boy with spikey hair and black-rimmed glasses at Capital. Jiaqi had frequently skipped night studies since the end of eleventh grade. He did not go to school on the weekends even at the height of exam pressure, when his peers voluntarily stayed at school until late every night. In twelfth grade, I often saw Jiaqi skimming through car magazines while other students studied in the same classroom. The reason was, as he put it, "Since I'm not going to beat [outperform] those high-achieving kids whether I study or not, I'm just not gonna study." I asked why he hadn't consider working harder to get higher test scores and improve his rankings. He shrugged and grinned mischievously, "No reason. I thought about it. I just stopped working hard in the end."

Although Jiaqi was rarely seen working in school, he secretly studied and with considerable effort. He asked me to practice English with him and go through his short essays (tested on the gaokao) in empty classrooms multiple times. His mother, Mrs. Xu, also reported that Jiaqi spent his weekends studying at his desk at home, which I later observed. I conducted a home observation with his family on a Sunday afternoon. Jiaqi picked me up at the bus station, and we headed straight to his home. Mrs. Xu greeted me and ordered Jiaqi to give me a tour of the apartment. I noticed that he had an open textbook on his desk, suggesting that he had been studying before we met. The tour ended in three minutes, and he told me that he was going to do work. I sat in a corner of the living room taking notes; Jiaqi was at his desk with his bedroom door open. Throughout the five hours I was there, Jiaqi left his room twice for a total of less than five minutes: once to go to the bathroom and another to fetch a glass of water from the kitchen. Jiaqi sat at his desk for the entire afternoon. He did not move, did not eat, and did not talk to anyone. The apartment was silent except for the sounds of Mrs. Xu chopping Chinese cabbage in the kitchen and Jiaqi flipping pages of his textbook. I wandered into the kitchen and chatted with Mrs. Xu as she made dinner, during which she informed me that Jiaqi had always studied at his desk all afternoon over the weekends.

Underachievers such as Jiaqi demonstrate ease under the public gaze at school but spend much time and effort studying alone. The secrecy of their efforts implies that they try to stay in the underachiever group and are careful not to fall into the loser group. The swan strategy also shows that the underachievers are an important group and play by the rules. Being perhaps the largest group on campus, the underachievers who do not care about test scores could challenge the rules of the status system. At the very least, they could threaten the stability by setting up alternative rules that bestow status.[14] However, rather than truly being at ease about test scores and test-based competition, they only pretend. Their carefree attitude serves as camouflage to hide their true intentions, and the swan strategy is effective because they wholeheartedly participate in status competition according to the preexisting rules. Consequently, as the underachievers maintain a carefree image, they support the status system. By paddling under water to keep themselves afloat, they sustain a system that drowns those at the bottom.

Losers and the Strategy of Looking Ahead: Mark Goes to Canada

Unlike the other groups, losers have few options in navigating the status system in school. Losers are often individuals who fail to pursue studyholic or underachiever status. Being stuck at the bottom, some losers hope to change their status by refusing to identify as one. The refusal approach often backfires. For one, the lack of self-identification does not prevent other students from labeling them as losers. Failure to demonstrate expected behavior as losers also leads to ridicule and mockery that hold the reluctant losers in their place. Losers who accept their position in the school status system thus employ a future-oriented strategy. They give up on status competition in high school and commit to early preparation for the next round of competition.

Mark was a tall, cheerful boy in Capital who did not have high test scores. He did not identify as a loser, but he once admitted that he fit the definition. Mark worked hard to prepare for the SAT and took the test five times. Despite his hard work, his combined score of 2180 was below average at his school, and he later attended the University of British Columbia. At first glance, Mark employed a questionable strategy. Specifically, he often pretended that he was hardworking when he was not. On a sunny Friday afternoon, I sat in the middle row beside the window in Mark's eleventh grade classroom. Students were at their desks waiting for the teacher to start class. Mark, who sat in the front corner of the room, suddenly picked up his seventeen-inch black laptop and slid into the empty seat next to mine. Surprised, I looked toward him and saw that he was playing games on his laptop. I must have frowned as I asked him, "What are you doing?" Before he could answer, the teacher walked into the room and announced that class had begun. Mark quickly put on his headphones. With his eyes still glued to the screen, he leaned over toward me and whispered, "I'm not in this class. But just so you know, I'm sitting beside you so that they'll think I'm studying when I'm not. See, you're my cover-up." He proudly squinted at me and went back to gaming.

Mark's decision to mask ease with effort was counterintuitive. Playing games counted as demonstrating ease. If he had let other students know that he was at ease, he could have been upwardly mobile and become an underachiever. But instead he concealed ease with effort. Mark routinely missed these golden opportunities to ascend to underachiever status and stayed as a loser toward the end of high school. One possible explanation for Mark's behavior could have been failure to understand the status hierarchy. However, Mark was one of the students who explained to me clearly the rules of the system. He knew what determined status and shared the same understanding of which students belonged to the four status groups. Another possibility is that Mark wanted to avoid the teacher's wrath for not paying attention to class. Yet he did not take the class ("I'm not in this class") and had no need to participate. Alternatively, Mark might have pretended to be studying to not disturb the lecture. However, his violent mouse clicking evidently bothered the girl beside him, as she periodically shot glances of annoyance at him. A more likely explanation was that Mark had simply given up on moving out of loser status. In this incident and others, he did not care to grasp the opportunity for upward mobility because he accepted his bottom position. Instead of demonstrating ease, he habitually maintained the studious image of a loser and did not strategize for upward mobility.

Rather than pursuing higher status, losers who acknowledge their status instead approach the system by planning for the next round of competition. Unlike his apparent lack of strategy in high school status, Mark consciously planned his college placement with an eye toward status competition. He decided to go to Canada instead of the United States, where almost all his high school peers went. I met up with Mark during his trip to Philadelphia two years after high school. As we talked about his days at Capital, Mark told me that he had been "crushed" by his consistently low SAT scores in high school, and he ended up applying only to universities in Canada. I asked him what led to this decision.

"That's because I couldn't compete with all those study gods. They were applying for places like Cornell or Penn, with SATs above the 2300s." Mark frowned, "I had no chance. I wouldn't have made it to a top university in the U.S. But I could still go to a top university in Canada because Canadian universities were easier to get into. Sure, it's Canada and not the U.S., but hey." He paused and then loudly concluded, "Some Canadian universities are also among the top-ranked in the world!"

This example shows that losers are not without strategy in navigating high school life. Yet while the other groups focus on pursuing status during high school, the losers prepare for future competition. Mark's strategy of looking ahead led him to apply to Canadian universities. This decision was future-oriented in two ways. First, he distanced himself from status competition in high school, which he perceived as a hopeless battle ("I couldn't compete with all those study gods"). Canadian universities were not on the radar of study gods and studyholics. Since these high performers paid little to no attention to the rankings of Canadian institutions, Mark avoided direct comparison and withdrew early from the competition. Second, Mark planned for a fresh start after high school. In his calculation, the students who outcompeted him would have gone to other universities in the United States. By turning to Canada, he would nonetheless attend a top university ("top-ranked in the world"). Most importantly, he would face a new and hopefully less-competitive pool of rivals, thus increasing his chances of having high status in college.[15] In other words, the losers accept the fact that they already lost in the fight. Being few in number, they do not try to change the rules, nor do they have the power to do so. They simply strategize for a fresh start in the next round. Yet by anticipating that the next round will operate on the same set of rules, they not only submit to the rules of status competition but also sustain them.

Justifying the Status System

In most social groups, status is determined by one's family background, ethnicity, work schedule, school resources, or a combination thereof.[16] By comparison, the elite students in this study commonly emphasize test scores. To justify the status system, they explain why some of them consistently outperform others and why others consistently fail to improve their test scores despite observed effort. Yet explaining variation in test scores can be difficult in such a homogenous group. The students come from comparably affluent families in Beijing. They also share identical schedules in school and spend as much as fifteen hours together each day. Using the card game metaphor, the elite students perceive each other as having comparable cards. Because the statistically salient factors such as effort and family background fail to explain variations in test scores, these students disregard the commonly attributed factors and instead subscribe to the idea that test scores reflect innate ability.

The Innate Ability Argument

The innate ability explanation argues that study gods are innately superior and losers are innately inferior. While this argument is politically incorrect and goes against the narrative of meritocracy in the Chinese Communist Party, elite students across status groups generally embrace this explanation and uniformly draw on it to justify the status system in school.[17] Mingjia, a high performer at Pinnacle who later went to Tsinghua University, was one of the students who supported this argument in our interview. I asked Mingjia what determined the status system, starting with the losers. However, she instead brought up the study gods and emphasized the importance of innate ability in differentiating status groups:

"What do you think about [the losers]?" I asked.

"I feel that effort is somewhat of a related factor, but I think it's probably genes," Mingjia responded in a matter-of-fact tone.

Hearing that, I raised my voice and repeated, "Genes?"

Mingjia immediately toned down her claim by saying, "Maybe not all because of genes. It's related to thinking habits, living habits."

I quickly quieted myself and asked her to elaborate. Mingjia answered, "Just, I think, there are people who are born smarter. Maybe they had better development in school or they had parents who educated them better. I have no idea how they became like that. Many people, they just have the ability to think."

In this example and others, students attribute status to innate abilities. By freely switching between examples of losers and study gods, Mingjia's response shows that the innate ability argument justifies the entire status system because it accounts for outcomes from top to bottom. Furthermore, Mingjia was insistent on the explanation despite audience disagreement, as shown by my bewilderment toward the idea that losers were born intellectually weaker ("it's probably genes"). In response to my reaction, she quickly toned down the argument by mentioning the social factors (habits, school, and family) that a socialist would agree with. Yet the shift in direction was short-lived. Mingjia returned to her initial argument and attributed status to innate ability ("born smarter," "the ability to think") in the very next sentence. Considering that Mingjia was high-performing, one might think that the high performers are motivated to justify their high status by arguing for superior innate ability. While this might be partially true, Mingjia made clear in our interview that she was nowhere close to becoming a study god and that she was at most a studyholic. This suggests that students such as Mingjia consider themselves to be innately inferior to the top performers in school.

Effort Plays No Role

Students insisting on the innate ability argument is related to their inability to formulate other possibilities. Seeing that students routinely failed to adopt alternative explanations, I presented alternative hypotheses in later conversations but was rebuked each time. Jianmin, a loser at Pinnacle, was a strong defender of the innate ability explanation despite his status in school. I had lunch with Jianmin in summer after the gaokao, when we talked about test scores and college plans. I asked him why study gods had good test scores.

Jianmin explained without hesitation, "Study gods are like, you're studying hard, but not this person. He might be online gaming or something. He has superior ability. [You] can't do anything about it, can't explain it. It's just like that, it's [being] very smart."

I suggested that effort was also key to gaining test success, but Jianmin sneered at my argument. He leaned toward the table. Putting both hands on the wooden table, he chuckled and said, "If effort were equivalent to [test] success, then success would be way too easy. If effort meant success, then I could just work hard. If everyone worked hard, then everyone would succeed. But that's not possible. So, there's no way effort led to success. There are a lot of other things, such as luck." He took a sip of tea and added, "And IQ, or intelligence."

Jianmin was among the many others who focus on innate qualities and reject other explanations, including time management, study habits, and past experiences.[18] Like Mingjia, Jianmin strongly supported the innate ability argument ("superb ability," "luck," "IQ, or intelligence"). Furthermore, Jianmin refuted my alternative hypothesis that emphasized hard work ("not possible") and offered himself as an example to illustrate the nature of the system. Conversations like these show that the losers are familiar with the rules that govern the hierarchy. They acknowledge that they have low status given the classification criteria and simply accept their low status.

Importantly, Jianmin's statement demonstrates the degree to which low-status students defend and justify the system. One possible reason for the low performers supporting the system is that they need to explain their relative low performance in a direct manner. By attributing low test scores to uncontrollable factors, namely, innate ability, these students avoid taking responsibility for their poor performance in school. It is also important to note that although the students share the same vocabulary and describe study gods as "smart" or having "superb brainpower," innate ability remains an abstract concept in these discussions. The students do not directly measure innate ability, nor do they have evidence to directly support this argument. They infer peers' innate ability from test scores and demonstrated effort. However, by treating this unobservable and unmeasurable trait as the only plausible explanation for variation in peer performance, the students create an unsurpassable gulf between the study gods and the others. As the students justify the system, study gods become an elevated group that is entirely distinguished from the rest. Consequently, the study gods became "gods" in school.

Innate Disability, the Flip Side of Innate Ability

Students believed that gods are "born" talented and distinguished from the rest. Following the same logic, the losers are "born" untalented. One among the students who bluntly expressed the idea that losers were "inferior" to the rest was Xiaolong, an eleventh grader at Capital. I sat beside Xiaolong in one of my observations. At the end of the daylong observation, he suddenly struck up a conversation by asking if I knew about the four status groups. He then explained the groups to me and revealed that he was an underachiever. At the time I had not yet understood the system and how it shaped students' daily lives. I asked him whether he had considered working hard in his studies to improve his test scores. In other words, I was challenging him to pursue high status and become a studyholic.

Xiaolong drew in a breath and looked at me in disbelief. He snapped at me with a furious frown, "I'm not a loser! Hell no! Studying that hard and still not getting good test scores means there's something wrong with that person's brain. It's just bad. It's always better to be an underachiever than a loser. I'm an underachiever. See, I don't study that much, that's why I don't do well. It's not because I'm stupid!"

Students draw a clear distinction between the losers and all others. In many instances, students hint that the loser is a category to be avoided at all cost. Such a distinction is especially important to underachievers such as Xiaolong. When faced with the question of status mobility, he instinctively marked boundaries by harshly criticizing the losers for lack of intellect ("something wrong with his/her brain," "stupid"). While the underachievers likely do so to keep themselves afloat, even the study gods and studyholics bash the losers. In my observations, the students frequently made degrading remarks and verbally abused the losers.

In an interview, I asked Tony, a study god at Capital, what he thought about the losers. Tony answered in a matter-of-fact tone, "They're retarded." As if he had fully answered the question, he then looked at me and waited for the next question. In another observation, I asked Joe, an above-average performer at Pinnacle, what he thought about the losers. Without hesitation, Joe replied bluntly, "[They've] got problems with their brains." An exception was Ashley, a study god who chose alternative terminology to explain losers' performance. In Ashley's words, the losers "didn't find the [right] way, or they had psychological issues." However, while this answer potentially pointed to behavioral and psychological factors, Ashley returned to the innate ability argument by adding, "Actually, smartness is a way of studying." Together, these examples show that students commonly attribute loser status to innate disability ("problem with their brains," "retarded").[19] With this narrative, losers are distinguished from the rest not simply because they have the lowest status in the hierarchy; their low status is justified as they are "innately inferior" to the other students.

A Fatalistic View of Status Outcomes

Students are so fearful of falling down the status ladder that they often refuse to pursue higher status. However, some underachievers in every cohort rise to high status by hard work, and underachievers certainly have witnessed others who tried and succeeded in becoming studyholics. Despite the cases of mobility around them, the students often express that status outcomes are unchangeable and beyond individual control. The innate ability argument creates among the students a sense of powerlessness that prompts them to take a stoic approach in understanding status outcomes in school. The students frequently attribute status outcomes to fate. In an earlier example, Jianmin implied that test scores were determined by destiny when he claimed that study gods were unchallengeable ("you can't do anything about it"). Similarly, Jiaqi and other students expressed similar feelings. I overheard Jiaqi comment on a loser's poor performance during break to a few friends. I joined in the discussion and asked if the loser under discussion could do anything to improve his situation. Jiaqi paused and tilted his head, appearing to be deep in thought. After a short while, he sighed heavily, waved his right hand, and said to me calmly, "It's a problem of IQ. They study all day long but there's no effect. These people are hopeless." Jiaqi concluded that the losers were destined to be losers ("hopeless"), with no hope of moving up the status ladder in school.

Many students talked about peers being "destined" to low status in a lighthearted manner. However, Shuhua, an athletic girl at Capital with above-average academic performance, was not one of them. When asked about the losers, Shuhua turned the casual conversation into a serious discussion and reported that she had been pondering status outcomes throughout high school. On a sunny afternoon after the gaokao, I went skating with Shuhua at a skating rink. When we sat down to take off our skates, I asked how her classmates did on the gaokao. Shuhua responded by sharing information on the study gods and studyholics who did well, and then the names of underachievers and losers who did poorly. She expressed pity for the latter group, who would be heading to provincial universities. She sighed, "It's sad, but it was expected." I asked her what these students could have done to improve their test scores or change their situations.

Shuhua straightened her back and shared her thoughts earnestly. "Seriously, I've been thinking about this question for quite some time. Why some people just don't do well on tests, no matter how hard they tried." She shook her head and said sympathetically, "I realized that it's all fate. There's a certain degree of inevitability. Right? If you think about it, it really is like that. There's nothing you can do about it. Nothing at all."

Like the others, Shuhua embraced the perception that status is determined by fate. Shuhua was among the few who admitted to thinking about the status system, yet she could not think of any other justification. Her narrative represented that of an apathetic fatalist to a larger degree than those of her peers. Although she put considerable thought into delineating the determinants of test scores, she arrived at the same conclusion as the others ("nothing you can do"). This response also points out that students in this study adopt the apparently illogical innate ability argument in an attempt to rationalize observed differences in test scores. The students thus attribute status outcomes to an unobserved characteristic, which they call "innate ability," and defend the system regardless of their positions. In doing so, they essentialize innate ability, reject the potential significance of effort, and develop a fatalistic view of their positions in the status system.

Beyond High School: Change and Continuity

For these elite Chinese students, life after graduation had been understandably different from high school. University was worlds apart from what they had been used to. Test scores and GPA were off limits from public view. They no longer shared identical schedules with schoolmates, and the pool of competition expanded considerably. The students who stayed in China found themselves facing top performers from all over the country; those who left China were against top performers from around the world. While some of the new encounters were like external shocks, the students were able to apply their understandings and strategies for status competition.

"Rural Kids Are Crazy": Temporal Changes to the Game in China

The elite students who were accepted to Peking and Tsinghua universities faced competitors from around the country. At first, these students upheld the status system and believed that the top performers were innately superior. Jun, a study god at Capital, said he had experienced "IQ suppression" by college classmates who outperformed him. Like Jun, other students expressed the same perceptions during their first year in college. For example, Kaifeng, the study god at Highland, became an above-average student at Peking University. He shook his head when asked about the high performers in his department. He let out a sigh and said those people were "true great gods, they're just too smart. They don't seem to be working at all, but you simply have no way to keep up with them. It's like they're not even in our dimension."

It soon became clear that the elite students were systematically losing in academic competitions against students from populous provinces.[20] Test-based competition became so intense and their efforts so in vain that many stopped competing for top status. Allowing themselves to have a shot at winning, the elite students developed alternative rules to obtain high status in college. Study gods and losers remained at the two ends of the hierarchy, but they degraded the studyholics to below the underachievers for reasons of ease.

In other words, instead of purely focusing on test scores, they elevated the importance of ease until it had equal importance with test scores.

Shuhua, who later went to Fudan University, was one of the elite students who participated in changing the rules for student status. I visited Shuhua regularly in college. In the fall of freshman year, she told me over snacks at the student cafeteria that university was reminiscent of high school. The only difference was that "the studyholics [in Fudan] were super hardworking," even more so than the studyholics back in high school. This showed that Shuhua, like the others, remained committed to the same status competition in college. However, as college life progressed, many study gods and studyholics had difficulty keeping up with their extremely hardworking peers, who mostly hailed from rural China. Simultaneously, the students' narrative about the status system began to change. I visited Shuhua around the end of her sophomore year. We had dinner at a restaurant, where she complained about the studyholics for the first time. She acknowledged that Beijing students like herself were low-performing but nonetheless argued that they were "better" than the studyholics.

"I realized that urban kids are usually well rounded. There's more to life than studying, right?" Shuhua proudly announced. "Students from rural, populous provinces are more competitive. All of them study like this." Shuhua tightened both fists and placed her wrists at the edge of the table, lowered her head, and pretended to be reading. Two seconds later, she sat up and continued, "We're also like this. But they don't move at all when they study. Those kids from like Jiangsu, Shandong, Henan, they're always studyholicking!"

Shuhua then used herself as a comparison to the studyholics. "I was in line for a health checkup, playing plants versus zombies on my phone." She reemphasized, "It was totally fine. There was nothing else to do. But my classmate beside me said," Shuhua mimicked the classmate's voice and said in a high-pitched voice, "'Oh, I wish I could play too, but I don't have time.'"

I asked, "What was she doing in line?"

"Studying." Shuhua rolled her eyes and replied with a fake smile. She then raised her voice, almost shouting across the table, "Those kids are crazy! Yeah, my grades aren't as good as theirs. I do the course requirements and maybe a paper that's extra reading. But they would read entire books for supplementary info! Oh my God!"

This example and others showed that, by end of their sophomore year, the domestically bound who stayed in China found themselves losing to the point where they temporarily changed the rules that governed status in college. Instead of focusing on test scores as usual, Shuhua claimed that ease, or well-roundedness, was key ("There's more to life than studying"). This led to the elite students fundamentally altering the status regarding studyholics. While the students used identical definitions of studyholics, namely hard work and high test scores, the studyholics as a group had anything but high status in college. The elite students, who were predominantly underachievers in college, mocked the studyholics for their study habits (mimicking their postures). They criticized the studyholics for their lack of well-roundedness, which signaled ease, something that would not have happened in high school. The students showed signs of disdain when talking about the studyholics (mimicking voices, rolling her eyes, fake smile, "oh my god"), which was a sharp contrast to what I had observed earlier. Finally, the fact that the elite students across schools were able to change the rules of the status system signaled that the studyholics in college seemed powerless to defend their positions.[21]

While the elite students changed the status system, such change was temporary. After college, they returned to the rules with which they were familiar. I visited Lili, a studyholic while at Capital, at Peking University in the winter of her sophomore year. Like Jun and Kaifeng, Lili was not high-performing at Peking University. As with Shuhua, Lili believed that Beijingers knew how to "have fun" in college and were thus superior to the rural, hardworking studyholics who "only knew how to study." As part of "having fun," which was essentially having ease, she bought a scooter to travel around the city and often hung out with friends at strip malls near campus. She shrugged over her slightly below-average grades in her department and spent more time with her boyfriend than studying. With this performance, Lili also used ease to elevate the status of the below-average Beijingers above the studyholics in college.

Lili flew to New York to start her master's program a month after she graduated from PKU. I met her a few days after she landed. As Lili happily showed me around her dorm room, she told me that she planned to "work hard to keep up" in her program. Pointing to a locked room beside her bedroom, she said, "That's my roommate's room. I moved in two days ago, but still haven't seen her. My other roommate says she's a PhD student who's always working in her lab." Smilingly, she added, "She's a studyholic for sure. I'll look up to that." An hour later, Tony and Daniel, who were high school friends with Lili and who interned in Manhattan that summer, joined us to show Lili around the area. As we walked toward the subway station, Daniel talked about his PhD program and mentioned doing well on the GRE.

"How much did you get on the GRE?" I asked.

Lili, who was about ten feet in front of Daniel and me, immediately turned her head and looked at us. She and Tony slowed down until they were beside us, the four of us forming a line that blocked the sidewalk. Daniel said in a matter-of-fact tone, "I got 336." Upon hearing that, Lili took in a breath and stared at him with widened eyes for a split second but then quickly looked aside. Seeing her dramatic reaction, I asked Lili how she had done on the GRE. She gave us an awkward smile and answered in a very small voice, "I got 332;

336 is really high." Lili lowered her head. She avoided eye contact with the three of us and remained silent until Tony and I tried to lighten the mood by switching topics.

Less than two months after college graduation, Lili already reverted to the original rules she abided by in high school. She no longer cared for the guideline she insisted on in college, which emphasized ease above test scores, and went back to assigning higher status to the studyholics than the underachievers. Specifically, she made plans to regain her status as a studyholic in grad school. This involved making her roommate (whom she had not yet met) a studyholic role model. Lili not only seemed determined to become a studyholic, but she also demonstrated a lack of ease. Her reaction upon hearing the word "GRE" showed that she was instinctively competitive about test scores (looking back and slowing down). Lili was visibly tense when knowing that a friend received high marks on the GRE (taking in a breath, staring, looking aside, awkward smiles). She also showed signs of embarrassment after revealing that she did not do as well compared to Daniel (avoiding eye contact, becoming silent). Instead of putting on a carefree attitude and claiming that ease was most important, which was what she had done in college, Lili picked up her old habits of being extremely anxious and competitive over test scores.[22]

Just as Lili started a new chapter in graduate school from the studyholic perspective, Xiaolong planned for the next stage after graduation using the underachiever approach. Xiaolong had been mindful of distinguishing himself from the losers back in high school. He later went to a provincial university and remained an underachiever there. I met up with Xiaolong in 2019, in the spring semester of his fifth year in college. The boy who had been the same height as me was now a foot taller but remained as thin as he had been in high school. He took me around campus and said that he wanted to do another year of college to prepare for graduate school in Tokyo. I was surprised since he was among the few who had not thought about going abroad.

"It's not worth it to compete for grad school in China," Xiaolong chuckled. "There are only a few good universities, and people study like crazy for the graduate school exam. It's too hard to get in; I'll never be able to compete with those people." He then said excitedly, "Japan is a better choice! Their universities are acceptably ranked in the world, and they have so few admission requirements!"

I asked how he planned to realize this goal. He answered confidently, "The main thing that's a bit hard is passing the language exam. I'll spend a year studying Japanese. I'll work hard, probably harder than I ever have, to learn the language within a year."

I thought this was a memorable moment in which a boy who had been primarily concerned with demonstrating ease decided to work "harder than ever." However, before I had a chance to respond, Xiaolong immediately toned down his claim. "Maybe not *that* hard. I'll read manga to learn Japanese." He smiled broadly, showing his teeth. "You know me. I don't work hard. I haven't in high school; I still don't. I know I could do better if I did, but I won't. I should've tried to develop the habit of hard work back then. Well, too late now!" He shrugged, "I want to avoid the intense competition [for graduate school] in China. It's just too much work."

Xiaolong was one of the few students who stayed in the same status group in high school and in college. He knew that putting in effort would result in better outcomes and that focusing on demonstrating ease had detrimental effects on his future. Yet he attributed his habit of demonstrating ease to status consistency since high school and decided that the habit had become un-changeable ("too late now," "I won't"). By expecting low test scores and em-phasizing ease, Xiaolong continued to compete for status reproduction using an underachiever approach. In fact, his approach of risk avoidance ran parallel to his behavior in high school. Five years ago, twelfth grader Xiaolong con-sciously demonstrated ease by watching manga during night studies at the expense of having low gaokao scores. In 2019, Xiaolong decided to learn Japa-nese by reading manga, at the expense of having low language exam scores.

"Americans Are Dumb": Playing the Same Game in the United States

Whereas those staying in the country anticipated playing the same set of rules but did not, the internationally bound students often did not know quite what to anticipate in Western countries. Before moving into their dorms, the stu-dents thought they would participate in escalated levels of competition on campus. They imagined a bleak situation in which they would be new players facing experienced players who were naturally advantaged. They were anxious to learn the new set of rules as soon as they arrived, and many were prepared to fight an uphill battle. To the students' surprise, they often found the status system the same as the one they had in high school. The threatening feeling from international students and foreign language disappeared in a matter of months, which was all they needed to become comfortable with the new environment.

Robert most clearly described the practice of using the same hierarchy in universities from the West Coast to the East Coast. I visited Robert in the summer after graduation, before he left for graduate school. We sat at his apart-ment to catch up and talked about the study gods and studyholics back in high school. I asked him if things had been different in college. Robert thought for a moment and said hesitantly, "I don't know of any study god here [at George

Washington]." He then quickly added, "But students who get good grades are respected, and it's even better if you have fun getting them." In Robert's words, the determinants for status were identical to those in high school. The students who had good grades were respected and had high status, and those who achieved high grades with ease were particularly respected ("better if you have fun getting them"). Robert saw himself and his peers participating in the same competition with a different set of players, with no one clearly in the lead of having top status.

Other students who studied in the United States shared Robert's perception. They not only upheld the rules that governed status allocation but continued to use the innate ability argument to explain these outcomes. Stacey, an average student at Capital, visited me in Philadelphia in the second semester of her freshman year at Claremont McKenna. I picked her up at the train station. Much had changed since she had left Beijing. She grew her shoulder-length hair long and no longer had braces. Importantly, she was no longer the average student at Capital but was among the top students in college. I asked how she had been as we walked on the concrete sidewalk toward the Penn campus.

"Oh, you need to hear this." She said enthusiastically. "When I just got here, I was a bit worried, you know? Everything's in English, I was worried about whether I could keep up."

I nodded, thinking to myself that this was going to be a conversation about her improvement in English. I was wrong, as our chat took a radical turn. "But then, I found out that Americans are dumb!" Stacey turned toward me with widened eyes and raised her voice with hurried excitement. "They just talk in class, and it totally scared me at first. So, I listened to them. I paid attention to what they were saying, and I realized that they weren't saying anything meaningful! They often said stuff that wasn't related to the course materials, or they said things that just showed that they didn't do the readings!"

Stacey burst out in laughter and said proudly with her chin up high, "I knew that because I did all the readings. Honestly, I swear, I read every single page. That's how I knew those Americans were definitely talking nonsense!" Stacey then concluded by wondering why her professors allowed students to freely discuss unrelated topics and expressed discontent about the "waste of time" during discussions.

The students who studied in the United States frequently referred to American peers' academic performance as a response to questions about everyday life in school. Just as Stacey delightfully found herself at the top of her class, others reported similar experiences. One among them was Tracy, whom I visited in her junior year at Johns Hopkins. Tracy and I walked through a busy cafeteria with students in discussion with open textbooks while eating. I commented that these students seemed to making efficient use of time. Tracy shook her head. She told me that her American classmates "don't seem to do well in school at all." She said amusedly, "I can't figure it out. Aren't they supposed to be at an advantage?"

Similarly, Joe visited Philadelphia before college graduation. We sat down on the banks of Schuylkill River and chatted about his college years. Joe recalled that his peers in Boston College were "not as good" as he was: "There's no way to see other people's GPA, so I thought everyone got straight As, like me. But I saw one classmate's, and it was not an A. I thought this fellow was very good, judging from class discussions and assignments. But he only got a B. Since then, I realized most people get Bs."

Together, these reports suggest that the elite Chinese students used the same rules to sort peers into different status groups. The narratives of Robert, Stacey, Tracy, and Joe provide a timeline throughout college. Upon arrival, students quickly learned that they outperformed the Americans academically. They repeatedly outperformed the Americans, especially when the native speakers supposedly had an advantage over them. Seeking to explain this phenomenon, the students invoked the innate ability argument that they had been all too familiar with in high school. They described the American students in college as "dumb" or "stupid," much like how they talked about the losers in high school.[23]

In addition to using the same rules and justifications, the elite students deployed identical status-based strategies to navigate the status system in college. Claire was a study god at Capital who later went to Yale. Her counselor was happy for her but expressed worries about Claire's adjustment to "becoming a small fish in a big pond [Yale]." The counselor's worries came true, and Claire was the only international-bound student who reported being academically low-performing in college. I visited Claire in her sophomore year. As we walked through the campus, she choked back her tears and told me that she had "developed an inferiority complex" at Yale. Claire said that she had been consistently below average since her first midterm, when she got the first C in her life. She studied more diligently than ever but still scored below average in the general elective course, which is supposed to be easy. Having low grades with high levels of effort, she saw herself as being on the verge of falling into the loser category. As a response, she rectified the situation by devoting herself to dance and becoming heavily involved in extracurricular activities the next semester. Additionally, she went on a yearlong exchange program to Cambridge University. Because she took a few courses that were graded as pass/fail, she freed herself from competition against her high-performing peers at Yale. These strategies worked, and she never fell to bottom status at school.

Claire deployed the same strategy to navigate the job market. I visited Claire and her boyfriend in New York, where the three of us had dinner at an

Indian restaurant. Claire had just graduated and started working at a company ranked in the top twenty globally. She seemed slightly embarrassed about it when I congratulated her over dinner. She waved her hand in embarrassment, explaining that she took the job "only because the offer came early, [and] saved me the trouble of job hunting." It later turned out that Claire's humility reflected the unspoken understanding that the position was unsatisfactory. In other meetings, Claire's high school friend, Selena, bluntly told me that Claire's pay was "quite low" in the field. Tony, who had been close to Claire in high school, commented that he "would never have taken the job." Stacey, who started the same position in the following year, left within a few months for a better one. Intrigued by these reports, I browsed the company website and found that Claire was the only Ivy League graduate in her department.

Claire's trajectory shows that, like other elite Chinese students, she was familiar with the rules that governed status reproduction. She was attentive to her test scores (GPA) and found out early on that she did not qualify as a study god at Yale, upon which she instinctively tried to maintain her high status by becoming a studyholic and studied diligently. When her strategy of hard work failed, she immediately sought to demonstrate ease to avoid falling to the bottom status group. Upon graduation, Claire knowingly took a job that was not comparable to those of her friends who had attended Yale or Capital. Despite knowing that others thought she was overqualified for the position, Claire accepted it without hesitation as part of demonstrating ease ("save the trouble of job hunting"). Claire's decisions to focus on extracurricular activities, go to Cambridge, and take a position that others did not approve of were all made in an attempt to demonstrate ease.

A closer look at Claire's trajectory shows that she had in fact adopted a strategy that fit her new position as an underachiever. She employed the swan strategy, a hallmark of underachievers. Claire focused on dance and became one of the leads in the dance club at Yale. However, since she had little training, she revealed to me that she had spent considerable time practicing in front of a mirror, out of sight from her peers. Her exchange trip to Cambridge involved intense competition since many students hoped to spend a year there. To land the position, she studiously prepared for the application and "was lucky" to get the opportunity. Even her offer did not come as easily as implied. Claire had spent summers as an unpaid intern for the company in New York City, working until late at night every day. The company was pleased with her performance and thus made her an offer before job hunting started. Yet Claire made no mention of these efforts in public or in front of her boyfriend, also a Yale graduate. Her façade of ease concealed her frantic paddling beneath the water.

Summary

The elite students in this study compete for status reproduction as if playing a game. They agree on a set of rules as soon as they take their seats. Very quickly, they distinguish four tiers of players using test scores and ease: study gods, studyholics, underachievers, and losers. They justify the rules of the game, arguing that status outcomes reflect innate ability. Then, the students formulate strategies according to their respective positions. The fact that all students uphold the status system and its sorting criteria indicates that the system is considerably powerful. Furthermore, with these practices, high schools serve as training grounds that prepare the elite youths from China to engage in future status competition.

Statuses change, but rules and strategies persist. In college, the students experience status mobility, sometimes crashing from top to bottom, other times rising to stardom. Yet their approach to status competition remains unchanged. Understanding the setup of the status system remains crucial. The students instinctively try to figure out the determinants of status before entering new environments in China, the United States, and elsewhere. As new players join in, the students prepare themselves for different rules. Some situations call for rule changes, others do not. Yet even the changes stay within the system. As shown in this chapter, the students in Chinese universities flipped the importance between test scores and ease for the sake of maintaining their competitive edge, but never considered criteria beyond the two. After taking their places in the new hierarchies, the young adults adopt the strategies they learned in high school and deploy them to maximize status outcomes as they engage in global competition.

3

Worshipping the Gods

In summer 2014, Mingjia and I sat by the window in a busy coffee shop in Beijing. The sun shone through the window onto the wooden table between us, the soft light in dissonance with the rigid features of the status system she was describing. Mingjia smiled and folded her arms: "Test scores are like money in society. I'm not saying that rich people are the most respected, but those with money have a bit more respect than those without." Five years later, Alex echoed this statement in a noisy tavern in Boston. He sipped his cocktail and said flatly, "People, society, respect those who have money. This is a simple dimension." He added humorously, "Maybe something else, like if he's cute, or if he's done something good. But in general, the mainstream idea is that."

ON A HOT, sunny afternoon, a month before the gaokao, Lili, Wanru, Mei, and I came back to Capital from lunch at McDonald's. It was time to return to the classroom and get back to work. The school walls were decorated with slogans such as "Every second counts" and "Time is money," but the three twelfth graders were in no hurry. The girls dragged their feet in the hallway and excitedly discussed the matcha McFlurry that had just come out at McDonald's. At the turn of the corner, a row of light pink posters about fifty feet ahead caught their attention. Their chatter died instantly; their smiles were immediately replaced by stares.

Wanru pointed to the posters and suddenly shouted, "Let's go worship the gods!" Before I realized what was going on, the girls dashed forward. Lili dragged me by the arm to keep up.

The girls stopped in front of the pink posters and craned their necks to read them intently. On the posters in a large black font were lists of names and test scores of students who did well on the previous mock exam. The three of them became silent as they shared a moment of admiration. A minute or two later, Wanru and Mei slowly lowered their chins. Without looking at each other, they turned away quietly and walked toward the classroom. Lili stayed behind and studied the posters with pursed lips. After what felt like forever, Lili slowly said to me with her eyes still fixed on the posters, "These kids are in the cohort below us. The eleventh graders took one of our mock exams." She took in a deep breath. Then, she stretched out her index finger to point to a boy's name listed at the top of the poster. The boy had scored about 650, which was lower than Lili. However, Lili looked defeated. She let out a sigh of admiration and said, "This kid is so good. I was nowhere near his level back in eleventh grade." Shaking her head, Lili smiled faintly at me. She concluded softly, "He's a true study god."

When I entered the schools, I pictured high-status students as popular cheerleaders and quarterbacks in Hollywood movies, or the jocks and cool kids in ethnographic studies. My imagination was not entirely correct. Without a doubt, high-status students are famous on campus. However, their fame cannot be simplified as popularity, and their impact on peers goes beyond what popularity entails. High-status students are not always personally known or recognized by peers, nor do they need to be physically present to exert their influence on others. These students sometimes even avoid peer associations. A good number of high-status students walk by themselves on campus, conceal their whereabouts from classmates, and study alone in seclusion. The friendlier ones do not stay within their status group but freely befriend others at all levels of performance. In fact, some of them hang out only with low performers.

Nonetheless, high performers, especially the study gods, are special people. They are at the center of attention in daily conversations. Their names and test scores alone powerfully transform students' collective emotions. In this example, none of the girls knew the top performer in eleventh grade. They would not recognize him if they crossed paths on campus. Yet, the mere sight of the boy's test scores changed the girls' behavior. While the girls had been chatty and lighthearted, they instantly fell silent and turned serious. They were previously slow to return to the classroom; after seeing the boy's test score, they made a beeline back to their seats. Lili's reaction was particularly interesting. Lili herself was a studyholic with high status in school. She scored thirty extra points on the additional test for Peking University, which she later attended. Considering her status, Lili could have cared less about the boy's performance. After all, she did not know the boy, nor were they in direct competition by virtue of being in different cohorts. There was no guarantee that the boy would stay as high-performing in twelfth grade either. Yet Lili instinctively recognized him as potentially higher performing than herself and awarded him study god status. Although she expressed feelings of being outcompeted (sigh, shaking head, and smiling faintly), she simultaneously articulated greater feelings of admiration.

Lili's behavior and emotions are the typical reactions students have toward high performers. To put it mildly, students respect the high performers. From Mingjia's perspective, test scores are analogous to money: the higher the scores, the more the respect. In this analogy, test scores define the elite student's worth in top high schools, just as money or wealth defines an elite's net worth in society.[1] Furthermore, elite students admire and "want to be like" the high performers, just as adults often express the desire to be like the wealthiest individuals in their country or the world. Respect is thus an understatement that fails to capture the elevated status of top performers. Peers' profound respect for them takes the form of celebrity admiration, and the special treatment top performers receive is more adequately described by the catchphrase "worshipping the gods." It is in this sense that having high status is more than simply being popular. Having high status is being respected. Essentially, it is about being worshipped.

Daily Interactions: General Friendliness and Peer Relationships

While students demonstrate status-based behaviors such as "worshipping the gods," they nonetheless construct a pleasant campus atmosphere in which all students are welcome. Breaks are marked by cheerful chatter in the classrooms, and meal times are filled with laughter. Student friendship networks consist of mixed-status groups, and there are no spatial boundaries separating groups of students. In the United States, students typically mark spatial boundaries by sitting with friends of the same status group in the classroom, cafeteria, and auditorium.[2] However, students in Chinese high schools walk to class and to the cafeteria with peers of different status. In terms of seating choices, teachers in the schools I visited assign seats for the students and shuffle them around periodically to foster friendships in the classroom. Even when students could decide on their seats, they did not do so. In Lili's classroom, for example, students selected seats at the time of their arrival to the first class and stayed there for the entire semester. Students in the international departments also shared the same rules for seating assignments. Brandon usually sat at the back of the classroom, but he was at the middle of the first row in biology class. When I asked him about the change of seat, he explained, "I arrived early on the first day, so I sat there the whole semester." He then complained that "it's too much pressure to face Mr. Eland [the biology teacher] all the time. I should've arrived later that day!"

Cohort and school meetings in the auditorium and on the sports field share the same guidelines. The school designates specific rows of seats for each classroom and cohort. In the meetings I joined, students took their seats as they arrived without regard to who was sitting where. Students do not save seats and do not switch places, and I never heard anyone complain about where they sat. The same goes for finding a table in the cafeteria. Three cohorts of over one thousand students pour into the cafeteria for lunch and dinner within the first few minutes of meal breaks.[3] Anticipating a crowd, students scramble for a table and try not to lose each other during the hunt for seats each day. They are unable to pick and choose where the table is; they are simply lucky to find a seat. In general, there is a lack of spatial boundaries, and students choose seats without concern for status distinctions.

Students openly identify peers of other status groups as their close friends and date people of higher or lower status. One way to observe peer networks and close friendship ties was to see which students shared meals. The lunch groups I observed all consisted of cross-status friendships.[4] One classroom in the domestic department at Capital had two study gods: Shiying and Dapeng. The two were friendly but not very close, and they had different lunch buddies. Dapeng hung out with Sinian, an average performer who later went to Renmin University. Shiying usually had lunch with Liwa, an underachiever. The status difference between Shiying and Liwa was significant. Shiying was the "superstar" who teachers hoped would be the highest scoring student in Beijing. By comparison, Liwa's test scores were far below the admission cutoff score, and she did not apply to THU or PKU. During my observations, Shiying, Liwa, and other average and low performers shared meals and walked to PE class together, and Shiying's mother gave them rides home after parent-teacher meetings. The same types of friendship patterns are visible in the international department. Samantha was a study god who scored 2330 on the SAT and later went to Columbia University. She shared the same classroom with two other high-status students: Tony, a study god, and Tracy, a studyholic. The three chatted and sat together in class, and they considered each other friends. Tony regularly went to lunch with Tracy and some others, but Samantha never joined them. She was not close with either Tony or Tracy. Samantha's good friends were other low performers, with whom she shared meals, did homework, and walked to class.

Even the dating relationships were often cross-status. High-status students sometimes dated within their groups. Some of the known couples were study gods and studyholics, such as Tony (study god) and Tracy (studyholic), or Dapeng (study god) and Jina (studyholic). However, high-status students also dated low-status students at an equal rate. One of the campus love stories was Claire (study god) and Bob (underachiever), who dated briefly until Bob called off the relationship and broke Claire's heart.[5] Gao (studyholic) spent years pursuing Aiya, an average performer who was close to being an underachiever. Robert (underachiever) pursued Samantha (study god) for some time. Samantha did not go out with him, not because of the status gap between them but because she was not interested in developing relationships at the time. Robert later dated Stacey, who had higher test scores than he did.

Taken together, students form inclusive friendship circles on campus. Status groups are rigidly defined, but friendship networks span multiple status groups. Being visibly together all the time with someone of another status group is unrelated to status in school, and close associations do not carry status consequences.[6] With these practices, students construct a campus atmosphere that is welcoming, warm, and friendly.

Peers Are in It Together

In top Chinese high schools, the overall inclusive peer relationships are also reflected in students' strong levels of group solidarity. Students share a sense of togetherness as they collectively focus on college outcomes. Yet college admissions are a zero-sum competition. After all, students are ranked against each other and compete for limited slots in top universities. A student receiving admission to PKU or THU means one less spot for the others, and the Ivy League schools are not likely to admit more than a few students from the same high school each year. Nonetheless, the campus atmosphere seems to outweigh the intense academic competition. Despite engaging in publicized competition on a daily basis, students do not see each other as competitors. Rather, they consider each other to be comrades fighting the same battle—the gaokao and college applications.

One of my visits to Pinnacle illustrates the sense of togetherness that students share. I was shadowing Fei, a study god, on a bright sunny day in 2013. Soon after the bell rang for lunch break, I followed Fei to the student cafeteria at Pinnacle. We joined a group of five boys who were devouring their bowls of rice. The boys discussed the outcomes of a mock exam as they gulped down their food. They first shared their test scores and then exchanged information about other high performers. I asked Miao, a sturdy boy who sat beside me, "You guys compete against students in different classrooms like this all the time?" The boys who overheard stopped eating and looked at me, seemingly stunned by my comment. Miao quickly explained, "No, actually, we don't see it as competing against each other." Fei added, "We don't feel that way." The other boys seem relieved to be in agreement. Miao concluded, "There's no competition here. We're all friends." Having made their point, the boys returned to their serious discussion and reviewed each other's incorrect answers on the mock exam.

In general, the students I observed were friendly toward each other. The example of Fei and Miao represents students' overall sentiment about peer relationships. In their minds, peers are all "friends"; they are "not in competition." Elite students in Beijing share a collective focus on college preparation. They routinely discuss and comment on each other's answers. While these discussions sometimes lean toward interrogations, such as demanding that a peer explain why he or she made a certain mistake, students do so with good intent. They review test answers to help each other improve, as good friends should. They demand explanations for incorrect answers to determine the source of the problem because they see this as key to preventing future mistakes. They encourage and sustain each other through the seemingly endless tests because that is what friends do. These conversations exist precisely because students care about each other. Thus, in their minds, the harsh discussions about individual performance do not serve to weigh a student's performance against another's. Instead, they are meant to lift each other up and bring out their best performances on college assessments.

Peer Policing

Identifying as a group, students share a sense of what constitutes adequate behavior and how they should interact. They correct each other's behaviors in the classroom on the spot, such as sleeping during class, and enforce corrections through peer pressure. The degree of policing that peers are subject to is considerably high, to the extent that students feel entitled to interfere with each other's personal or family decisions, such as trying to change each other's college choices. In the last class period of the day, Mrs. Wu, Fei's homeroom teacher, brought attention to their college admission lists. She said worriedly, "Five of you in this very classroom want to major in physics at Tsinghua University. But that department is only taking in seven from Beijing this year. You [five] need to reconsider." She then dismissed the class, picked up her books, and walked out briskly.

Immediately, groups of students left their desks and surrounded the five who had listed this choice. They closed in on them and built elaborate arguments, forcefully persuading the five to make alternative choices. Feng, one of the five who sat in front of me, was surrounded by four students: two standing at his left, one sitting on his desk, and one taking over the seat to his right. Qiang, who sat at his right, said to Feng forcefully, "Choose physics in PKU. You do physics, I'll do physics." Feng replied, "I can't use my extra points for PKU!" Feng packed his black backpack and tried to leave the room. However, the students standing at his left did not move. Qiang loudly told Feng to sit down. Feng held on to his backpack and reluctantly sat back down. Qiang started lecturing him about how wonderful the physics department in PKU was, stating that it had "broader scope" compared to "the narrow focus" of the same major at THU. Another echoed, "Most of the faculty in PKU are Western educated!," meaning that the department at PKU offered top-notch undergraduate training. Feng, however, resisted by saying, "My dad wanted me to go to Tsinghua." Qiang, with one hand holding his water bottle, immediately replied with confidence, "I'll convince your dad to let you go to PKU instead!" Feng smirked, "Yeah right." He then grabbed his things and pushed his way out the classroom. Undiscouraged, Qiang shouted behind, "You want to do physics? Go to PKU!"

Tangyi, a girl with rosy cheeks and a short ponytail, was another of the five. She clutched her textbooks at the back of the room, surrounded by anxious-looking peers, including Fei, who stood between Tangyi and the back door, blocking the exit with his six-foot figure. Fei gently but firmly directed Tangyi to change her list by pointing out her unviable backup plans.

"What is your second choice?" Fei asked gently.

"I don't know, my parents decided them for me." Tangyi replied with a frown.

"Not the university," Fei said. "I mean the major."

"I don't know!" She shouted impatiently, "It's all physics [majors]!"

Fei analyzed her possible alternatives as the group listened. He listed out the universities that had physics departments that might have been on her list and their respective cutoff scores, and he concluded, "You can't list these four together. No matter the sequence, if you don't get into your top choice [physics at Tsinghua], you won't get into your second and fourth choices either."

Tangyi frowned deeper. She angrily replied, "How do you know if I won't get into my top choice?"

Fei looked speechless as the others burst out in laughter. Tangyi tried but failed to move closer to the back door. She gave up and scooted toward the middle of the classroom, followed by students telling her to reconsider. Qiang walked over and patted Fei on the back and said, "She's okay, her test scores are high enough. You should know by now the power of parents in college choices." Fei, looking defeated, left the classroom hunched over. I quickly followed. As we walked out the school gate, he murmured that Tangyi "made a big mistake" in her college lists. Still concerned, Fei mapped out all her possible college outcomes in his mind and analyzed the chances of Tangyi to transfer once in college.

In this example and others, the students rushed to correct each other when they sensed certain peers had made incorrect college choices. Failing to get into one's top choice was a real threat to college outcomes, as elite students considered the top choice to be the *only* choice and the four subsequent choices as undesirable backups. If they failed to get into their top choice, the worst-case scenario was they would not get into any university, which would in turn damage the classroom's overall college outcome ranking. It is likely that the students reacted in an effort to help their peers achieve the best possible college outcomes. While they may have meant well, the forceful persuasion and insistence on peers changing course suggested concerns that went beyond peer support. A more likely explanation is that the students took Mrs. Wu's hint at the potential risk of having students without a placement in the classroom. As a group, the students tried to eliminate such risk factors. Feng and Tangyi both cited parental decisions in their reasons to maintain their college choices. Considering that parents play an important role in college choices,[7] the students could have retreated when they sensed parental influence. However, this was not the case, as the students invoked the teacher to pressure the five into switching their college choices. Students informed Mrs. Wu of their failure to change the five students' minds. Mrs. Wu ended class the next day by addressing the class in a serious tone: "Remember, your college choices are yours. Don't leave everything for your parents to decide."

Whether the five students would be admitted to their top choice had very little to do with the others. Yet when a 100 percent college admission rate is seen as the norm, not receiving any placement is a serious transgression. The students thus did whatever they could to fix the situation. Qiang was willing to go the extra mile to change Feng's mind. He promised to change his own college choice with Feng ("you do physics, I'll do physics" at PKU) and even thought he could persuade Feng's parents ("I'll convince your dad"). Fei mapped out Tangyi's possible college choice combinations on the spot and highlighted her lack of viable fallback plans ("won't get into other colleges either"). Altogether, these policing efforts seem to have made a difference. When the exam results were publicized, every student in the classroom had a college placement. Fewer than five of them went to the physics department at THU, and at least some of them, including both Feng and Tangyi, had changed their minds.

Keeping Status Boundaries

Cross-status relationships and solidarity notwithstanding, students remain mindful of status in their interactions. Students insist that others behave in accordance with their status position. They do not tolerate individuals who attempt to cross over to another (higher) status group, nor do they allow others to mistake a student's low status for high status. Because these interactions that clarify status boundaries are nonconfrontational, students maintain harmonious campus atmospheres while they uphold distinctions between peers.

One of the students who sometimes presented herself as having higher status was Lili, a studyholic at Capital who later went to PKU. Lili was extremely diligent. I rarely saw her rest or take breaks, and her conversations with friends were usually about test answers. Even her teachers were worried that she would be "stressed out about the gaokao." In a daylong observation, I shared lunch with her, Wanru, and Mei. Lili proudly announced over lunch that she did not finish her homework. Mei raised an eyebrow but quickly lowered her head and played with her food. Wanru quickly replied in a challenging tone, "Oh yeah? I haven't been doing my physics homework the whole semester." Mei looked at Wanru in disbelief. Lili turned her head ninety degrees toward me, her long ponytail swaying to the other side. Looking horrified, she yelled at Wanru about the possible consequences of annoying the physics teacher with statements like, "You won't be able to get away with this!"

Lili made another attempt to present herself as being at ease (and thus a study god rather than studyholic) on the second and last day of the gaokao. I ran into Lili and a group of students who were standing in a circle outside the gate, where friends and families were dropping off the exam takers. Somewhere in the group conversation, students asked each other if they would study at the test site. Lili announced that she would not because she planned to "just hang around at the exam site." The group broke up a few minutes later. I bid Lili good luck, but instead she held my arm and led me into the exam site. As soon as we walked past security, Lili headed straight to a classroom and joined a few other students for quiet last-minute cramming. The others left about eight to ten minutes before the start of the exam, but Lili stayed behind. Seemingly worried, a boy turned back and hesitantly reminded Lili, "It's time to go to the exam room." Lili nodded but didn't move, her nose buried in a textbook. The boy sighed, adding, "Don't be late!" Lili nodded without looking at him. Lili studied a bit more until it was almost the start of the exam. When she joined her friends lining up to enter the exam classroom, some said in relief, "Whew, you're here!" Others joked, "Memorized more formulas, eh?" Lili smiled and did not answer.

The only thing Lili, being solidly studyholic, needed in order to acquire top status was demonstrating ease. However, her effort at cultivating a lighthearted image always fell flat. In these examples and others, her peers kept her in her studyholic status by flatly rejecting her claims of having ease. Wanru intentionally challenged Lili by offering herself as a "true" case of ease (not turning in homework once versus regularly). Mei clearly did not approve (raised eyebrows). Other students at the test location knew that her actions betrayed her words and did not hesitate to point out that she had been studying ("memorized more formulas"). In both cases, Lili responded with typical studyholic behavior (warning Wanru and staying in the classroom), which further affirmed her status. In short, Lili's peers knew perfectly well that she was no study god. They refused to let her pretend to be one and shot down her every attempt.

Just as Wanru and Mei marked distinction between studyholics and study gods, students keep peers in their respective status. Study gods take a backseat and watch as their peers draw status boundaries for them. However, very infrequently, a student will unintentionally elevate an individual beyond his or her actual status. In these instances, study gods take immediate action and lay claim to distinction. Such an example took place in spring 2013 when I shadowed Shiying. That day happened to be Muhan's birthday. When we congratulated her, Muhan, an underachiever, smiled broadly, showing her teeth. She cheerfully told us that she was blessed to receive birthday gifts from her friends. To my surprise, she then suddenly compared herself to Jina, a high-status and widely admired studyholic in the same classroom. "But this is nothing compared to Jina. She got gifts from just about everyone in the cohort on her birthday. You should've seen it, she had so many gifts that she couldn't close her locker." Muhan gestured an explosion by drawing half a circle with her hands. She said dramatically with widened eyes, "It was like gifts bursting out from her locker! She's definitely the most admired person on campus."

I nodded and took mental note of Jina's popularity. Seeing me take note of this piece of information, Shiying gently interrupted us, "Well, Jina gave birthday gifts to a lot of people, including me. People were returning the favor."

Muhan clammed up. I attempted to combine both girls' arguments by asking, "But [to the point that] gifts burst out from her locker?" My question implied that Jina might have been receiving presents in return, but the number of gifts was too many to all be returned favors. In other words, Jina was indeed admired by peers, just not as many as it seemed.

Both Shiying and Muhan understood my implicit argument. Muhan slightly nodded and looked at Shiying. Shiying gave us her usual sweet smile and responded amusedly, "Then you know how many people she gave gifts to in the past year." Not wishing to argue further, Muhan quickly left the conversation by walking away.

Students often expressed admiration toward those with high status, including both study gods like Shiying and, to a lesser degree, studyholics like Jina. Shiying nodded in acknowledgment of Jina's high status in other instances, but she quickly dismissed Muhan's statement in this example. These different responses suggested that Jina being admired was not the issue that spurred Shiying to put Jina in her place. Instead, she dismissed Muhan's unrightful elevation of Jina's status to the top in school (seeing a studyholic as "the most admired person"). Using but a few sentences, Shiying, who had top status in school, re-created Jina's image. Jina was no longer "the most admired student" on campus but an ordinary student who put significant effort into making friends. Being a studyholic, Jina could enjoy peer admiration. But other students could not elevate her status to compare her with a study god, nor was she allowed to trespass into study god territory. Finally, as a top-status student, Shiying had the final word and settled the debate.

Students could have easily engaged in conflict, hostility, or bitter arguments when they corrected and denounced each other. Yet these instances share a low degree of tension and are marked by pleasant group atmospheres. The students deliver these comments with laugher, jokes, and smiles. They have smooth communication as they hold each other in their respective positions. With these interactions, the elite students in this study cultivate close friendship ties. They perceive peers as helpful, considerate, and agreeable. Most report that their friends genuinely care about each other and are grateful for having a supportive peer environment.

High Performers Enjoy Peer Adoration

The students in this study were generally friendly, warm, and supportive toward each other. However, to the extent that status shapes peer interaction patterns, not all peer interactions exhibited the same level of closeness, and students often did not share the same degree of mutual association. Classroom observations and interviews showed that peers systematically treated the high performers with respect and showered them with adoration. The high performers, in return, frequently demonstrated high levels of entitlement toward peer attention. These behaviors included routinely ignoring friendly schoolmates, being free of peer policing, and demanding peer respect.

Center of Attention: Claire Has a School of Followers

High-status students are easily noticeable—they are the ones at the center of attention in peer groups. Study gods and studyholics have a strong presence on campus without being physically present. Claire was a girl with loose curls and a taste for elegant dresses. Her exceptional grades and SAT score of 2330, said to be highest in the cohort, secured her position at the top of Capital. Claire was a well-known study god. In my visits to Capital, almost the entire student body in the international department claimed to be on friendly terms with Claire. She was indeed generally friendly toward most, but the number of students who self-identified as her friend greatly exceeded the number of people whom she hung out with.[8] Students knew her application list by heart and waited anxiously for her admission outcomes. On any day during admissions season, students in the international department would tell me whether Claire had heard back from a certain university. In midspring, Claire received many rejections but no acceptance. Her schoolmates rose to her defense and claimed that it was normal for her to receive only rejections so far because

"Claire only applied to the best universities" and "she used other people's dream school as a backup." Upon hearing these explanations for the second or third time, I paused to wonder whether they made sense, with an unintentional frown. Seeing my facial expression and nonresponse, one of the students quickly shouted, "It's the truth! Claire's safety net was Wesleyan University, that's Monica's dream school!" The student stretched out one arm and pointed toward a girl, presumably Monica, who was twenty feet away.

Students' anxiousness turned into relief and joyous celebration the day Claire was accepted to Yale. Her peers in the international department openly expressed admiration toward Claire as if it were a group accomplishment.[9] In the weeks afterward, many students had an opening line of "Did you hear that Claire got into Yale?" Students in the domestic departments also rejoiced in her Yale acceptance when they heard the news. Soon afterward, the school fueled student excitement by unabashedly celebrating Claire's achievement. The international department at Capital showed each student's name and admission outcome to visitors on a large flat screen at the entrance of the building. Claire appeared first in a full-body shot, wearing a white dress in what appeared to be a garden, with "Yale University" in a large font beneath her picture. Other students' headshots and their admission outcomes appeared later in no specific order. To tout Claire's achievement, Capital asked Claire to make a life-size poster of herself for public display. The poster was completed around the time of graduation and was placed in front of the conference hall, where school gatherings and parent-teacher meetings were held. With all the buzz and celebration, younger cohorts certainly knew about Claire. Students talked about Claire's achievement as the highlight of the department for multiple years. I returned to Capital the following year after Claire had graduated. Students in the next two cohorts recounted Claire's college placement and SAT score. Her name sparked conversations, and students commonly referred to her as the "superstar" whom "everybody knew."

Students could have paid attention only to Claire's admission outcome. Yet they had closely followed the developments of her application results and were emotionally invested in her college outcome. They had trusted that Claire would be successful in the face of rejections and had vehemently defended her when an outsider showed signs of doubt toward her academic ability (defending her and offering explanations or excuses). They also collectively celebrated her individual achievement as group success (spreading news, with tones of admiration). Being at the center of attention, Claire facilitated collective peer attention. When Capital asked the graduating cohort to provide personal pictures, Claire instinctively turned in a full-body shot instead of a headshot, which all other students submitted. Claire did not consider the poster to be an unnecessary burden but willingly took on the task and asked her mother for help. Receiving and generating collective celebration of her achievement, Claire became a legend.

Celebrity Treatment: Xijun Is the Star of the School

Not all high-status students mingle with peers on campus. Many distinguish themselves, intentionally or unintentionally, by being physically and psychologically distant from other students. Xijun was a thin, fair-skinned girl at Pinnacle who occasionally worked as a model. I shadowed Xijun on a sunny spring day in twelfth grade, after she had landed in first place on a top arts university admission exam. It was PE class, and Xijun joined her classmates in various athletic activities on the sports field. I stood in the shade to one side and spectated. A short boy with spiky hair approached me from behind and asked the reason for my presence. I replied that I was shadowing Xijun.

Immediately his eyes brightened. "Xijun's the star of our school. You know that, right?" The boy said in a tone of noticeable admiration, "Xijun got into [the top art university]! Before her, the last person in our school who got in was [a director]; you know, he's now famous. And that was ages ago, nobody else had gotten in since then!"

The boy went on excitedly talking about Xijun's achievement at an accelerated pace. I smiled and listened to him recounting Xijun's achievements in the past year. About ten minutes later, the bell rang and Xijun walked over. She wore a faint smile and looked tall, with her shoulders back. She gestured to me with a tilt of her chin. The boy had still been talking about his admiration toward Xijun, but he clammed up upon seeing her. He looked at her with shining eyes as she approached us.

Xijun did not make eye contact with the boy. She stopped at least five feet away from us and softly announced, "Class is over, let's go."

"Oh, we were just talking about you!" I cheerfully pointed to the boy.

Xijun glanced at him and lifted the corners of her mouth. The boy's eyes widened. He seemed to want to say something but did not. He looked anxious or in disbelief. Xijun looked me in the eye and said again, this time more firmly, "Let's go." She then turned and walked away. Following her, I looked back and saw a flash of regret in the boy's look. He was looking toward Xijun's direction with dropped shoulders. I later asked Xijun if she knew the boy. "Yeah, he's a kid from another classroom. I've never really talked to him." She shrugged, "Ignore him. A lot of people are like that."

Xijun and many other high-status students were both celebrities and lone wolves. As a celebrity, Xijun could have had peers celebrate her many achievements. She published two volumes of prose, won a national award for her film project, and was the top scoring applicant on the admissions exam of an art university that ranked within the top five in the world. Xijun's achievements received attention from the media, which even showed a mini documentary about her on TV. However, she refrained from talking about her achievements with other students and did not inform them of her award ceremony, which she attended with her parents.[10] Students turned their heads to look at her when she passed by in the hallway, but she passed by them as if she had not noticed their gazes. I rarely saw Xijun hang out with her peers on campus.[11] She went home as soon as the bell rang and avoided interacting with peers much like the way she did in this incident. The anonymous boy was enthusiastic about her achievements and shared his passion with visitors to campus. He was excited see her (as shown by his clamming up and shining eyes) and wanted to talk to her (looking anxious). Yet Xijun ignored him. She drew a clear social distance, being physically apart (five feet apart and walking away) and emotionally unresponsive (announcing her wish to leave, no eye contact, glancing, and "ignore him").[12] Despite her routine nonresponse, Xijun's peers never withdrew their attention. They distinguished her from others and self-identified as her fans.

Freedom to Misbehave: Luna Never Completes Any Assignment

While peers policed each other regarding adequate classroom behaviors, high performers could behave in ways that lower performers could not. In a group interview, I asked Pan and Haochen, two students with respectively low and high status, if they thought any student was special. Pan immediately brought up Luna, a high-status student. Pan raised her voice and listed what she knew about Luna in a tone of admiration: "This girl was the top student on the tenth grade test. Since then, her test scores have always stayed like that. Luna is always sleeping. She can't get up in the morning, so she rushes to class without eating breakfast. She sleeps through classes, never completes assignments, like that. But she has always done exceptionally well!" With awe in her voice, Pan looked at me with wide eyes and added excitedly, "She transferred to the international department, and she later got into Yale!" Haochen silently but dramatically nodded in agreement.

Luna's behavior differed drastically from that of other students. In my fieldwork, I was impressed by students' attentiveness to classroom instructions, as I had not seen anyone fall asleep during class. In cases where students dozed off, their peers nearby would wake them up immediately. Students also criticized peers who were late to school, which suggested that punctuality was a norm in the high schools I visited. However, while Luna did not follow normative classroom behavior ("always sleeping" and "never completed assignments"), she was free from peer policing and not reprimanded. Luna's example can be compared with an earlier example of Wanru, an underachiever who admitted to never turning in assignments. The two demonstrated similar behaviors, with Luna's transgression being greater than that of Wanru. However, while Luna's peers excused her for her violations, Wanru's peers did not. Even mild misbehavior generated peer admiration for the high-status students like Luna. Pan and Haochen found Luna to be exceptional, while Lili and Mei considered Wanru to be in big trouble. This example and many others show that high-status students have considerable freedom from peer policing, to the point where they can break normative classroom behaviors that others are corrected for.

Demanding Respect: Julie Is "Quite Famous"

Being constantly showered with peer adoration, high-status students often become entitled to special treatment and take for granted other students' attention. This mentality is most clearly demonstrated when they encounter unexpected inattention. Julie was a tall, athletic girl at Central who self-identified as a study god. Julie texted me on a chilly spring afternoon and invited me to have coffee together at a coffee shop near her school. We sat across from each other, and I listened to her complain about an "unacceptable" incident that had happened earlier. Simply put, she had talked to boy in the eleventh grade cohort but found out that he did not know her.

I was puzzled and asked, "He's not in your cohort. Why should he know you?"

Julie put down her drink, glared at me angrily, and raised her voice, "You probably don't know, but I'm quite famous at school. I'm the top-performing student. Maybe not always the top, but I'm always in the top 10 percent. I'm also captain of the girls' basketball team. How could anyone not know me?" Later in the conversation, Julie concluded, "I need to tell my friends to talk to him and keep him informed."

With Julie at the top of the status system, her entitlement to peer attention was strong. She informed me of her high status in the first few meetings by casually mentioning that she spent only about ten days preparing and took the SAT just once, while others studied for months and took the test multiple times.[13] She also reported that she continued to attend basketball practices and organized the school's Christmas party when her peers were scrambling to meet application deadlines. Julie strongly self-identified with her position in the status system and expected to receive the corresponding level of respect. While most students do not anticipate being known by students in other cohorts, Julie expected all students on campus to know her, hear about her achievements, and recognize her in person. To Julie, distinction had become her due. As a result, when a student did not give her the attention she felt she deserved, Julie reacted as if the younger student had deprived her of her right. When faced with such a violation, Julie drew on peer support (her friends) to correct the violator's offense and framed this decision as an act of benevolence ("keep him informed").

Taken together, the selected students at the upper end of the hierarchy receive and often command unwavering attention. Study gods and studyholics carry themselves with poise in daily interactions and enjoy high levels of peer admiration. They grow accustomed to having peer admiration at their feet. As they stay within high status, they put minimal or no effort into making friends on campus and are accustomed to peers flocking to their sides, eager to befriend them. With these behaviors, the high-status students become the legitimate elite on campus and have elevated status. The high performers learn to highlight their distinction from their peers, and as I show below, many continue to employ this approach when interacting with peers in college and at work.

Low Performers Do Nothing Right

While study gods and studyholics command peer attention without pursuing the limelight, underachievers and losers are unable to position themselves to receive peer attention. Study gods like Clair are remembered even after graduation, but underachievers and losers receive no credit for their talents and are quickly forgotten. High-status students are celebrated by peers for their achievements. By comparison, low-status students often find themselves the target of peer derision for miniscule mistakes. When they do something worthy of celebration, peers instead respond with mockery. And while a few study gods or studyholics ignore other students, some underachievers and losers are ignored even when they approach peers with friendly gestures.

Quickly Forgotten: Brandon Receives No Credit

Low performers are often buried in the crowd regardless of their nonacademic talents. Brandon, a quiet boy of medium height, was Claire's classmate in the international department. Brandon scored 2140 on the SAT and later attended the University of California, Los Angeles. He was talented in sports and music. When other students stayed in the classroom to study, Brandon and his friends often spent their breaks on basketball courts. In my scorekeeping, he was often the highest scoring player or tallied the most assists. Brandon was also skilled at the violin. An American teacher commented that Brandon was the most musical in the school and praised him for playing a violin solo. Although his overall test scores were average, Brandon was a high performer in his favorite course, psychology. His classmates perceived him to be the most knowledge-able student in the subject area and approached him for help with assignments. I shadowed Brandon a day before the deadline of an assignment for his Advanced Placement (AP) course in psychology. His classmates surrounded him at every break throughout the day. Brandon sat at his desk and pleasantly held the Q&A sessions as if he were the teaching assistant for the class.

Brandon was sociable and had many friends in high school, but his peers never talked about his music talent. They could not recall him playing solo or even that there had been a school concert. They were unconcerned about his basketball skills. Brandon was accepted to UCLA, which his peers treated as a nonevent. I returned to Capital the following year after his graduation. When I asked a few students in the next cohort if they knew Brandon, they looked at me with blank faces and shook their heads. Without high performance, Brandon did not have high status. His peers thus saw his extracurricular accomplishments as nonachievements, and he was forgotten soon after graduation.

Brandon's experiences contrasted with those of Claire. She enjoyed peer admiration for an individual achievement, but Brandon enjoyed no such recognition despite his multiple talents (sports and music). The school celebrated Claire's academic performance and called her to publicize her achievements. Brandon was not given such a task. Students remembered Claire's college application process in detail and could list the rejections she had received; they did not know where Brandon applied or the acceptances he received other than UCLA.[14] Being undistinguished in academic performance, Brandon received no credit for his extracurricular activities. He became a faceless figure in the crowd and was quickly forgotten.

Shamed in the Classroom: Sarah Fails to Answer a Question

Low-status students usually are not at the center of peer attention. When they are, they often find themselves the target of peer-initiated shaming events. I observed Sarah's eleventh grade physics class in the international department at Capital. The physics teacher, Mrs. Zhang, was reviewing test questions. She walked to the right side of the room to check students' answers. She then went back to the front and asked Sarah, a low-status student, for the answer to the next question.

Sarah fearfully stood up and answered in a faint voice. Hearing an apparently incorrect answer, a couple students gasped. Joseph, a boy sitting next to me at the far back of the classroom, frowned and swore audibly, "What the fuck?"

I immediately looked at Mrs. Zhang when I heard the swear word. It was clear that Mrs. Zhang had heard Joseph, as she glanced at him. Sarah had also heard him and instantly fell silent. Mrs. Zhang looked back at Sarah and asked her to go on. Sarah anxiously tried to explain how she had arrived at her answer, but William, who sat three seats to her left, cut her off by giving his own answer loudly and eventually took over. The teacher commanded attention by checking with Sarah, who was still standing, to determine where the problem had lain. Seemingly embarrassed, Sarah pouted and held her pen tightly as she stood blushing. Seeing that Sarah was unable to provide a satisfactory answer, the teacher told her to sit down and moved on to the next question.

In shaming events like this one, the initiators do not necessarily have high status, but the shamed individual almost always has low status in school. Joseph and William were above-average performers but did not have high status. On the other hand, Sarah's classmates and friends reported that she fit the definition of a loser. Joseph, like many other boys, sometimes used foul language to joke with others. Yet he was serious when he swore at Sarah, which Sarah noticed and took offense to (by being silent). William could have been trying to help, but his offensive behaviors strongly suggested otherwise (cutting her off, talking loudly, and taking over), and they embarrassed Sarah (who blushed). The two broke classroom etiquette, such as no swearing, responding only when called upon, and raising a hand before speaking, to mock Sarah. In the process, they not only directed student attention to Sarah's low status but also impeded Mrs. Zhang's efforts to focus on helping Sarah correct her answer.

While peer shaming is usually directed toward low-status students, their test mistakes should not be a surprise to any student familiar with the status system. Considering that low status is defined as having poor test scores, low-status students predictably have wrong answers on every test. However, these expectations notwithstanding, the students refuse to let low performers off the hook. None of the students defended Sarah, no one offered any excuse, and no one pardoned her for the mistake. Her peers treated her as if she had committed a serious offense and publicly humiliated her until she was ashamed.

Not Leadership Material: Ruolun Is Mocked for Service

Low-status students often learn that they are better off avoiding peer attention, as even celebratory gatherings could turn into mocking events. On a sunny morning, I joined the twelfth graders in a flag-raising ceremony toward the end of the school year at Capital. During the short meeting, a teacher on the podium asked students to applaud the student council members for their service.[15] A line of students, all members of the student council, boarded the podium. As the teacher called out their names, each took a step forward and took a bow as the students applauded mechanically. However, when the teacher called out "Ruolun," the students did not immediately respond in applause. Instead, there were audible chuckles, gasps, and mockery. Students around me commented with noticeable disapproval, "*He's* on the student council?" Seeing that Ruolun had bowed and was stepping back in line and the teacher had moved on to calling the next council member, some of the faster reacting students sparsely applauded Ruolun. The ceremony ended within a few minutes. I slowly exited the sports field with the students. Although most of them did not make further comments, several walked back to their classrooms with a smirk on their faces.

When Ruolun came back to his classroom, the students had become disinterested in the topic. None of them approached him to talk about his experiences on the student council, nor did anyone probe how he obtained the position.[16] Certainly, no one congratulated him or thanked him for his yearlong service to the cohort. I casually mentioned this incident in conversations later that day, but none of the students I talked to had known that Ruolun was on the student council. His group of friends had been clueless about it, as they laughed when another underachieving boy joked, "If he's on it, I could've been on it too!"

Ruolun's case was an exception that proved the norm. His peers clearly disapproved of his presence on the student council. The students rejected his qualification as a member in a leadership position (with chuckles, gasps, and smirks) and responded to his yearlong service with mockery ("He's on it? I could have been . . . !"). In addition to disapproval, Ruolun's schoolmates were also disinterested in him. While his unexpectedly holding a leadership position generated buzz in the classroom, interest in him dwindled within a few minutes. Ruolun did not bring peer attention to his accomplishment either. As a council member, he needed to participate in regular meetings. However, the fact that his friends had not known about it suggests that he either had kept it secret or forgot to mention it. Alternatively, his friends might have simply forgotten about his routine absence when hanging out. Being an underachiever, Ruolun was given different treatment from his high-status peers for the same achievement. Instead of being applauded like the other council members were, he was mocked for holding the same position.

Getting the Cold Shoulder: Kangwei Is Avoided

While the students were generally friendly toward each other in school, occasionally a student, usually one at the bottom of the status system, was shunned by peers. Kangwei, a skinny boy with pale skin and narrow eyes, was seen as the "worst student" in school. When I first entered Capital, Kangwei sometimes approached me for small talk. However, my conversations with

Kangwei were always short-lived. The students around me would quickly cut in and end the conversation abruptly. After I became closer to many of the students, they physically guided me away from Kangwei. The boys led me away upon seeing him approach, warning me on the way, "Ignore him." The girls dragged me in the opposite direction when they saw Kangwei walking toward us from as far as the end of the hallway. One such example took place when I shadowed Lili two weeks before the gaokao. Lili, Wanru, and I waited for Mei at the entrance of a school building to have lunch.

I stood inside the entrance, facing out toward Lili and Wanru. The three of us were jokingly complaining about Mei's tardiness and how hungry we were. The two girls suddenly stopped talking and glanced at each other. I saw them quietly turn around and walk outside, when someone tapped me on the back. I looked over my shoulder. It was Kangwei.

"Hey! I haven't seen you for a while!" he said enthusiastically, with a broad smile.

"That's right!" I responded.

Lili and Wanru looked back at me with sullen faces. The two of them then exchanged looks. Kangwei shot me questions such as "How have you been?" and "How's your research going?" I answered him with very short sentences, saying, "I'm okay" and "It's going well." The more I responded, the further away Lili and Wanru moved, turning their backs to Kangwei and peering at me out of the corner of their eyes. I tried to follow the girls outside and answer Kangwei's questions at the same time. However, the girls backed away with each step Kangwei and I took.

All of a sudden, Mei rushed over from the hallway, shouting, "Sorry I'm late! Let's go!" She pushed me toward Lili and Wanru with her shoulder, creating a clear space between me and Kangwei. Lili and Wanru smiled in relief and gestured for me to join them by waving their hands. I left Kangwei with a "Bye!" and ran toward them immediately. Kangwei might have said goodbye and seen us off, but none of us looked back.

Throughout my fieldwork, I observed multiple incidents of students avoiding, shunning, and sometimes showing blatant disgust toward Kangwei. I interacted with Kangwei for less than one minute, but this brief encounter already gave me a taste of what it felt like to be ignored. The girls signaled at least three times that I should not have engaged in conversation (by moving away, exchanging looks, and pushing me toward them). My response to Kangwei was hardly welcoming, even rude, compared to his friendliness.[17] Nonetheless, the fact that I had responded to his questions was sufficient for the girls to show disapproval (sullen faces, peering, and moving further away). In this incident as well as many others, students made clear that the appropriate interaction norm with Kangwei, who had very low status, was no interaction.

Given that Kangwei was among the only two students who I knew were avoided by peers, I thought that the students must have had a special reason to do so. I asked many students what they thought about Kangwei and why they treated him harshly in follow-up interviews. The students criticized him for frequently getting into fights or aggressively pursuing girls or said that he "looked hideous" and had a "gross smile." While some of these accusations might have been true, other students who had comparable behaviors were not shunned. Furthermore, even if the students' criticisms were true, peer policing to the point of shunning an individual student seemed too harsh considering the transgression.

It finally became clear in a follow-up interview with Yulang, a high-status student, that none of the behavioral issues that students cited accounted for students' collective hostility toward Kangwei. Yulang reported not knowing about Kangwei's transgressions but nonetheless thought he was an "oddball" and minimized contact with him. After failing to obtain a specific reason for labeling him as "odd," I finally asked whether Kangwei would be treated differently if he had very high test scores.

"Of course!" Yulang immediately nodded and answered in a matter-of-fact tone. "We'd be more tolerant of him. People wouldn't talk about him like that [as negatively]."

Yulang's response pointed out that Kangwei's greatest "flaw" was not his fighting and pursuing girls but that he was very low-performing and had bottom status at school. Seeing that this was a possible lead, I then asked a few others the same question. The students I later interviewed shared the same answer as Yulang but often rejected my hypothetical scenario and insisted that "it was impossible" for Kangwei to become a high performer. However, regardless of whether Kangwei's situation in school could be salvaged, students would have forgiven him of all the accused behaviors if he had had high test scores. The degree of peer policing toward Kangwei, with his very low status, became sky high. Students scrutinized his every move and accused him of an increasing number of problematic behaviors, which in turn sustained the high level of peer policing. The cycle of peer policing and taking issue with his behaviors escalated to the point where even Kangwei's smile was problematic ("gross").

I last saw Kangwei on graduation day, when proud parents swarmed to campus with their cameras. The graduating cohort wore black graduation gowns, joyfully taking group pictures. There were jubilant shouts everywhere, and laughter filled the air. At a corner of campus, Kangwei quietly posed solo for his mother. When a few students and I walked by, I paused and congratulated the mother and son. Kangwei responded with his usual broad smile. His mother looked surprised and asked, "Would you . . . ?" But the other students, who were already a few steps ahead, called me away before she could finish the sentence.

Taken together, these examples show that low performers and high performers have different patterns of peer interactions. Underachievers and losers do not occupy peer attention, nor do they get credit for their achievements. When they find themselves under the spotlight, they are shamed for wrongdoings as insignificant as a test mistake. They are not given the chance to serve in leadership positions. Even when they are given the opportunity, they receive peer mockery in return. In extreme cases, their friendliness toward others is met with opposite levels of enthusiasm, to the point of receiving no peer response at all. These interaction patterns in school are reproduced in college and job settings. As I show later, students who consider themselves to have average or low status continue to admire the high performers. They learn to blend into the crowd and do not publicize individual achievements.

Student Recognition of Differential Peer Treatment

Students recognize the systematic differences in patterns of peer interactions. For example, Jiaqi explained that test scores and status were critical in determining peer interactions. In his words, "Many high performers aren't sociable. If their grades fall, their friends might stop talking to them. Fewer people would talk to them; they'd get less audience." However, while some students were critical of these practices, they nonetheless followed the norm. Those who have experienced status mobility during high school held an especially pragmatic view of status-based interactions.

Peer Discrimination: "If You Study Well, You Can Do Anything"

Tony, a high performer, was critical toward these systematic differences. In particular, he disagreed with the practice of appointing high performers to leadership positions. I joined Tony at the empty student council room in a daylong observation. A pile of books neatly lay on the ground at a corner of the room. The books were titled *Winning at Capital*. The coversheet was a picture of a confident boy standing under a bright blue sky. Tony sat in a black leather chair behind the desk, relaxed. Putting one hand behind his head, he pointed to the pile with another and said sarcastically, "I contributed to that." The books were student biographies that Capital published to boast of student achievement. He then said that the book project was only one of the many errands that fell under their responsibility. Tony rolled his eyes and said, "There were lots of miscellaneous tasks."[18]

"Wow, you guys are impressive," I complimented.

"No! This is discrimination!" Tony shook his head and said, "It you think about it, this is basically discrimination! In [many] schools, if you study well, people think you can do anything. We have this kind of discrimination at Capital, too."

Tony saw the prejudicial treatment of students with different statuses as discriminative practices based on test scores. His perception came from his observations of how tasks were distributed in school. Having high status in school, Tony undertook many tasks for the cohort and complained bitterly about them. For example, he unwillingly wrote a biography for a book he did not care for, and he regularly led student discussions over readings in the social sciences club even though he wanted to skip every meeting. In our conversations, Tony admitted that he was good at studying, but the tasks he shouldered were unrelated to academic performance. He argued that students should not have entrusted these nonacademic tasks to a small group of high performers but should instead "let those who want to do these things do them." Unfortunately, the latter situation almost never happened. Students generally had "blind faith" in high performers, believing that they excelled in all sorts of tasks. Simultaneously, they "discriminated" against the low performers, thinking they were "worthless" and "incapable" of doing anything.

While Tony was critical toward peer discrimination based on test scores, he nonetheless neglected the advantages he enjoyed as a high-status student. Tony focused on the burdens that he grudgingly shouldered. He did not mention the attention he received and seemed unaware of the fact that he was free from peer policing. Tony's entitlement to peer attention and freedom of behavior is especially clear when comparing him with Kevin, a low performer who scored "1000-something on the SAT." Neither boy was gregarious, and both often disappeared from the classroom. Yet Tony's classmates forgave him for leaving the classroom unannounced but criticized Kevin as someone who "never talked, never was a gregarious guy, [and who] disappeared from the classroom during class." Additionally, Tony and Kevin both had imperfect appearances. The classmates criticized Kevin for "growing his hair super long, with bangs over his eyebrows," commenting negatively with statements such as, "Think about it. A guy, looking like *that!*" Although classmates also joked about Tony's "dumb-looking" smile, they used these comments to contrast Tony's "simple-minded appearance" with his "superior intelligence." Tony was respected and admired, and other students wanted to be like him; Kevin was ignored and spoken ill of. Other students avoided him and needless to say did not want to be like him.[19] Even the ability to explain patterns of peer interactions depended on status. In later interviews, students admitted to making sure that I "never meet" Kevin. By comparison, Tony was free to hang out with the researcher and call students out on discrimination.

The Need to Shine: Dehong's Self-Reflection

While some students are critical of the differential interaction patterns, others support these systematic differences and perceive them to be legitimate. Dehong, a studyholic who had been an underachiever in the first year and a half in high school, belonged to the latter group. I invited Dehong for coffee at the Beijing Center of my alma mater after he was accepted to Fudan University. We sat in the white faux leather chairs across a white marble table beside the French windows that oversaw a busy street. In our conversation, he was at first relieved that the gaokao was over but changed his mood when we talked about his peers in high school.

"People need to shine at something. And they need to shine to a certain degree to get my attention." He chuckled, holding his white paper cup in both hands.

"What do you mean by shine?" I asked. "High test scores or something?"

Dehong immediately sat up straight and nodded. "That would be a very big shining point." He explained in a serious manner, "I'm the type who isn't talented at anything. Even at studying, I can't compete in the Olympiad. I have no talent in music, art, or things of that sort, [nor] in sports. I can only get people's attention by hard work. I study hard to get people's attention. If I had gotten poor test scores, there wouldn't be me. I'd be buried somewhere in the crowd. I wouldn't exist."

"No way, that's not true," I objected, but Dehong cut me off.

"This is how things work." He said flatly, "It's been about a month since the gaokao. I've already forgotten many [schoolmates] who aren't important, like those who aren't good at tests, those who don't excel. If you're not better than others, it's normal for you to be forgotten. Why should anyone remember you? There's no reason for that."

I sat across the white marble table, speechless at his statement. Dehong continued by offering himself as an example. "I'd say something like this: 'My high school friend Dehong, he got really good grades and went to this [good] university, I think he's great.'" He paused and looked me in the eyes. I responded with a nod, thinking that was an accurate description of himself. He then continued, "[But not], 'My high school friend Dehong, he got average grades and went to this ordinary university.'" I looked at him, puzzled. Dehong said with a sneer, "Why on earth would I say that? Why would I even remember him, right? I have no reason to remember him." Looking as if he had explained the obvious, Dehong emotionlessly put down the paper cup on the table between us and slouched back into the chair.

Dehong took an exceptionally harsh view in explaining peer associations. Dehong's understanding of the reality in peer relationships might have been shaped by his upward mobility experiences in school. His peers paid little attention to him when he was an underachiever; but peers took notice of him and followed him after became a studyholic. Having experienced differential treatment, Dehong learned that the high-status students stood out ("shine") and that peers were a forgetful crowd who remembered only those with high status. While Dehong mentioned extracurricular activities as part of individual talent, his point was not that these traits made a student "shine." In the elite Chinese student status system, Dehong and other students knew too well that nonacademic talent was unrelated to whether one "shined" in front of peers.[20] Instead, he was emphasizing the inevitability and necessity for him to achieve high test scores to attract peer attention. As he explained, he was willing to "work himself to death" because it was "the only way people would notice me." His efforts paid off, and he successfully crossed the high and low status boundary. The transition from nobody to somebody taught him that test scores, status, and peer attention were inseparable. He learned to accept the fact that peer interactions differed based on test scores and supported the system as natural, practical, and logical ("normal," "no reason to remember"). Adopting a pragmatic approach, he declared the systematic differential peer treatment as unchangeable reality ("This is how things work").

Beyond High School: New Friends, Same Interactions

If making friends in high school was something that came naturally, building relationships beyond it, in college and at work, was a different story. The students no longer met with the same group of friends every day and certainly did not stay together in the same room for as long as fifteen hours each day. College friends and colleagues might have been as reliable and supportive as high school classmates, but they were not groomed in the same environment with the elite students. Six years after high school graduation, most study gods and studyholics still kept in touch with high school friends, who in turn stayed on top of the study gods' trajectories.

Students closely followed Dapeng, a study god. They shared details of Dapeng's transition to Goldman Sachs and how he married his high school sweetheart Jina,[21] and they made educated guesses about his income without prompting. Not all study gods and studyholics had peer admirers. Few of Yulang's high school classmates knew that she enrolled in a PhD program ranked among the top in the world after graduating from THU. On the other hand, underachievers and losers have lost touch with classmates from high school. Xiaolong, an underachiever, stayed in Beijing for college but no longer associated with his high school friends. When Mark, a student who fit the definition of a loser, proudly announced on social media that he "finally received an A" in his last semester at the University of British Columbia, few of his friends who liked his post were from the same high school.

By 2020, all except one of the twenty-eight students graduated from college. I visited most of them after college graduation.[22] I was interested in knowing about their current peer relationships and whether they maintained ties with their adolescent friends. Interesting patterns emerged, namely that students' friendships primarily consisted of peers who lived nearby and had the same ethnicity. The students who remained in China unintentionally befriended peers based on residential location. They found the rural students who "focused on studying" difficult, while the urban dwellers who "knew how to enjoy life" were agreeable. The students in the United States and Europe reported being in a "diversified environment," and most found refuge in the Chinese international community. Many outside of China tried desperately to befriend their local peers, only to gravitate toward intraethnic networks a few years later for reasons such as shared interests, similar culinary tastes, and cooperation on test preparation.[23] Yet the basis of peer interactions has not all changed. Students continue to admire high performers in college. They keep an eye on each other's individual performance and award elevated status to those who outperform others. Low performers remain invisible. These patterns of associations suggest that the former adolescents, who later became college students and are now in the labor market, employ a status-interaction principle to govern peer interaction, as they have since high school.

In twelfth grade, Lili and her friends "worshipped the gods." Shuhua expressed similar emotions toward the study gods throughout college. I visited Shuhua at her university in her freshman year. She revealed to me over dessert that she deeply admired Shiying, her high school classmate and study god, and then bemoaned the lack of "people like that" in college. "Studyholics are very good at studying and maybe one or two other things. But study gods like Shiying are good at everything." Shuhua then rested her chin on her left hand. She looked into the air and said with dreamy eyes, "I really admire Shiying. I admire her from the bottom of my heart." I visited Shuhua annually in the first three years of college. She landed an internship at a luxury whiskey company in her junior year but remained disappointed toward her peers in college for their insufficient competition in the process. I texted to congratulate her on her college graduation in her senior year. In our text exchanges, she told me that she was "doing well" and had been focused on job hunting. She then said that she had given up on wishing for a study god to appear, to the point where she "didn't talk about these things anymore." However, she quickly followed up with a text that read, "But if there were study gods, I'd still think they're awesome. Haha!" Shuhua admired the study gods since the start of her freshman year to the end of her senior year. She adored Shiying and wished there were more effortlessly high performers in college. Her dreamy eyes and tone of admiration ran parallel to Lili's: both saw study gods as superior to others and figuratively bowed down to "worship the gods."

The young adults with high status had followers who admired them and commanded peer attention to a degree that others students did not. After graduating from Cornell, Tony joined a financial firm in New York. A few months after moving to Queens, he threw a birthday party at the rooftop lounge of his building. I visited him the morning after the party. He told me cheerfully that some two dozen friends joined the celebration. The attendees included friends from high school, such as Stacey and Daniel, college friends who were nearby, and colleagues at work. Tony reported being a good host and "socializing" at the beginning of the party. He greeted the guests, fixed drinks for them, and introduced them to each other. He was pleased that they seemed to enjoy themselves that night. He chuckled and described that, toward the end of the party, the international group had switched to speaking in Spanish; the Americans were on autopilot and many got drunk; and the Chinese friends were having a ball playing card games.[24]

While most students reported celebrating birthdays with friends, Tony's birthday party was considerably larger and more diverse in peer composition than those of other students. These differences might reflect personal preferences, but the ability to gather peers at short notice is exclusive to young adults with high status. Tony was a study god in high school and a top performer in college. He was also a high performer at work, where he was given the freedom to join various teams based on personal interest. The attendance at his party showed he had a very strong command of peer attention, considering that it was inconvenient for many to participate. Stacey took the train in from Boston late in the afternoon and left early the next morning for a meeting. I met Stacey in Boston a few days after the party, during which she jokingly complained, "I made that trip just for him! I wouldn't do that for other people!" His college friends traveled from nearby cities and suburbs. Although his colleagues lived in New York, coming to the party was not as convenient for them as one would think. The day before his birthday, Tony and his colleagues had just returned from a two-week work trip. Tony described the trip as he loaded the washing machine with a basket of work clothes, having two more baskets in the queue. "It was basically two weeks of intense socializing at [another city], after which you kind of just want to be alone, lie down and unwind, or something." In other words, the event was analogous to Tony's call to worship, to which his peers jumped through hoops to respond. The fact that other students could not command peers to do so, and that they were unwilling to do so for others, demonstrates that the high-status individuals continue to receive special treatment and remain at the center of attention at work as in high school.

Students interact with peers in different ways that reflect their relative standings in each peer group. Alex was an underachiever at Capital who later attended Boston College. I visited him in late summer 2019, when he was two years into his job as a software engineer at a multinational ecommerce company. Alex had not changed much. He still had short, curly hair and a few pimples on his cheeks. He greeted me at the entrance of his company after work hours, holding a black laptop in one arm, with earphones in both ears. He was wearing a red checkered shirt and khaki pants, which let him blend into the flow of people exiting and entering the building. We drove to dinner at a tavern near Fenway Park in his red SUV. Commemorating his college life, Alex first reported that he had a 3.77 GPA. In his assessment, he was "about average" in the Chinese student community, where "the lower [performers] got 3.5" and "the higher ones got 3.9." However, Alex was a high performer by university standards. The university website states that students can make the dean's list with a 3.4 GPA. And although Alex never mentioned it, he had graduated magna cum laude.

Being differently positioned in the status system depending on the comparison group, Alex adopted two sets of interaction patterns according to his relative performance. Alex had little to say about the Chinese group. When I asked him about whom they were, his main comment was that he deeply respected "a girl who got a 4.0 GPA and went to Harvard law!" When we talked about other friends in the university, many of whom were Kenyan, he smiled and said that he talks to them frequently despite being scattered around the world. Alex was fond of his non-Chinese friends who were lower performing than himself but nonetheless maintained distance from them. He commented, "All of us here are pretty smart. We've been through selection." But he immediately added with a sigh, "There are always some who can't keep up. They can't do the work, but we try to help." I asked if he had helped those friends. Alex responded succinctly, "I try to keep to myself." I raised an eyebrow, wondering whether this went against his claim of being friendly and close to peers. Sensing that I was unconvinced, Alex quickly added, "But if they come to me, I'll help out if I can."

Alex considered his peers to be two separate peer groups: the Chinese nationals, half of whom outperformed him, and the other (international) students, who generally did worse than he did on coursework. Being an average student in the former group, Alex addressed those peers from the perspective of the crowd. He analyzed the ranges of GPA (3.5 to 3.9), assessed his relative position in the group ("about average"), and expressed admiration toward the top performer (girl with 4.0 GPA). By comparison, Alex adopted a top-down perspective when mentioning his friends who were low performers. He had a tone of superiority (sigh, coming that others "can't keep up," "can't do the work"); he also marked boundaries, which was a hallmark of high status. He did not help despite sensing peers' need of assistance ("keep to myself") and only conditionally responded to their requests ("if I can"). These narratives revealed that Alex had kept a distance from peers who were low performers, like Xijun's behavior toward peers in high school.

By and large, peer interactions in high school resemble interactions with those in college and at work. An example that clearly presents these parallel relationships is how Xijun, the distant celebrity at Pinnacle, continued to be one in college and at work. I met Xijun in early winter 2019. It was her last semester at the London School of Economics (LSE), but she had finished all required coursework, completed her thesis, and was simply waiting to graduate. While she could have stayed in London, Xijun decided to return home for good because London was "boring" and winter there was "too cold and gloomy." Xijun offered to pick me up at the arrival lobby at Beijing airport. She arrived promptly, dressed comfortably in a hoodie, dark-colored sweatpants, and a puffy black parka. She took me to dinner at a five-star venue that was usually reserved for weddings in a black Jeep, which cost over $100,000.[25.]

On the way, Xijun updated me about what she had gone through since college. Xijun started taking on commercial ad cases in her sophomore year. She sought out schoolmates who specialized in lighting, script writing, and other areas, to form a crew. In Xijun's words, "I set up my own company" and was profiting to the point where "I could buy all the luxury goods I wanted with my own money." I responded by saying that it was nice to start a company with friends. Xijun corrected me immediately, "Oh, no, I'm not friends with them." She added, "They're colleagues, more like employees." Xijun took a leave of absence to get the company on track, and I suspect some of her colleagues did as well. A year or so later, one of the most successful commercial ad producers in the country invited her to be his apprentice. Xijun jumped at the opportunity and left the team behind. As a result, the team dissolved and the company evaporated.

After she "learned the ropes" of the trade through apprenticing and learned how to "produce the quality films her team could not" earlier, she started taking cases as a freelancer. Xijun avoided the 2018 media recession in China by going to graduate school at LSE. While students usually go to graduate school to receive further training, Xijun's needs were simply "to rest for a while but not leave my CV blank," something that LSE "completely fulfilled" by offering a master's program that was "way too easy," was "mostly common sense," and "hardly required any effort." In other words, her time at LSE served the sole purpose of letting her chill for a few years. Xijun traveled frequently, alone, during her master's studies. She sent me postcards from various European countries, but I had not seen her post pictures with classmates and friends on social media. She had "so much time" that she wrote a novel in school and published it within two months after returning to Beijing. When asked about the novel, she tilted the corners of her mouth and said, "I wrote it pitched to the market; I knew it was bound to generate interest. As I expected, a company bought it and is turning it into a movie." Although she had resettled in Beijing, Xijun was not in touch with her college schoolmates, nor did she work with them. As we made a right turn into an alley, she shrugged, "I have no idea what they're doing." She then added with a cavalier attitude, "No matter anyway."

Many of the elite students in this study who stayed at the top of their career trajectories were oblivious to peers who had lower performance. Xijun was a top performer in her field of expertise, which shaped her subsequent interaction with others. In high school, Claire was the center of attention of her followers, who defended and supported her; likewise, Xijun was at the center of attention among her college peers, who followed her to the point of leaving school to become her "employees." In high school, Julie felt entitled to peer attention; in the labor market, Xijun also felt entitled to attention by companies ("bound to generate interest" and "as I expected"). Granted, Xijun's sense of entitlement stems from her professional training and top performance in her field. However, while workers are often confident about their work results, Xijun's high sense of entitlement toward job success was unmatched by other professionals.[26]

While many elite young adults build friendship relationships with their peers, it appears that harmonious peer relationships are not necessary for those on their quest to become global elite. Instead, they distinguish themselves and maintain a distance from peers. They not only draw physical boundaries (ditching peers at a moment's notice, or not keeping in touch), but are also emotionally detached from others. Xijun's ambivalence toward those whom she considered beneath her was remarkably similar in 2013 and in 2019. She ignored her peers and was indifferent toward their outcomes ("not friends," and that they "don't matter"). Xijun's lack of interaction and boundary-marking behavior reminded me about her interaction patterns with peers in high school. Just as she was nonassociational with colleagues ("I have no idea what they're doing"), she had delivered the same comment about her high school peers: six years earlier, I walked with twelfth grader Xijun out of the school gate in the late afternoon. When I asked about her peers' activities that night, she unemotionally responded, "I have no idea."

Shuhua, Tony, Alex, and Xijun are four among the many who continue to uphold the interaction norms they learned in high school. Elite young adults habitually locate each other in different status groups using test scores and later job performance, as they did in high school. Because these assessments shape peer associations to no small degree, students instinctively approach, respond to, and interact with peers using the same set of norms later in life. As a result, peer interactions during adolescence become precursors to their interaction patterns with peers from around the world in young adulthood.

Summary

While the students in this study were similarly elite, their peer relationships in high school differed from each other. They were supportive toward each other, but students from high-status groups enjoyed more than friendly interactions. These exalted individuals were at the center of peer attention and were admired for anything they did, even if they went against normative classroom behavior. Students from low-status groups enjoyed none of these privileges. Having systematically experienced differential treatment, students learned that test scores and status were inevitably connected to treatment by peers. They habitually favored individuals with high status and discriminated against those with low status and expected to be treated likewise. In the process, students supported and policed each other so that all acted within their respective status boundaries.

The findings in this chapter highlight the power of status in shaping interpersonal relationships and interaction patterns. Students have different levels of sociability and gregarious tendencies. However, personal characteristics are not as consequential as status in determining peer interactions. Many study gods and studyholics are agreeable companions; others are distant and unwilling to associate with peers. In the same regard, many underachievers and losers are friendly and cordial; others less so. However, even the coldest and most distant high-status students have admirers who try to befriend them. By comparison, the harmless and sociable students at the bottom of the status system are shunned, and their schoolmates do not make eye contact with them, let alone build relationships.

In 2019, the students had transitioned to work and graduate school around the world. Many things had changed, but patterns of peer relationships endured. To the extent that these young adults continued to carry themselves in social groups as they had in high school, adolescent peer groups played an important role in shaping how future elites associated among themselves and with others. It is likely that these elites self-identify as having high status in society and subsequently behave accordingly. In such a context, the elite young adults expect to be excused of misconduct and have strong feelings of entitlement to various privileges. After all, they have learned since they were young that, just as study gods deserve to be worshiped, they deserve the freedom to do anything.

4

Hanging Teachers
on the Blackboard

As soon as Mrs. Tang entered the teacher's office, she approached me with folded arms to talk about Weicheng, a study god. "Weicheng wanted to hit the gym last Tuesday, but it was after hours. When people see that a gym, or anything, is closed, they usually just walk away, right?" I nodded in agreement. Mrs. Tang rolled her eyes, "But not Weicheng. He got angry. He kicked and shattered the glass door. He was caught on security camera in school uniform. The gym contacted the school, so now *we* have to deal with it. We told the gym, 'He's a twelfth grader stressed out about the gaokao.'" Furiously, she added, "I saw him the next day—he wasn't apologetic at all! He even looked proud! Clearly no one talked to him about this!"

ON ONE CHILLY winter morning in March, I joined a classroom of thirty-two Capital students at nine o'clock for Mrs. Mao's geography class. The students were quietly hunched over their cream-colored desks, ready to take notes. Mrs. Mao briskly walked into the classroom. This class was a test review session in which the teacher stood by the blackboard and discussed recent test questions. One question was about how the Xiamen-Shenzhen Railway was constructed. Mrs. Mao explained that the railway, originally designed to be along the coastline, had to be moved inland due to military concerns.

"But it only moved one kilometer inward! This explanation is too far-fetched!" Gao, a boy with spiky hair and dark-rimmed glasses who sat near the front, loudly interrupted Mrs. Mao. "It should've been like that other railway that moved a lot further!"

Another girl piped up in agreement. There was a hustle in the room as students refuted Mrs. Mao's answer.

Mrs. Mao tried to give a more thorough explanation. But before she could say anything, Dapeng, a boy who sat at the far back of the room (in front of me), lifted his head, looked at her, and said quietly but firmly, "Let me [answer]. I can talk about this for a bit."

Mrs. Mao froze for a split second, bewildered. "Fine," she said, awkwardly putting down the piece of chalk she was holding.

Dapeng rose from his seat and murmured, "I can explain this more clearly anyway."

Both the students sitting by him and I were stunned. The girl to Dapeng's left looked up from her desk and dramatically took a breath, her eyes wide with anticipation. Mrs. Mao was stone-faced. The students silently stared at Dapeng with their chins lowered as he walked toward the blackboard. In the manner of a teacher denouncing a student's incorrect answer, Dapeng quickly erased what Mrs. Mao had written. He then drew a map of the coastline and lectured us: "The railway was designed early on, but other intersecting railways were completed before it started being built. . . . So this is basically it. It's actually socioeconomic reasons that led to changes in the construction of this railroad." With a tense look and straightened back, Mrs. Mao watched Dapeng walk assuredly back to seat. Emotionlessly, she nodded and said in English, "Thank you." She then continued class as if nothing had happened.

This episode greeted me on my first day at Capital. I expected to see similar manifestations of elite student entitlement in every classroom. However, I soon realized that these outbursts of student entitlement were infrequent and observed only among the top performers. The top performers evidently enjoyed an elevated status at school. In the incident above, Dapeng was one of the few study gods, the top-performing students who demonstrated low levels of effort. He was the highest-scoring student in a districtwide mock exam. He received sixty extra points for Peking University through the principal's recommendation, which is available to one or two students in a few top high schools each year.[1] In fact, Dapeng was so academically stellar that he did not even make use of the extra points—he later attended Peking University as one of the top 50 students out of some 72,000 exam takers in Beijing. With such high status in school, Dapeng demonstrated a strikingly high degree of entitlement and disrespect. He openly suggested that Mrs. Mao was incompetent by denouncing her answer (she had told the class that the railway moved due to military concerns, but Dapeng said it was for socioeconomic reasons). He ignored her visible signs of annoyance (stone-faced, tense, emotionless) and took over class. Finally, he publicly treated her as if she were the student by erasing her answer on the blackboard.

Dapeng's behavior was not unusual among the study gods. There was even a special phrase for Dapeng's behavior: "hanging teachers on the blackboard" (ba laoshi gua heiban shang). I first came across this phrase in a magazine article describing Pinnacle as "the school where students hang teachers on the blackboard." The article did not explain what the phrase meant, so I asked Mr. Hu, my key informant and the head math teacher at Pinnacle, for an explanation. He smiled and said proudly, "It means that our students are so smart that they will prove you wrong in class." Shaking his head, he then added, "But that was a very long time ago. Nowadays our students don't do this anymore. I wish they could." Mr. Hu's positive response to possibly being "hung on the blackboard" shows that teachers respond differently to this phenomenon.[2] Regardless of teacher reactions, however, the fact that there is a popular phrase describing this particular style of interaction suggests that this pattern of student-teacher interactions observed among top-performing elite students is widely recognized.

Daily Interactions: General Respect and Overall Entitlement

Behaviors such as "hanging teachers on the blackboard" are uncommon and noteworthy especially when considered in the context of Chinese classrooms, where students are generally always respectful toward teachers. Regardless of academic performance, students stop and greet teachers in the hallways. They make sure to be quiet when passing by the teacher's office so as not to disturb the teachers inside. If they need to talk to a teacher in the office, they knock on the door lightly, walk in gingerly, quickly approach the teacher they are looking for, and talk in a very low voice. In short, student compliance is normative. Study gods and losers alike run errands for teachers, such as delivering things to other students or making posters for the school, without complaint. A teacher's mere presence in the classroom is sufficient to command student attention. When a teacher enters a classroom, he or she needs only to stand in front of the room. The students quickly hush each other. Some teachers initiate a ritualistic greeting at the beginning of class by simply uttering two words: "Class [has] begun!" or "Class leader!" Upon hearing this, the class leader immediately orders every student in the classroom to stand up, bow, and greet the teacher by chanting in unison this formulaic greeting: "Good morning/ afternoon, Mr./Ms. So-and-so [teacher's surname]!"

Teachers reprimand students whenever they are seen doing something wrong. Once, when I was sitting in a classroom waiting for class to start, Mrs. Nie walked to the center of the room toward Shiying, a study god at Capital. Shiying was responsible for delivering handouts. I overheard Mrs. Nie tell Shiying, in a serious tone, that she was being "inconsiderate." Shiying stood stiffly. She stayed silent as Mrs. Nie angrily said, "Not everyone received their handouts. Without them, they won't be able to follow in class, they wouldn't know what's going on at all. But you didn't check, you didn't even notice. Now go make it right." Shiying nodded obediently and softly replied, "Okay." She then actively sought out and delivered the handouts to the individuals, including myself, with a smile. In this example (as in many others), the student obediently accepts the teacher's correction regardless of test scores and school status.

Overall, the students in this study are well-behaved. Elite students in Beijing need minimal teacher supervision and are quick to respond to instructions. Even the exception proves the rule: during a twelfth grade meeting at Pinnacle, a teacher publicly criticized a girl for sending a one-line text message to ask for permission to skip class. The student had texted, "I don't feel well, I'm not coming to class today." Many of the students in the room gasped or tittered upon hearing this. It was clear that this behavior was disrespectful and unacceptable to both teachers and students. Instead, an appropriate text message would have greeted the teacher, apologized, explained the situation, and then asked for permission or forgiveness.

Teachers Are the Experts on College Preparation

There is good reason for students to be respectful and fully compliant to teacher instructions. For those preparing for the gaokao, many of the extra points mentioned in earlier chapters require teachers' endorsement. Students in top high schools have an additional reason to closely follow teachers' instructions: teachers are the creators of mock exams. These students identify teachers as experts who have unparalleled knowledge of exam content. Furthermore, students widely believe that their teachers are often enlisted as exam creators for the gaokao. One of these students was Yulang, the first girl I got to know at Capital.

Yulang was close to her history teacher, Mr. Yang, and kept in touch with him after she went to Tsinghua University. I met up with Yulang during her first year at Tsinghua. She asked me over coffee, "You know Mr. Yang?" I nodded. She then leaned over and said in a hushed voice, "He went missing over the summer. Nobody could reach him, nobody knew where he went. I tried to contact him a few times, but he never answered." Although this sounded like the beginning of a horror story, Yulang quickly clarified that it was not. "We all think that he got enlisted to be one of the people who write gaokao questions. Actually, we're pretty sure of that." I was surprised and asked how she obtained this information. "Because the time that he went off the radar totally fit the timeline. It started a few weeks before the exam, when the exam questions are submitted and finalized. He was unreachable until a few weeks after, which is when they need to grade the answers." She then went on to explain that exam givers were brought into isolation altogether and that cell phones were definitely not allowed. I probed further by suggesting that it might have been a coincidence. Yulang shook her head and explained patiently, "Our teachers take turns to write those questions, everyone knows that." She reached for her drink, sat back, and said, "Of course, twelfth grade teachers can't do that the year their students are taking the exam. Two years ago, Mrs. Zheng wrote questions for the gaokao. Mr. Yang is eligible this year." She leaned against the chair, looked me in the eye, and said assuredly, "That's what happened."

Convinced that teachers hold critical information about the exam, students such as Yulang closely tracked their teachers' movements. Yulang's educated guess turned out to be true, as teachers at Capital and Pinnacle later confirmed that high school teachers were indeed enlisted to create exam questions. Furthermore, the teachers clarified that only the most experienced teachers in top high schools were enlisted. Yet regardless of whether the students guessed correctly, Yulang's explanation provided a calculated, rational reason for students to follow their teachers' instructions. While a cultural explanation for student compliance emphasizes the Confucian norm, elite students' narratives offer an instrumental reason for them to respect and obey teachers—after all, there is no better way to prepare for the gaokao than to follow its creators' test prep instructions.

Students applying to American universities also had reason to follow their teachers and counselors. Schoolteachers provide recommendation letters and determine a student's GPA, both of which are part of the application package. Additionally, these students trust their counselors to send them to top universities in the United States. One of the most trusted counselors was Tom, a middle-aged white American and former admissions officer in the United States. In 2013, after application results came out, Capital achieved its record high of sending eight students to the University of Pennsylvania in one year. The number of students admitted there was so high that Capital alumni would have accounted for over 10 percent of Chinese freshmen at Penn that year.[3] Students gossiped that Tom had single-handedly contributed to this record high and that "he must have had connections with that university." Not surprisingly, students in the class of 2014 were devastated when Tom left Capital for Pinnacle the next fall. They were utterly convinced of Tom's importance when it became clear, in spring 2014, that not a single Capital student got into Penn, but four from Pinnacle did.

While this story spread quickly and convinced many students, those who were admitted to Penn in 2013 and other counselors at Capital declared it a rumor. One of the eight students who had enrolled in Penn was Selena. Selena frowned in disagreement upon hearing me repeat this gossip during our interview. It was the summer after her high school graduation. She explained that her advisor was not Tom but John, a Chinese national. Selena commented that John was "not particularly helpful, but he occasionally gave good suggestions about my essays." She could not recall receiving extra help from any other counselor, including Tom. The other counselors at Capital also rebuked the story as nonsense. John, in particular, sneered and said that students were "imaginative." He acknowledged that Tom had left Capital, but Tom's departure and Capital's sudden drop in Penn admissions the following year "were coincidental, not causal [relationships]." He argued that there was no way to pinpoint why Penn did not admit any student from Capital that year, but that this shouldn't have been a concern because, as he proudly declared, "Even though none of our students went to Penn this year, they got into many other very, very good universities."

While the counselors refuted this gossip, the students continued to be certain of it. In spring 2014, I had lunch with Tony and his friends at one of his favorite noodle places near campus. Tony decided to accept the offer from Cornell. While he was satisfied for himself, he was upset with his cohort's overall placements and attributed it to Tom's resignation. Slurping his noodles, Tony brought up the rumor about Tom and his record student placements. "Tom sent so many students to [the University of Pennsylvania] when lots of other high schools sent none." He said with a frown, "This year, nobody in my cohort got in. Nobody! And look at Pinnacle, four of them got admitted!" The others nodded in agreement. I suggested that it might have been a mere coincidence or that Capital might have sent too many students to the university in 2013. Tony sneered at my suggestion, "No way!" His friend explained, "Remember when our school hosted that [admissions] event last year? Many admissions officers visited. Tom got students to show the officers around, one on one, each with an officer from the school they applied for. My friend got asked. Many of them got in to their dream school a few months later." Tony nodded and added, "Nothing like that happened for us this year." He then ended the conversation by asking, "If it wasn't Tom, what was it? Magic?"

While Tom's role in Penn admissions remains debatable, studies show that high school counselors do play a part in students' college admission outcomes. Counselors who build relationships with university admissions officers are able to establish their high schools as feeders for those universities.[4] It is likely that Tom connected students with admissions officers from the universities to which they applied in order to strategically cultivate relationships with those universities. While it is unclear how beneficial this strategy was, top-performing students such as Tony identified it as part of the necessary support they were entitled to receive. When these students did not receive the expected help, they not only dismissed other counselors' explanations of admissions outcomes ("What was it, magic?") but also saw themselves as being deprived of

educational opportunities. By comparison, I did not observe any low performers discuss Tom's resignation. In fact, as I show later, the low-performing students had a different relationship with admissions counselors, and this difference precluded them from being entitled to counselors' strategic support.

Teachers and Students Are in It Together

In addition to seeing teachers as college preparation experts, students trust
teachers because they share a common interest. The students want to be as
high-performing as possible in order to get into the best universities. The
teachers want as many high-performing students as possible because although
teachers refrain from talking about it, it is public knowledge that top high
schools give teachers bonuses if their students perform well, especially if a
good number of them get into top universities. Performance pay, however, has
caveats. Students and parents know that teachers must choose one of several
strategies to maximize their rewards. They can improve the average performance of all students by helping the low performers. Alternatively, they can
focus on the middle-range students, in the hope that some of them might become competitive candidates for top universities. Regardless of the approach,
one thing is clear: top performers must remain as high-performing as possible.[5] For this reason, teachers often allow high performers to do as they please,
especially as the gaokao or application season approaches. There is a tacit
understanding among students that teachers favor those who are likely to get
into top universities.[6]

Students know that the additional income gained from sending students to
top universities is important to many teachers. When asked directly how they
felt about the emphasis on producing top students, students would smile and
say something such as "Teachers don't earn much," "[The teacher] has kids to
feed," or "Teachers need to make a living too." Given that these students
seemed understanding, the teachers did not conceal their calculations of
bonus pay. During a daylong observation at Capital, I overheard a group of five
or six girls talking about admissions chances. It was around noon. Shuhua and
her friends were chatting at their desks. Two other girls briskly walked into the
room and headed straight toward Shuhua. They had just returned from the
teachers' office after talking to Mrs. Nie, the homeroom teacher of a top-
performing classroom in Capital. She had been "counting how many in our
classroom would go to Peking or Tsinghua." One of the girls announced that
"Mrs. Nie came up with seven. You know." The others nodded. The fact that
no one asked for names suggested that they all agreed on whom the anointed
seven were. The girl continued, "Mrs. Nie said she really needed an eighth one.
But nobody knew who." Some of the girls seemed confused, and a few looked

at each other inquisitively. The girl then loudly announced, "Mrs. Nie suggested Shuhua *might* be able to [get in], and she asked what we thought of Shuhua's potential!" At this point, all of the girls turned toward Shuhua, who shook her head dramatically and shouted in horror, "No way! Don't count on me for that! That's too much pressure! Seven should be enough for her!" The group burst out in laughter. The girl who made the announcement patted Shuhua on the back and said, "We told her that you might, but it's not certain. Mrs. Nie seemed a bit bummed, but at least she can count on seven." Shuhua let out a sigh of relief and dropped her shoulders. Another girl in the group asked, "How much exactly do teachers get for that, though?" The girls shrugged. Nobody knew the amount. "It's probably a lot," they agreed.

While the teachers I spoke to neither confirmed the amount nor talked about this practice, the linkage of teacher income to student performance is a type of performance-related pay (or merit pay) endorsed by government policy.[7] User input information on kanzhun.com (the equivalent of glassdoor .com), which allows users to post their income anonymously, shows that teachers in Omega could potentially receive performance pay exceeding their annual income. Knowing that teachers' interests are aligned with their own, students see teachers as collaborators and trust them to have their best interests in mind. Awareness and tacit support of bonus pay calculations reassure students and encourage them to obey teachers' gaokao instructions and rely on them for college applications. Furthermore, in the eyes of students, performance pay justifies why teachers often treat them differently based on test scores.

Building Relationships through Gift Giving

Recognizing the role of teachers in their quest for top university placements, students express appreciation through gift giving, an exchange behavior practiced in Chinese business and government sectors.[8] Teachers are well aware that they would receive gifts on holidays, events, and birthdays.[9] They also know what *not* to expect. For example, cards seldom contributed to building teacher-student relationships. When I told Mr. Long that American students sometimes wrote cards to their teachers, he responded with a serious frown. "Cards? What kind of gift is that?" He asked, "Why would anyone want that?"

All teachers in the schools I visited had received gifts from students (and parents). This was made clear to me when I bumped into Mr. Hu at Pinnacle during a daylong observation. Mr. Hu saw me in the hallway and invited me to his office, which he shared with three other math teachers. He courteously asked if I would like to have some tea. I gladly accepted. However, his next question—"What type of tea do you want?"—was harder to answer. I stood there and stared at him blankly, not realizing that there were even options.

He smiled and led me to a table in the center of the room, where an assortment of teas was piled. As I marveled at the collection of pricey teas, Mr. Hu pointed to a few and suggested a type of green tea that was especially nice. I quickly agreed and watched him put a few tea leaves in a paper cup. As he poured hot water into the cup, he explained that most of the teas were gifts for the teachers who shared the same office. Since the office mates together had an "endless" supply of high-quality teas, they developed the habit of sharing these gifts with each other.

In the schools I visited, students customarily maintained and built relationships with their teachers by giving gifts. These gifts convey different intentions depending on content and occasion. Students like Shiying thought about them as occasion-appropriate ways of expressing gratitude. For example, she had prepared individually wrapped apples as Christmas gifts for every teacher.[10] Others had more instrumental motivations, such as catching the attention of and help from teachers of certain subjects.[11] While teachers always receive gifts on holidays and special occasions, it should be noted that not all students give gifts. One example is Jiaqi, an underachiever. When I asked whether he had gifted teachers anything, he frowned and asked confusedly, "No, why?" This response suggests that the practice of giving gifts to teachers, despite its normativity, was absurd to some students.

Teachers also have different reactions to gifts. Mr. Long was unenthusiastic about his elaborately wrapped birthday gift from a student, but Mr. Hu and his office mates' cheerful tea collecting suggests appreciation. Regardless of these different responses, the potential educational benefits obtained through teachers' attention and support outweigh the costs of gifts for elite students and their families. After all, students see teachers as critical to achieving college placements and, by extension, their futures. In other words, while gift giving is primarily understood by students as a way of showing respect, in light of its very high benefit-cost ratio, it is also a way for elite students to strengthen mutual ties of obligation with their teachers.

Praising and Empowering Students

Teachers routinely expected a lot from their students. Capital teachers often told students they would "change the world"—implying that they would assume leadership positions in the future. I have heard teachers tell a classroom full of students, "All of you have the potential to be the prime minister. See, you guys gave good answers to the questions that even our prime minister couldn't answer." Similarly, Pinnacle teachers constantly reminded their students that they were superior to students at other schools. These teachers would frequently say, in casual conversations with students, "We are Pinnacle," "We are clearly much better than others," or "We are still top in the district." I observed teachers telling students more than once a day, "The goal for [others] is too low for us, so we've set a more adequate, higher standard for you." These "standards" included normative student behavior, such as efficiently lining up for school-wide meetings on the sports field and being quiet in the hallways. Oftentimes, the standard for test scores was surprisingly high, as teachers in many subjects told the students in test reviews, "Your average score should be the full score."

In addition to teachers, school principals also took the lead in praising students as exceptional. When I first went to Beijing, I met with the principal of Capital to ask for permission to conduct research on campus. After listening to my research agenda, he called in two teachers to introduce the school. He then announced, "Capital is doing great and we're getting even better. Our students are exceptionally talented. We have absolutely nothing to hide." The teachers nodded in agreement and a male teacher echoed, "Of course." Similarly, when I conducted a pilot study in another high school, the vice principal pointed to the students passing by and proudly declared, "Other schools in the States and Australia consider our students to be geniuses!" School principals also frequently listened to student concerns. Pinnacle students reported frequently seeing their principal roaming the hallways and felt free to voice their concerns on the spot. Capital held weekly student-principal meetings, where a group of seven to ten students could voice their concerns to the principal directly and make recommendations on school or classroom policies and facilities. According to interview responses, the students who attended wholeheartedly trusted that school leaders and administrators would make improvements according to their suggestions.

Teachers and principals at Capital and Pinnacle, as well as at the other top high schools I visited, repeatedly told students that they were special and superior to nonelite students who had failed to test into these schools. These routine comments to the student body highlighted and legitimated a need to self-distinguish from the unnamed nonelite masses. The practice of direct communication between students and principals further led students to believe that their opinions were important and should be addressed by adults. On the whole, the general pattern of student-teacher interactions—in short, the expectation that authority figures and adults in power would fulfill their demands on a daily basis—created an environment in which teachers intentionally or unintentionally developed students' strong sense of elite entitlement.

High Performers Deal with Teachers

Student-teacher relationships in this study were generally characterized as respectful, comrade-like, and working toward a shared goal (success in college placements). However, while the elite students had a general sense of entitlement, not all asserted the same level of entitlement. Closer observations reveal that the level of student entitlement aligned with their test scores and thus status in school, as teachers systematically distinguished between high- and low-performing students and consistently granted favors to the high per- formers. In response, the high performers—study gods and studyholics— frequently demonstrated very high levels of entitlement that did not adhere to the generally respectful and cooperative student attitude. These behaviors include refusing to carry out teachers' demands, negotiating with teachers, and expecting them to provide assistance at any time.

Even if the Teacher Says No: Xijun Wants to Film the Classroom

Clashes between students and teachers almost always involved a high-performing student in school. Xijun, a slender, long-haired girl who was at the top of the student status hierarchy at Pinnacle, got into an argument with her homeroom teacher. She wanted to film the classroom for a project she was preparing for an art school application. Xijun did not have a very good rela- tionship with her homeroom teacher, Mr. Liu. In Xijun's words, "My relation- ship isn't that good with him . . . we often trash-talk each other, Mr. Liu and I. I would trash-talk him, and he'd trash-talk me."[12]

Mr. Liu confirmed that the feeling was mutual. In a separate interview, he stated that his relationship with Xijun was marked by conflict and tension and that he had serious reservations about Xijun documenting daily interactions in the classroom for her portfolio. Xijun was surprised to encounter pushback from teachers who did not wish to be on camera. Mr. Liu recalled, "I reminded her [that] it's good to be filming things, but it's better to communicate with the teachers before you do it. Maybe she talked to some teachers. Some teachers didn't [want] her to do that. But no one can stop her if she wants to do some- thing. Not even when the teacher forbids it. She is still going to do it. I got into an [intense argument] with her for this, and I yelled at her. I really did." At this point, Mr. Liu paused and looked into my eyes, making sure that I understood the seriousness of the incident. He then concluded the story with a faint smile, leaned back against his chair, and sighed, "But that was useless. Useless."

I was able to obtain the student's perspective of this story a few days later, when I walked with Xijun around campus on a hot summer afternoon. She took out her camera and started taking pictures of classmates and the campus without asking anyone's consent. I casually asked if she had done the same in front of her teachers. She replied, "Yeah, I did. Most teachers were fine with it. But Mr. Ye [the history teacher]! Him! He wouldn't allow it without a reason! Mr. Liu scolded me for that. At one point, Mr. Ye just stood there and refused to lecture when I had the camcorder on. But who cares. I did it anyway. They were against it for no good reason."

It was clear that Mr. Liu failed to keep Xijun's behavior in line with teacher expectations. While Mr. Liu could have contacted her parents, publicly criticized her, or initiated other punishments, he chose to reprimand Xijun in private, even though in vain, and later excused her behavior as strong-mindedness. Xijun might indeed have been iron willed, but she could have explained her decision or clarified that the project was crucial to honing her artistic skills and useful for her college application. Rather, she shrugged off Mr. Liu's reprimand and decided that teachers who disagreed with her were unreasonable. Despite the tension and disruption in classroom instruction (with the teacher "standing there and refusing to lecture"), other students in the classroom were uninvolved in the conflict between the star student and the visibly angry teacher. In this instance, Xijun, a student who was expected to be respectful to teachers, instead disrupted classroom activities to the point of forcing the teacher into silent protest.

Negotiating One's Way: Tony Wants to Drop the Project

While study gods and studyholics could straightforwardly refuse teachers' requests, they usually negotiated with teachers. Tony, a study god at Capital who was later admitted to Cornell, complained bitterly about participating in a school project that paired top students with faculty all over Beijing to facilitate student interest in research. Handpicked by his teacher, Tony participated in a biology lab. However, he wanted to drop out halfway because "it was a waste of time" and did not help with college applications. He only grudgingly finished the project because his biology teacher "pleaded with me to stay." However, he later found out that he had to prepare a project defense at the end of the semester. Glaring, Tony said to me firmly, "To hell with going to my project defense. It's such a waste of time." I asked if he had consulted his teacher. Frowning, he replied, "I called and said that I'd rather die than go. I already did what I was told just so Mr. Fang [his teacher] wouldn't look bad."

Tony spent every break that morning contacting Mr. Fang and telling him about his decision to withdraw from the project. Around noon, Mr. Fang came looking for him in the student study lounge. Mr. Fang swiftly sat down across from Tony and said softly, "I talked to [teachers in the project] last night. They were concerned. I'll thank you if you go. You don't need to prepare anything. You already have a PowerPoint from an earlier presentation, right?" Tony responded with a nod but stayed silent. "Then just read what you have. You can leave immediately after you're done. I'd do you wrong if you were to spend more time. This is the last time, I promise." Tony was still silent. Mr. Fang quickly left the room, the corner of his black windbreaker flapping behind him.

As soon as Mr. Fang was out of sight, Tony banged his head against the back of the chair. Mimicking Mr. Fang's soft voice, Tony said in a high pitch, "'This is the last time. I promise this is the last time.'" He then barked, "It's already been the last time for three times!" When I commented that Mr. Fang looked sincere, Tony glowered at me. "These teachers know how to fake [their feelings]! He was totally faking it! [Teachers] fake it to get kids to do what they want!"

Tony spent the rest of the day drafting an argument against going to his project defense. By the end of the afternoon sessions, Tony had spoken to other students and another senior teacher about the issue at hand. He reached a resolution, which was to "play dead. Just don't go [to the defense] no matter what." Eight hours after Tony's nonstop complaints, his triumphant moment finally arrived when he cornered Mr. Fang in a noisy hallway. After hearing his petition, Mr. Fang said angrily, "I can't do anything if you are determined not to go." As I watched Mr. Fang storm away, Tony let out a sigh of relief. "Everything's fine now," he said. He smiled broadly in relief and looked proud.

Although Tony initially performed the unwanted task, he negotiated with the teacher by speaking to Mr. Fang multiple times, building up increasingly elaborate arguments, and soliciting advice from others. When Mr. Fang persisted, Tony's reactions led to a reversal of typical teacher-student interactions. Instead of the teacher giving the student instructions, Tony gave a set of acknowledged but unspoken instructions to the teacher. One was that Mr. Fang would bear the consequences of Tony's decision, which included apologizing to the university faculty and lab mates, the research team, and the school higher-ups. Additionally, Mr. Fang would complete additional paperwork related to project abandonment. Tony's broad smile and proud looks marked the end of this episode with a personal victory: he had imposed his will on the teacher despite pushback.

Assistance on Demand: Tracy Wants Help, Now

Study gods and studyholics also feel entitled to teachers' on-call assistance. Tracy, an extroverted studyholic who later went to Johns Hopkins, reported having built good relationships with her teachers, especially with her counselor, John. Tracy had an anxiety attack a few hours before the application deadline. As she described the incident, "My ED [early decision] was Johns Hopkins, and I needed to hand in the main documents. The night before the deadline, I asked help from a teacher I was close with, and I revised about 60 percent, basically, all of my essay. And John got so pissed, because I had told him I was going to use [the old] version. Then, in the night, probably the middle of the last night, and then, sometime after ten o'clock PM, I called good ol' John. John edited my essay again, and John was so mad. He emailed it back and said, 'I think it is almost perfect. I'm gonna kill you if you revise it again.' Like that." She laughed, "What he really meant was, just stop revising it!"

John, who was also Selena's counselor, had about two dozen advisees in each cohort. He had a fixed schedule at work and usually went to bed around the time Tracy called him. However, instead of telling Tracy to use the old version they had previously agreed on, John stayed up late to edit Tracy's new essay. With John's help, Tracy was able to submit her materials right before the system closed at eleven o'clock that night. The timing of Tracy's request (after ten) and application submission suggests that John immediately worked on her essay as soon as he received her call. While most students would consider it rude to call their teacher's cell phone late at night for immediate favors, Tracy felt comfortable doing so. To Tracy, John's time and assistance were at her service. In other conversations, she reported scheduling appointments with John frequently and estimated that she met with him "about three or four times per month during application season." Tracy's frequency and length of meetings with counselors were much higher than those of average- or low-performing students, who often struggled to get attention from counselors. Most of them had to schedule appointments weeks in advance. Finally, Tracy completely disregarded her counselor's annoyance. She acknowledged that John was upset about being asked to provide last-minute editing on something he considered unnecessary (he "got so pissed" and "was so mad"), yet she nonetheless demanded his help and shrugged off his irritation.

In this and many other instances, teachers behaved as supportive and tolerant adults who obeyed the demands of the top performers. Study gods and studyholics interacted with teachers with confidence and felt free to do as pleased even when teachers disagreed. They imposed demands on teachers irrespective of opposition and pushback. As teachers routinely granted favors to high performers and systematically yielded to them in the classroom, top-performing students learned to regularly expect that their wishes would be granted. These students became the anointed elites among their peers and exerted a strong sense of entitlement toward teachers. As I show later, students learn that high performance grants favors from authority figures, and they continue to hold on to this same attitude after entering the labor force.

Low Performers Follow Teacher Instructions

While students with high status have the final say, students on the other end of the status spectrum, the underachievers and losers, are barred from enacting entitlement in their daily interactions with teachers. Study gods like Dapeng could go as far as to shame teachers in the classroom, but underachievers and losers often found themselves the targets of teacher-initiated shaming events.

Study gods and studyholics expect teachers to save the day in a timely manner, but others have to work just to secure a meeting time. Finally, study gods can force their way through, but underachievers and losers who do so face consequences for their misbehavior.

Public Shaming as Routine Events

For low-performing students who struggle to answer exam questions, "hanging teachers on the blackboard" is unimaginable. The consequences of failing to deliver correct answers in class are severe and often involve public humiliation. A typical interaction between teachers and low performers took place in Fei's classroom a month before the gaokao. I arrived early at Pinnacle and took my seat at the far end of the room. Class had not yet started, but Ms. Gao, the biology teacher, walked crisply into the classroom with a stern look. As soon as the bell rang at seven fifty-five, she glanced around the room without a word and the students quieted down. This class was a review of a test given in the previous class session, and Ms. Gao began by calling on students to answer each question. She called on Liang, a student at the right side of the room, for the first question. Liang stood but kept his head down and mumbled, "I got it wrong. I chose A."

Ms. Gao glared at him. "Why? Do you remember what we said about human cells? We used an example. What was it that moved in the example?"

"It was protein." The student looked ashamed and further lowered his head.

"This is a problem with your knowledge." Seeing that Liang kept his head down and did not respond, Ms. Gao continued, "If you saw A and thought it was correct, did you look at answers B, C, and D?" Liang responded in a voice so small it was inaudible. Ms. Gao looked at the sheet of paper in her hand and called on a girl in the middle of the classroom. Liang quickly sat down. The girl also reported having selected the wrong answer.

Ms. Gao then announced to the class with a frown, "Only three of you got question 1 wrong, so I'm not going to call on every one of you. No one got questions 2 and 3 wrong, so we'll skip those." Liang sat still in his seat as Ms. Gao turned her attention to other students and warned the others not to make the same mistake. He did not look at Ms. Gao or at the other students as they were called. After he sat down, Liang did not move for more than 15 minutes, when the test review was almost over.

Liang was far from the only student shamed by teachers. I observed similar interactions in every classroom I visited. Discussions about test questions take up half of all class activities in twelfth grade. In these review sessions, teachers regularly make public assessments about students' answers. While study gods and studyholics are able to immediately respond with the correct answers, others who cannot feel subjected to the public gaze. In this incident and many others, teachers like Ms. Gao turned test reviews into shaming events by knowingly asking students for answers they did not have and requesting them to provide detailed reasons for unintended mistakes ("Why?" and "What was the example?"). When I calculated these events in my field notes, I found that these incidents took place at an average of once every hour in class. In this example and many others, the students who reported having incorrect answers were singled out and publicly shamed. While each shaming event was short, about one minute each, considering the fast pace of daily conversation and being under public gaze, every minute felt very long.[13]

The routine frequency of this interaction pattern points to the importance of teachers in sustaining and validating the student status system. Teachers become daily providers of information on student test scores by repeatedly shaming certain students for their low performance and assigning them an esti-mated rank in the classroom. Liang and the other student whom the teacher exposed as two of the "only three" (out of about thirty students) with the wrong answer were assigned to the bottom 10 percent of the class. Furthermore, teach-ers make individual assessments of the students who are shamed. In Liang's case, Ms. Gao's concluding remark was that Liang had "problems with his knowledge," which suggested that he was ignorant. These interactions appeared to have an impact on the ashamed students. Liang and others showed clear signs of em-barrassment during the interaction process. After the event ended, Liang's dumbfounded response and dispirited stillness suggest that low performers take these events seriously and indeed feel singled out from their peers.

Help Needed: Alex's College Application

At Capital, every homeroom teacher has about thirty students per classroom, and every counselor has about twenty-five advisees per cohort. Counselors have limited time to work with each student. Low performers typically spend less time with their teachers and have to wait much longer to catch their atten-tion.[14] For example, Alex, an average student who scored 2150 on the SAT, often had trouble getting ahold of his counselor, Tom.[15] During my initial meeting with Tom, he bemoaned that many students "only wanted to apply for high-ranking schools" irrespective of the fit between student interest and university strength. Alex, however, had a different take: Tom had told him "not to apply to any Ivy League school" for reasons such as "they are too selective" and "it would be too difficult for you to get accepted." Despite this warning, Alex decided to apply to three Ivies anyway because they were his dream schools. When Alex informed Tom of his decision, Tom suggested that he go to another school counselor for advice.

"[Tom] said something like, 'Well, I can't help you. You can ask Andrew [another counselor] to go over your essays for those three universities,'" Alex recalled. He described this meeting with visible anger as we chatted inside the student common room. I later learned that Alex did as told and turned to Andrew for help on those three applications. Tom remained Alex's counselor and was in charge of all his other applications. He acknowledged outsourcing Alex's applications to colleagues, saying, "I reviewed many of [his application essays], and other staff members read some as well."

I grabbed lunch with Alex a month after he had turned in some twenty college application packages. He complained loudly about not having gotten the attention he needed from Tom. "The main issue was that I couldn't get hold of Tom," he said furiously. "There was one time I scheduled a meeting with him at four o'clock in the afternoon. I went to his office and waited for him for half an hour. I wrote a note and then I left. He sent me an email asking why I wasn't there at five o' clock. I told him our meeting was at four. He told me to check our emails." Alex took a deep breath, "Well, it was four. So we had to reschedule. I hate to complain, but Tom is unreliable. Like, getting him to go over my essays. He always said he was busy. Nobody knows what he was busy with, but I always had to reschedule our meetings to the following week. If you think about it, this was during application season. With deadlines coming up, you need time to revise essays . . . [and] I always sent my essays to Tom two or three days in advance so he would have time to look over them before our meeting."

Students often rewrote their essays after asking their counselors for suggestions about how to revise and perfect them. Each revision took many days, often weeks. Students such as Tracy produced up to five revisions in one application season until they were satisfied. With application deadlines approaching, Alex was understandably anxious. He reported being respectful toward his counselor, but despite these efforts, he did not receive the help he needed. Instead of being encouraged to pursue his dream schools, Alex was discouraged from even trying. When he decided to try his luck, he found himself handed over to another counselor whom he was not familiar with. Because he did not receive timely feedback on his application essays, he felt that he applied with substandard essays, which in turn may have shaped his admissions outcomes. He later went to Boston College, a school he had been so unenthusiastic about that he forgot he had even applied there.

Tom's refusal to help Alex seemed odd, as I had observed that Tom was an attentive counselor to many of his other advisees. Tom had a full schedule, and I often saw him meeting with students during my impromptu visits to the counselor's office. When I shadowed Robert, then an eleventh grader who demonstrated high potential by studying for the GRE in the hope of acing the SAT, Tom scheduled four meetings with him to go over his college list and gave him homework to push their meetings forward. Other high performers reported that Tom was an attentive counselor who met with them frequently and as needed. The reason why he and Alex had a different relationship may be multifaceted. One possibility was that Alex admitted doing what Tom had lamented (students applying for universities solely based on rankings). Another possibility, however, was that Tom, who was rumored to be the highest paid among all counselors, chose to invest in students who had better chances of going to top universities and gave less attention to average performers like Alex. Considering that teachers' attention and time are limited, and also that their income is greatly determined by students' university outcomes, it is understandable that they may choose to be more attentive to students with higher chances of getting into a top university.[16]

A Favor Lost: Haozuo Steps Out of Line

Not all low performers shy away from confronting teachers. A few try to enact entitlement by refusing to follow their instructions. However, rather than yielding to them, teachers publicly humiliate these rule breakers. One example of an underachiever or loser trying to enact entitlement by refusing to do as told took place on a warm summer morning at Pinnacle. The twelfth grade students were called to the sports field to do fifteen minutes of calisthenics. They lined up in rows and performed exercises as the music counted their movements in eight beats. Haozuo, a skinny boy with black-rimmed glasses, paced at the back and did not participate. I walked toward him and asked why he was at the far back. He replied with a confident smile, "Because I'm special, I do whatever I want."

A few moments later, a teacher walked toward him and asked why he didn't join the others. Haozuo said that he would do whatever he felt like doing. The teacher, however, kept probing. Finally, Haozuo shouted angrily, "Because I don't feel well!" "Why don't you feel well?" the teacher asked. Haozuo shook his head and did not answer. The teacher insisted that he get in line and join the others. Haozuo looked angry but stepped closer to his classmates. Soon after, another teacher came over and ordered Haozuo to join the exercise. With two teachers demanding and watching him until he stepped back in line, Haozuo reluctantly joined his peers and half-heartedly moved his hands and feet.

After the exercise, I brought up this incident as I walked back to the classroom with Fei, a top performer at Pinnacle. "Oh, him." Still sweating, Fei took a sip from his water bottle and shrugged, "He's fine. He's a transfer student from [another high school]. He's probably still not accustomed to our school." Gulping down the rest of his water, Fei added, "Our students are overall much higher-performing than other schools' students." Fei returned to his seat and ended our conversation.

Pinnacle and other top-performing high schools take in transfer students who are top students at their former schools. These transfer students often expect that they can achieve yet higher marks if given access to resources and teachers at other top high schools. In return, the receiving schools obtain higher average gaokao and SAT scores and better average college admissions outcomes. However, among the five transfer cases I encountered, four (including Haozuo) maladjusted and became low performers. It is likely that Haozuo did as he pleased because of his top performer status at his previous school. However, after he transferred, he became a low performer who no longer enjoyed the privilege he had grown used to. His attempt to enact entitlement failed, and by rebuking his request for a small favor (getting out of group exercise), teachers held him firmly to his new position in the school hierarchy.

Importantly, this incident did not simply end with Haozuo reluctantly joining the group. One week later, teachers publicly shamed Haozuo for his behavior. As I followed students to their cohort meeting in the school auditorium shortly after lunch one day, the head teacher of the twelfth grade cohort, a plump middle-aged woman with thin lips, commanded all students' attention as she named certain students and publicly criticized them for bad behavior. She yelled into the microphone, "In the third afternoon class last Wednesday, I saw a student from class number 4 walking out the school gate. I asked her where she was going. She said she was going [home]. This was PE class, and PE class is a regular class. Why are you not going? But she dared to say it in a matter-of-fact way!" She glared at the students. "Even during group exercise, when told to squat, a few of you still stood there looking around! If you can't even do this one simple thing, I don't believe you can do anything for society in the future!" The students were silenced by her rage. Even though Haozuo wasn't called out by name, everyone knew she was talking about him.

It was clear that the teacher was referring to what happened during last week's calisthenics, when Haozuo was the only one in the cohort who blatantly refused to participate. In this example, the fact that Haozuo eventually joined the others showed that he overestimated the degree of entitlement an average student like him could express. Haozuo later switching to saying that he was "not feeling well" might have been the truth, but the teachers nonetheless considered his excuse to be unacceptable and refused to accommodate him. Pinnacle students like Fei acknowledged Haozuo's maladjustment at school but were unsympathetic toward his enactment of entitlement ("he's fine"). Additionally, the teacher took Haozuo's minor offense so seriously that she broadcasted her doubt about his future role in society. The consequences of low performers trying to enact the entitlement to which they were not entitled included not only teachers' rebuffs but also public shaming.

In short, low performers and high performers receive systematically differ-ent treatment. Underachievers and losers cannot do as they please, nor do they succeed in negotiating with teachers for small favors. They have trouble getting the help they need, when they need it. Instead of forcing the teachers to yield to their wishes, these students yield to the teachers and avoid conflict with them. And when they do not, the result is public humiliation, whether in the classroom or at school gatherings. These dispositions learned in school are later reproduced in job settings. As I show below, students who self-identify as "ordinary workers" wait patiently for their supervisors' attention and do not ever defy them.

Making Sense of Student-Teacher Interactions

I was not the only one who observed systematic differences in interaction patterns between high and low performers and their teachers. Students them-selves also acknowledged these differences. However, the students understood these interactions differently depending on their performance and status at school. The study gods and studyholics preparing for colleges in the United States and China, such as Ashley, Tracy, Fei, and Mingjia, reported that the teachers treated the students equally and "focused on those [low performers'] test failures because they are trying help them do better." High-performing students believed that public shaming events were carried out "with good in-tentions," even though the shamed students "sometimes don't appreciate it." The underachievers and losers, however, disagreed. They not only recognized the differential treatment and carefully avoided breaking rules but also re-frained from talking about different student-teacher interaction patterns alto-gether. Very infrequently, and only once during fifteen months of fieldwork in the high schools, did a low performer muster the courage to voice his perspec-tive to teachers.[17]

Blatant Favoritism: "If I Did That, What Would the School Do?"

This rare incident occurred during a daylong observation at Capital. I ran into Mr. Long at noon, and he invited me to join him for lunch in the school cafete-ria, which was filled with hundreds of rambling students, metal spoons and chopsticks clanking together, and pop songs blasting from a TV on a pillar. We found a vacant table beside Jiaqi, an underachiever. Mr. Long sat beside Jiaqi and across from me. Seeing us, Jiaqi quickly swallowed a couple mouthfuls of rice and leaned toward me across the table, asking in a hushed voice, "Have you heard about the incident with Yulang?" Yulang was the top performer in his cohort, and other students often chatted about her stellar performance.

"What happened?" Barely able to hear him, Mr. Long and I leaned in to listen to the story. Jiaqi said, "Yulang had an argument with Mr. Luo in history class. Mr. Luo, you know him, he likes to push his ideas. But Yulang disagreed with him on his view of some historical event. So she slammed her books on the desk and stormed out of the room!"

I was taken aback. "What happened then?"

"Nothing!" Jiaqi rolled his eyes and continued, "The school allowed her to transfer to another history class the next day. Nothing happened."

I turned to Mr. Long and asked, "Really? Did you know?"

Mr. Long responded nonchalantly, "Yeah, I think I heard about it. But it's nothing."

Upon hearing Mr. Long's response, Jiaqi immediately interjected, "It might be nothing for her, but the rest of us, the students like us, we couldn't have done that!" He continued furiously, "Think about it. If I did that, what would the school do? They would figure out a way to punish me for disrespecting a teacher. I wouldn't be able to just transfer to another class. They'd definitely call my parents and ask them to come in to talk about my [problematic] behavior. And then who knows! But the school did nothing to her! They didn't even call her parents! She just transferred like that!"

Mr. Long did not respond. He looked into the air as if trying to distance himself from Jiaqi's accusations. I asked Mr. Long, "Doesn't every student have his or her own opinions?"

Looking at me as if I had said something stupid, Mr. Long said, almost laughing, "Oh, but that's not the case for her. Miss Yulang would *never* back down from her opinion!"[18] Jiaqi vehemently nodded his head in agreement. Not wanting to discuss this further, Mr. Long changed the subject.

One year later, I had the opportunity to ask Yulang what really happened over tea at a coffee shop on her college campus. Yulang, then a math major at Tsinghua, shared a different interpretation of the events. According to her, she sat in the first row and raised her hand to express an opinion, which was a perfectly normal classroom behavior. The incident ended with her staying in the classroom and leaving immediately after class ended. She later transferred to another history class because she had a schedule conflict, and she never talked to Mr. Luo again.

While the rumor was much more melodramatic than the actual incident, Jiaqi's fury—especially his use of himself as a hypothetical counterexample—revealed that underachievers and losers were keenly aware of teachers' favoritism and the privileges enjoyed by top performers. Yulang's rumored behavior was unusual in being highly disrespectful, even for study gods. Even so, Mr. Long attributed this behavior to individual stubbornness ("she would never back down"). Additionally, Mr. Long confirmed Jiaqi's perception by dismissing the incident as not noteworthy ("it's nothing"). This lukewarm reaction suggests that the teachers attempt to tone down the anger of low-performing students while refusing to change exactly what they are angry about. By doing so, they tacitly corroborate students' claims of unequal treatment.

Unexpected Favors: Dehong's Gratitude

Teachers do not always or only favor high-performing students. Some also grant favors to average and below-average students. These instances, however, are extremely rare, and recipients never take them for granted. One midwinter day, eleventh grader Dehong suddenly texted me, asking me to meet him at school the next day. As soon as he saw me, he quickly led me to the near-empty student study lounge. He immediately started summarizing his performance in school. He said that he worked hard but was never high-performing. He then spent thirty minutes talking about how he intended to improve his test scores over the academic year. As I listened and wondered about the purpose of this conversation, Dehong revealed that a teacher who did him a favor had inspired him to try to improve.

"I really needed to apply for the exemplary behavior component to get extra points on the gaokao," he said. "These might be the only extra points I can get. I narrowly qualified for the application, but I needed a teacher to vouch for me. I didn't know who would. I'm not a top student, I'm just ordinary. I barely made the cutoff [for this application]. I talked to Mrs. Wu about this a few days ago. She said she'd look into it, the regulations and stuff, but I wasn't sure. I didn't know what to think." He lowered his head and bent his upper body toward the desk. This well-built boy was at the verge of tears. "But three days later, she told me that she took care of it, so I could apply because she figured everything out for me. I am *so* thankful. Really, I never thought she would do this." Dehong let out a sigh of relief as he slouched against the sofa.

This event was so significant that Dehong, an adolescent boy who usually tried to play cool, became emotional discussing it. While Dehong did not end up getting the extra points, he remained grateful to his teacher for helping him and was motivated to work hard in his last year of high school. The following year, Dehong's test scores improved significantly and he got into Fudan University, which nobody would have predicted when he was an eleventh grader.

Dehong saw this incident as an important lesson. He reported that Mrs. Wu's favor taught him to take everything in school very seriously and to be helpful to others whenever possible. However, Dehong remains an exception that proves the rule. He saw this experience as *extraordinary*, and he was overwhelmed with gratitude. His high-performing peers who actually received the extra points exhibited entitlement by attributing the points to their good grades alone. In fact, the study gods and studyholics in this study who received these extra points all failed to mention that a teacher's recommendation was part of the requirement.

Teacher Reactions to Student Entitlement

Teachers who anoint the top performers as elites among elites do not consciously do so. Neither do they see themselves as suppressing the low performers. In fact, teachers dislike how top performers interact with them. Regardless of how they feel, however, the teachers tolerate and support top performers, citing their academic performance. The same is not true for low performers who, after attempting to enact entitlement, fail as anticipated. Teachers step aside and watch them fail, even to the extent of not getting into any college.

Complaints about the Study Gods

More often than not, teachers are bitter about high performers' entitlement. While teachers allow them to demonstrate their entitlement, they also report feelings of annoyance. One example is the relationship between Shiying, a study god, and her middle-aged homeroom teacher Mrs. Nie. When I first joined the classroom, Mrs. Nie made it clear to me that she was very fond of Shiying by indicating that Shiying was a wonderful student whom she could trust and with whom she could easily communicate. In my observations, Shiying had good relationships with her teachers. However, Mrs. Nie's opinion of Shiying totally changed after the gaokao, when Shiying ghosted them. I interviewed Mrs. Nie the summer after Shiying was admitted to Tsinghua. Mrs. Nie reported, "I must say I am very disappointed with Shiying. She never came to visit the teachers or to say thank you after the gaokao. Even other students whom I didn't expect to come, came. But Shiying didn't, not even after the placements were out for so long. I am quite disappointed."

It is customary for students attending college in China to visit their high school teachers after receiving their college placements. In these ritualistic visits, students report on how they did on the gaokao and update teachers about where they are headed. Importantly, students who did well on the gaokao are expected to thank teachers for three years of preparing them for exams. Shiying, a study god, was expected to visit her teachers to express gratitude. However, she neither visited nor thanked her homeroom teacher and was out of touch all summer. When I later asked Shiying if she had plans to visit her teachers at Capital before starting college, she responded that she had no plans to do so, but she might "if the occasion arises."

In our interview, Mrs. Nie thought that the school had given Shiying ample support through heavy investment and many leadership opportunities. Yet, being a study god, Shiying likely considered her high performance to be an individual achievement. Her taken-for-granted attitude toward exam success should be interpreted not simply as a lack of gratitude but instead as a strong sense of entitlement.

In addition to feeling annoyed and disappointed about study god entitlement, and despite going easy on study gods, teachers often complain about them. One such teacher is Mr. Sun, Yulang's Olympiad coach. I had asked Yulang to identify her closest teacher and invite him or her for an interview. She texted me to tell me that Mr. Sun was available and had agreed to participate. When I met with Mr. Sun, he immediately asked me why I wanted to interview him. I thanked him and said, "I asked Yulang to identify her closest teacher. She told me to come to you." Mr. Sun immediately gave a disclaimer, "Hah, I'm not her closest teacher. She's much closer to [another teacher]. She only asked me because she thinks it's okay to trouble me." He then said that because he was Yulang's Olympiad coach, Yulang "knew" that he would say yes to her many requests, including agreeing to an interview (over her text message notification) with a researcher he had never met. For the rest of the interview, Mr. Sun offered many examples of Yulang's entitled behaviors. After his unfavorable comments, however, he was always quick to emphasize that Yulang was a top performer who had a good chance of winning the Olympiad.

Since his tolerance of Yulang seemed to be based on the expectation that she would win the Olympiad (which she did not), I asked Mr. Sun how he felt about Yulang's early elimination. Mr. Sun sighed, "She lost motivation after hearing that winning the Olympiad no longer guaranteed entry to Tsinghua. She took an instrumental approach to the Olympiad, which I think is totally disagreeable. She saw the Olympiad as a means to an end, so she lost motivation when it didn't deliver the benefits she wanted. She stopped working as hard for it, and so she failed." Although he was disappointed in Yulang, Mr. Sun nonetheless helped her obtain additional points by signing her up for winter camps hosted by Peking and Tsinghua universities. Students who behave like Yulang reveal that teachers consciously tolerate the study gods' and studyholics' entitlement based on their high performance. Despite how they personally feel, teachers swallow their anger and help these students pursue their dream schools.

Letting the Losers Fail

Similarly, teachers are displeased when losers and underachievers behave in entitled ways. Their reactions, however, are very different: they simply allow low-performing students to fail. Jianmin was a student at Pinnacle who fit the definition of a loser. He worked hard and was driven but was never top-performing and later scored poorly on the gaokao. I met up with Jianmin the day after college placements were announced, when he sadly broke the news that he did not receive any offer of admission and was at a loss about his next step. I was shocked because this was unheard of at top high schools. Jianmin attributed this outcome to having an unexpectedly poor performance on the gaokao. He scored forty points lower than he had predicted. His homeroom teacher, Mr. Hu, had a different take and practically anticipated this outcome. I met with Mr. Hu a few days after meeting with Jianmin. When I mentioned Jianmin's surprisingly poor performance and nonexistent college placement, Mr. Hu quickly corrected me.

"No, that's not the case," he said. "Jianmin has always overestimated his performance. He kept thinking that he did better than how he actually did. You might score about twenty points higher or lower, this is not unheard of. But forty [points] is way off. Jianmin did well on a mock exam. He maybe scored an additional twenty or thirty points. But that was just this one time out of all of the mock exams. He didn't take into account his performance in all those others, and treated those as exceptions. He kept focusing on that one time when he did very well."

I probed further by asking how it was that Jianmin had misperceived his abilities until the end of twelfth grade. Mr. Hu shook his head and shrugged. He then repeated what he had said earlier: "As I said, he kept overpredicting his test score."

In the high schools I visited, students had to consult homeroom teachers about college choices before applying. Capital teachers had every student's online password to check student decisions. Pinnacle teachers collected students' lists and talked to individual students who made seemingly risky decisions. For example, Mrs. Wu, another homeroom teacher, asked various students in the classroom to make alternative college choices, citing each university's admission quota for Beijingers. Jianmin's classmates reported that Mr. Hu had talked to some of them about their college choices. Mr. Hu also cared deeply about his students. He once had a dream in which a university lowered its admission cutoff score so that some of his students who had scored just two points below the cutoff were admitted, instead of being bumped down to their second-choice university. In our conversation, Mr. Hu pounded his chest with his fist and said, "I woke up, and I was so upset that it was just a dream."

Considering these reported interactions, Mr. Hu's lack of communication with Jianmin about his college choice was unusual. Pinnacle has a 100 percent rate of sending students to college, and Mr. Hu's classroom consisted of selected top performers. In a classroom in which half of the students were expected to enter Peking or Tsinghua, just the thought that *any* student failed to get into any college was unimaginable. Having perceived that Jianmin's college list was unrealistic, Mr. Hu could have corrected Jianmin's predicted exam scores or made alternative college suggestions. Yet he took a hands-off approach and attributed Jianmin's results to be the student's sole responsibility. One possible explanation is that the teacher and student simply did not get along. However, Jianmin had been one of six selected students that Mr. Hu had introduced to me when I first arrived at Pinnacle, meaning that they must have been on better terms at the time. Another possible explanation is that Mr. Hu had communicated with Jianmin about his overestimated test scores, but Jianmin refused to follow his suggestions ("he kept focusing on that one time"). If so, Jianmin's demonstration of entitlement led to grave consequences. Mr. Hu allowed Jianmin to submit a poorly conceived college list that resulted in no college placement whatsoever. The teacher's gestures (shaking his head, shrugging) further suggested a lack of empathy and implied that the low performer had only himself to blame. Simply put, after Jianmin demonstrated a certain level of entitlement, the teacher let him fail.

Beyond High School: Job Performance
Is the New Test Score

For the elite students in this study who had just entered the labor force, high school seemed like history. They had put away their uniforms and put on business suits. Instead of bowing, they now greeted authority figures with handshakes and confident smiles. The gaokao and SATs were distant memories; a few of them barely remembered their test scores. As of 2019, most study gods had embarked on a career trajectory that will allow them to claim membership among the global elite, with most of them earning in the top 5 to 20 percent of incomes in countries such as the United States and United Kingdom. Many low performers, however, had vastly different experiences—some delayed graduation or went through a prolonged job hunt (student outcomes as of 2019 are shown in Table A1). Not all study gods had higher-earning jobs than their lower-performing peers. Kaifeng, a study god at Highland, became a researcher; his income is comparable to that of Alex, an underachiever in Capital who is now an engineer. Huating, a high-performing girl in Pinnacle who found herself close to being a loser after doing poorly on the gaokao, worked her way up by transferring to Oxford and is now earning in the top 5 percent income bracket in the United Kingdom. However, other differences are present in the process of transitioning to employment. The study gods in this study typically had seamless transitions to the labor force and received offers before graduation. Underachievers and losers usually did not. Many of the latter group decided to postpone the job search until they had obtained a post-graduate degree at a highly ranked university.

When I visited the students two years after they had graduated from college, I was curious to know how those who had entered the work force were adjusting to life beyond campus. Of course, one of the most significant changes was that they had stopped comparing test scores. Yet despite the change in focus, these former students continued to perceive supervisor relationships through what they remember of their interactions with high school teachers. These young professionals see individual performance as inevitably linked to whether or not authority figures favor them. Although measures of performance differ by the type of work, those who are successful demonstrate very high levels of entitlement toward authority figures; those who self-perceive as low performers do not dare to defy supervisors. In other words, these former students, who are now high earners globally, subscribe to an entitlement-and-performance model of social status carried over from high school.

Recall how Dapeng "hung the teacher on the blackboard" by publicly criticizing his teacher and taking over class.[19] I was informed of something similar during my meeting with Xiangzu, an engineering PhD student and part-time counselor at an American automotive and energy company. Over dinner at a busy dim sum restaurant in Beijing in 2018, Xiangzu harshly criticized his American employer. In his words, the company was "completely irresponsible" because it sold products by withholding crucial information from its customers and was "evil" in that it perpetuated global social inequality by manufacturing environmentally hazardous products in developing countries. I was stunned and listened intently as he talked for fifteen minutes about what he had told company higher-ups, including his recommendations. Xiangzu reached the following conclusion: he could do a much better job than his employer and had a viable plan. Specifically, he aspired to start his own business using the skills and knowledge he acquired in school and at work and eventually take over the international market. Of course, whether Xiangzu's employer would agree with his suggestions and whether he would really succeed in "taking the company down" remain to be seen. While Xiangzu's plan has yet to materialize, twelfth grader Dapeng and recent college graduate Xiangzu exhibit parallel behaviors: both publicly criticized authority figures who had power over them and felt entitled enough to "hang their superiors on the blackboard."

Others who are not as high-performing on the job did not and dared not demonstrate strong degrees of entitlement at work. Selena, a top student who had been dismissive to her counselors, was no longer a top performer and had to work very hard at Penn. She later entered the financial industry in New York and perceived herself to be "ordinary" at work. Selena was consciously compliant with her supervisor's instructions despite being upset about them. I met Selena on a Saturday afternoon, after she had postponed our meeting throughout the day until it was time for me to leave the city. She then offered to walk me to the station and grab coffee on the way. During our coffee stroll, Selena told me she was stressed about working alongside colleagues who mostly graduated from "the top universities." When I reminded her that she had also come from a top university, she shook her head and said that she was not comparable to her colleagues who had arrived on the job with internships and other more relevant coursework under their belt. Feeling inadequate in comparison, Selena often canceled meetings with friends on weekends and glued herself to her laptop at home whenever she had the slightest suspicion that her boss "could be going over [her] work." She sighed and forced a smile as we squeezed through pedestrians on the busy streets. "There might be something, or a follow-up of something I did, for me to do," she said. Feeling pressured and outperformed by her peers, Selena felt on call at all times, subject to the whims of her supervisors. For her, as for many other non-top-performing professionals, meek compliance toward authority figures was habitual.

One of the clearest illustrations that reveals how the supervisee-supervisor relationship reflects snippets of the student-teacher relationship is how Tracy, the student who had been comfortable asking her counselor for immediate favors, built relationships with superiors. One sunny afternoon in Beijing, I met up with Tracy. She had graduated from Johns Hopkins and had completed an internship at a leading investment bank in Hong Kong; she was about to officially start her job as a trader at the same company. I asked to meet at a busy shopping district, once a historical residential alley, full of Beijing-style deserts, handmade shoes, and other local goods. Tracy arrived wearing a pair of stylish sunglasses, a tight-fitting black top, and gray shorts with a big bow on the front; her designer crossbody bag and studded gray flats were both straight from the latest American fashion blogs. She stood out from the crowd and the classic Chinese-style buildings. As we strolled through the area, Tracy entered a tea shop and decided to purchase gifts for her supervisors. She ended up spending about $100 on assorted flavors of herbal tea.

While we waited for the store clerk to organize the gifts into three large paper bags, Tracy explained to me in her usual fast-paced manner that gift giving was part of cultivating relationships with her supervisors. She had written them all thank-you cards before returning home for vacation. "I know that my supervisors talk about me in a good way when I'm away. They think I'm likable and very well-mannered." She then said matter-of-factly, "You know, it's important to have your boss like you. They'll give you better cases if they do. You have to get on their good side." I asked her what she meant by "better cases." She immediately replied, "The ones that bring in more money! If the boss likes you, they'll give you the cases that are profitable." Walking out of the store and back into the summer heat, she looked at me and smiled confidently. "My supervisors, all of them, like me a lot. I mean, why wouldn't they? I do a good job!"

Like many other elite students in this study who have just entered the workforce, Tracy recognized the need to deal with higher-ups as she worked her way up the career ladder. Young adults continued to use gift giving as a way of building relationships as they did in high school. Tracy carefully selected small but thoughtful gifts in 2018, like Shiying's Christmas apples back in 2013. In the twelfth grade, Tony and other students believed that counselors had a hand in their college placements; similarly, Tracy openly acknowledged that developing friendly relationships with supervisors would lead to better opportunities and a higher income. Considering that starting salaries are crucial for future income, elite students who value good relationships with their supervisors will enjoy long-term benefits as their careers develop.[20]

While the students who became high-performing professionals seek to develop positive relationships with their supervisors, it is equally important to note that they simultaneously express certain degrees of entitlement and expect favors. By claiming that they are high-performing ("do a good job"), they take for granted that supervisors "like" them and demand that the more lucrative caseloads ("better cases") be assigned to them. Tracy's description of her relationship with supervisors reminded me of the relationships she had built with her teachers in high school. Just as Tracy felt entitled to her supervisor's favors ("My supervisors, all of them, like me a lot. I mean, why wouldn't they? I do a good job!"), she had formerly claimed that her teachers liked her. In fact, she had once used almost the exact same words to talk about her relationship with her teachers. In our interview five years earlier, twelfth grader Tracy swung around in a black office chair and told me lightheartedly, "Teachers like me. Why wouldn't they? I'm such a good student!"

Xiangzu, Selena, and Tracy are but three of many former students who follow the interaction guidelines they learned in high school when interacting with supervisors. By identifying job performance as critical to chances of career advancement and income, elite young professionals willingly focus on job performance and interact with supervisors accordingly. This approach allows individual job performance to be loosely compared to test scores and the employee-supervisor relationship to be more or less understood in terms of the student-teacher relationship. Teachers' interactions with elite students become models for those students' future interactions with supervisors around the world.

Summary

These Chinese students from wealthy backgrounds did not have identical high school experiences. All students were respectful toward teachers, but study gods and studyholics were at times allowed to be strongly entitled in ways that underachievers and losers were not. Teachers sustained and reinforced the boundaries between high- and low-performing students. One consequence is that students understand that their performance in school significantly shapes their relationship with authority figures—their teachers. Top students can impose their will on teachers, while low performers must follow teachers' instructions. Teachers dislike rude and defiant behaviors but nevertheless allow them when top performers are concerned. In this way, teachers foster a particularly strong sense of entitlement among many academically stellar students and (unintentionally) reinforce the low status of academically mediocre students. This pattern, however, does not preclude the possibility of teachers granting unexpected favors to low performers. In many instances, these unexpected favors strongly motivate low performers and help them pursue their educational goals.

By focusing on student-teacher interactions in high school, this chapter carries implications for employee-employer interactions. In many ways, elite Chinese students interact with their employers and supervisors in ways that seem comparable to student-teacher interactions. The role of test scores in shaping student-teacher interactions also points to the possible meaning of job performance from the perspective of these rising global elites. For these up-and-coming global elites, cultivating relationships with superiors at the workplace often involves balancing respect and entitlement. While it takes time to master these skills, these youth did not enter the labor force without preparation. In fact, they acquired and practiced these skills by interacting with authority figures in high school. Teachers thus play an important role in the creation of the future global elite.

5

Grooming the New Elites

Mr. Wu sat comfortably in the brown leather chair in his spacious office and itemized the things he and his wife would do for their daughter, Xijun, on the day of the gaokao. "We'll make sure about the dates, what subjects are tested at what time, what might happen during the exam, and where to have lunch. All these things." Mr. Wu paused to make sure I was following. "Beijing is very big, you know. We'll also have to find her a hotel room nearby, to let her rest during the three-hour break between the morning and afternoon sessions. These are things we can take care of, so we have to get them done quickly, or else there's nothing for us to do." Seeing my astonishment, Mr. Wu jokingly concluded as he leaned back, "Chinese parents are all like this. We're all like nannies."

ONE NIGHT in April, Julie texted and asked me to meet at my earliest convenience. Julie was a top performer at Central from an elite family. Her father was a business school professor; her mother withdrew from the labor force when Julie was in twelfth grade to take better care of her. One indicator of the family's affluence was that Julie's monthly allowance for food and her cell phone was equivalent to a worker's monthly wage (about $300 at the time). Since students rarely asked to meet with such eagerness, I was intrigued and agreed to meet the following night for dinner. We met at a McDonald's halfway between her house and Central. We sat across from each other with our burgers and fries, as Julie hurriedly described to me an incident that happened at her house—her parents had refused to let her buy a particular cup to bring to school. Chinese high schools, including Central, had water dispensers and encouraged students to bring their own water bottles or cups by not offering disposable ones. It was two months before graduation, and Julie accidentally broke hers. "I needed a new one," she said. "So I looked for one that I liked." Julie emphasized that she had spent an entire afternoon searching online for a replacement and finally found the perfect one on Amazon. Julie brightened up as she described the cup: "It was an orange cup, not one of those ugly ones, but a pretty one. I mean, the cup looked like mine! It basically had [my name] written all over it!"

I nodded and inquired about the price. She said it was somewhere between 35 and 45 RMB ($6 to $9). I had purchased a cup at Walmart earlier that week for a dollar or two. She shrugged, "It's not that much. How expensive can a cup be? I needed to use one, and that one was perfect for me. I told my parents to get it for me. I told my mom to give me her credit card. But she wouldn't! They wouldn't let me get it!" Julie put both of her elbows on the table and leaned forward. She raised her voice, "They told me to bring a cup from home!"

"Then why don't you do that?" I asked.

Julie took in a breath dramatically and glared at me angrily. Seemingly in disbelief that I did not understand her resentment, she almost yelled, "Did you not hear what I just said?" Pounding the table with her fists, "I told you! The cup was a good one! It's not like those cups at home! None of them are good, they're all like those old, white ones, you know? I told them to get it for me, but they wouldn't! My mom wouldn't, so I held my patience and talked to her about it, but she still wouldn't and she told me to ask my dad. I did, but he refused!"

"Why don't you buy it yourself?" I suggested.

Julie frowned and said furiously, "My allowance is for food and phone bills. This was what my dad and I had agreed on. This is a matter of principle!"

Julie sank back into her chair. Still upset, she added that the family incident had taken place in the middle of the night and ended with her angrily and tearfully slamming her bedroom door in front of her parents. She had texted me when she was in her room.

A few months later, I brought up this incident in an interview with Julie's mother, Mrs. Jin. "Oh, I didn't know she called you to whine," Mrs. Jin chuckled. She described the night similarly to what Julie had said. However, the mother's point of view was somewhat different from the daughter's.

"We thought the cup was a bit expensive." Mrs. Jin elaborated, "I said that there are many new cups at home, they're never used, and she could use those. She said, 'How dare you want me to use those cups!' But, actually, those cups were perfectly fine. Think about it, if her dad and I were using them, why couldn't she? . . . [Julie] felt wronged. She got really angry. She instantly turned and went to her room." Mrs. Jin sighed, "Honestly, I don't know if Julie still hates me for that. I'm quite scared of Julie." The episode ended with Julie purchasing the cup she desired—her mother slipped her credit card under the door later that night.

The single-child generation in China is commonly perceived to be "little emperors," spoiled children to whom adults willingly concede and fulfill their wishes.[1] However, not all elite singletons are equally entitled at home. While some become little emperors, others do not enjoy royal treatment when the college entrance exam draws near but instead experience heightened stress due to shouldering the family's expectations.[2] Elite students' little-emperor-like entitlement is thus not simply due to their singleton status or the family's wealth. Rather importantly, it comes from excelling at school. Julie was not the average student but a study god in Central, where 90 percent of the students are accepted to universities ranked in the top fifty in the United States each year.[3] With her top status, Julie was comfortable exercising her entitlement toward her parents, who provided the resources she enjoyed. When her parents denied her pursuit of distinction (by the cup she used), her furious reaction (slamming the door) signaled her sense of entitlement and her feeling that she deserved better treatment. By insisting on distinction and demanding that her parents fulfill her wishes, even in buying a cup, Julie behaved like the stereotypical little emperor.

Creating a College-Focused Environment

The elite parents in this study shared many things in common. For one, they were influential people who had abundant resources at their disposal. They cared for, loved, and took pride in grooming their single child, regardless of his or her status at school or test scores. All of them had high hopes for their children and perceived that helping children focus on college applications was crucial. Parents treated the single child's college preparations as a family project and were determined to let the child perform to the best of his or her ability. The students witnessed parents making use of their wealth and networks to advantage them. According to the students, examples of parental influence in college admissions include "purchasing minority status" (which added five points in the gaokao), "soliciting recommendation letters from the principal" even if the principal did not know the child, and "publishing the child's writings as a book and having the principal write the preface." Of course, there were limits to parents' reach. I once joined a few parents for dinner at an upscale restaurant. A father who had connections with Highland, and whose child was not part of this study, sat at my left. He told me that he "used to be able to purchase admission to Tsinghua University in the nineties. But that's no longer possible after the government cracked down on these practices." He bemoaned this change and complained regretfully, "I can't even do it for my own child now."

Although elite parents did not have as much control as they would have liked in their children's college competition, they nonetheless assisted them by creating an environment in which they could focus on college admissions. Yet creating a college-focused environment involved more than caretaking and often entailed considerable sacrifice.[4] Many parents altered their behaviors at home to minimize the disturbance to the test-taking child. They made changes in their work schedules and residential locations to care for the child's needs.[5] Parents also provided emotional support for their children in ways they otherwise would not have.[6] While these practices might seem extreme, elite Chinese parents considered them nonnegotiable. For the parents, allowing their single child to achieve the best possible college outcome was a goal that trumped all other concerns. However, the multiple forms and very high levels of parental support carried the unintentional consequence of fostering elite children's general sense of entitlement.

Accommodating Behaviors: Parents on Mute

Many parents focused on constructing an ideal environment for the college applicant at home. Parents excused children from doing household chores during twelfth grade. Most elite students did not help with family chores, but a few reported doing the dishes or clearing the dining table for extra allowance in tenth or eleventh grade. Yet even these students no longer did so in twelfth grade. Parents not only encouraged children to behave differently at home to focus on college preparation but also changed their own behaviors to facilitate children's academic performance. In my home observations, parents intentionally put the family on mute to keep the apartment quiet when the child studied at home. I visited Fei, a high performer at Capital, and his parents at their apartment on three Sunday afternoons.

Fei spent his afternoons in the study room, which was converted from a dining room. He usually sat at a wooden desk beside the window, with his back facing the door. I took the seat at a dining table to the right of the door. These afternoons usually passed by with Fei being focused on studying for an upcoming test. There was little to document since Fei did not move, nor did he make any sound in the three to five hours I was there. Occasionally, the father would sneak in to peak at what the son (and even I) was doing. A typical example took place on the second Sunday when I visited, at about five o'clock. Fei and I were working quietly in our seats. The door creaked open. I looked across my left shoulder and saw Mr. Li carefully looking into the room. The father looked at me and smiled, putting his index finger across his lips. He then opened the door so slowly that it would not creak again. He took a few steps into the room quietly and fetched something in a drawer in the room. As he passed me on the way back out, he peaked at my laptop screen. Seeing my Word document and statistics software window, he lightly nodded as if gesturing approval. He then silently slipped out without uttering a word. Fei never turned around and did not seem to notice that his father had entered the room.

In all the homes I visited, parents talked in hushed voices and tiptoed when walking near or into the child's room. I sometimes heard clatters of pots and pans in the late afternoon at Fei's house and didn't realize that it was Fei's mother cooking in the kitchen adjacent to the study until she spoke on the phone. Even then, she spoke in such a hushed voice that I could barely hear her. After an afternoon of home observation, I asked Fei what his parents had been doing in the apartment. He said that his parents "usually watched TV in their room." I told him that I had thought they were napping because there was no sound at all. Fei shrugged and explained, "They muted the TV." By consciously minimizing disturbances to the studying child, parents expected children to ignore them, and the children indeed did so. When Fei's father walked into the room, Fei did not show any signs of acknowledging his father's presence. He did not turn to or peek at his father, but simply focused on solving test questions. Even if Fei's father and other parents exaggerated the family atmosphere due to my presence, these behaviors represented the ideal environment among the elite families in this study.

Adjusted Work Schedules: Decreased and Nonparticipation in the Labor Force

In addition to muting the household, parents often made changes to their labor force participation or work schedule to take care of their twelfth grade child. While the elite students might have been thankful to their parents, they did not explicitly acknowledge these changes as parental effort. Rather, the students saw them as trivial details of everyday life. Soon after I entered Capital, I noticed that many eleventh grade students stayed in school for dinner and night study, but a few did not. Intrigued by the difference, I asked Dehong, a key respondent, where he went at the end of my day of observation.

The bell rang at half past five, signaling the end of the school day. Students packed up their books and a few quickly left the classroom, while some stayed behind and chatted. Dehong was among those who swiftly gathered his belongings, showing no intention to stay. I quickly approached him and asked about his plans afterward.

"Oh, I don't know," he said as he packed up his black backpack. Without making eye contact, he explained, "I eat dinner at home because my dad cooks for me. His workplace is close by, so he can come home and cook every night."

"That sounds nice!" I asked, "Has your father always cooked for the family?"

Dehong shook his head, "Nah, it just started this year. He said it's healthier to eat at home."

Dehong's father went home early to cook for him starting in eleventh grade and continued to do so at least until the gaokao. I accompanied Dehong's mother outside the exam site on gaokao morning and went home with the family at noon. As soon as we arrived, Dehong's mother prepared his room for him to take a twenty-five-minute nap; his father quickly made three dishes and rice within half an hour. Dehong perceived his father's decision to cook every night as irrelevant to his exam schedule. He attributed his father's decision first to the company's proximity to home and then to his father's concern for the family's health. However, when I interviewed Dehong a few weeks after the gaokao, he revealed that his father no longer cooked dinner for the family. In fact, his father stopped going home for dinner and instead stayed at his office until late at night.

A clear indicator that parents had purposefully adjusted their work schedules to accommodate their children's college preparation activities was that these changes aligned with children's application timelines. Parents of students in the domestic department worked less until the end of high school, when the gaokao was over. On that same note, parents in the international department worked less until spring of twelfth grade, when college admission results were available. I met Selena at the beginning of twelfth grade, when she was busy preparing her application packages. Selena reported having dinner with both parents every day since the past semester. However, after she obtained a satisfactory SAT score of 2200, Selena's father started to have "a lot of work." When I interviewed her a few weeks after she was accepted to Penn in the spring, her father had become absent from dinner altogether.

If elite fathers worked less in crucial periods of their children's schooling, elite mothers temporarily withdrew from the labor force to care for their twelfth graders. One such example was Julie's mother. In an early conversation, I asked Julie about her parents' occupations. After saying that her father was a professor at a top university, she continued in a matter-of-fact tone, "My mom is a homemaker. She used to work, but she dropped out of work so she could take care of me this year. She wanted to do that." Julie crossed her legs and looked at me, waiting for the next question.

Julie acknowledged her mother's perspective, which was to have dropped out of the labor force primarily to support her. However, she nonetheless attributed her mother's decision to withdraw from the labor force as the mother's personal preference ("she wanted to do that"). Julie's mother went back to work the year after Julie graduated from high school, which Julie also reasoned was the mother's personal decision and unrelated to her application timeline. While the adolescents' explanations of parents' work schedules and labor force participation might have been true, the fact that none of these parents did so in any period other than twelfth grade (or only when they perceived the child needed care) suggested that these decisions were parental efforts to support their child.

Changed Living Arrangements: Out with Dad,
In with Grandparents

The Chinese parents in this study made changes to the extended family's living arrangements to accommodate their child's college preparation schedule. Many families rented an apartment that was close to school so that the twelfth grade child could minimize commute times. This was so common that teachers often helped solicit units for interested parents and announced the move-in dates at parent-teacher meetings. Parents decided not only on where to live but also on who could live together. One such example was Lili's father. On a hot summer afternoon in May, Lili and I walked to the cafeteria from her classroom. Her grandmother cooked dinner and her grandfather biked to school every evening to deliver her home-cooked dinner. When I saw her grandfather at the school gate, I jokingly asked Lili if her grandparents, by preparing and delivering her dinner every day, left anything for her parents to do. She smiled mischievously and said that her grandparents moved in because her mom sometimes worked late and that the family "thought I should eat well and stay healthy." Her father made room for the grandparents by moving away. She made it clear that this was a temporary arrangement, that her father would move back home and her grandparents would return to where they lived after she graduated. I asked why her father had to move out. "Well, my grans knew how to take care of me better," Lili explained. "My dad can't do anything. He's not helpful. My grans moved in and he moved out, so he wouldn't disturb my studies."

While Lili's father might not have been helpful to her college preparation, there was no indication that he held Lili back in her studies. Yet it was insufficient for the father to play a neutral role. When the father failed to contribute, his main contribution was to move out of the house and make way for the grandparents, who could help, to move in. The three-generational coresidence living situation was indeed temporary. When I conducted a follow-up interview with Lili after she enrolled at Peking University, her father had moved home and her grandparents had moved back to their original house in another province.

Even without the arrival of additional caregiving adults, some families decided that the "unhelpful" fathers nonetheless had to leave so as not to potentially disturb the child's studies. Shiying's family was one of the families who made such temporary changes in the father's residence location. I walked home with Shiying on the first day of intensive observation after school at ten o'clock. It was pitch dark. We passed by a few cars with their lights on and some parents waiting for their children, and then we saw someone with two dogs walking toward us. As soon as I saw them, one dog frantically dashed toward us. The dog stopped in front of Shiying while I froze. "Oh, that's my mom!" Shiying said as she picked up the leash of what looked like an over-weight Yorkshire. I greeted Mrs. Liu, who may have smiled back (I couldn't see her face clearly). Mrs. Liu told me in a cheerful tone that her husband had moved to another apartment. She said, "In the Mainland, many men work until very late, so they might as well stay there for a few days. This also makes things more convenient." Mrs. Liu then asked if I was tired, while Shiying made frequent dashes with her dog. Shiying waited for us at the intersections, but walked back toward us after a few seconds. Mrs. Liu suddenly raised her voice to Shiying, saying, "Your dad isn't coming home today!" "Oh," Shiying responded. There was no sign of surprise in her tone, just plain acknowl-edgment, as she walked back to us and passed a white lunch bag to her mother to carry for her.

While I suspected that the father might have moved out to accommodate my staying with the family, Mrs. Liu's explanation and Shiying's reaction both suggested that the father spending nights away from home was not uncom-mon. After we arrived at their spacious, three-bedroom apartment, Shiying picked up her cell phone and called her dad. She had no particular emotional expression in the twenty-second phone conversation, which consisted of "Hey, dad. . . . Yeah, I'm home. . . . It's fine, not really." I stayed with Shiying and her mother for four days. The father did not show up, nor did he call home after Shiying came home late at night. Later in the school year, I ran into Shiy-ing's mother on campus for parent-teacher meetings; her father did not ac-company the mother during these visits. Shiying's older cousin stayed with the family to support and accompany Shiying during the gaokao. I joined the mother, daughter, and cousin for a stress-relieving dinner on the first day of the gaokao, but the father was again absent. The absence of Shiying's and Lili's fathers, however, does not suggest that they were generally absent. Rather, these examples pointed to the norm of parents' relocation to support children's college preparation. Just as Lili's father moved home after the gaokao, Shiying's father soon moved back home. The parents moved to another apartment in Beijing when Shiying went to college and later to yet another apartment they owned in another province after retirement.

Conscious Indulgence: All-You-Can-Use Resources and Whatever-the-Circumstances Support

The elite parents in this study had ample resources. Many parents allowed their children to access an assortment of goods and gave them the freedom to pur-chase products they liked, regardless of test scores. Both Selena, a high per-former, and Bowei, an underachiever, boasted collections of designer sneakers, each pair estimated to cost over $100. Shiying, a study god, was free to make purchases online using her mother's credit card without supervision.[7] Claire reported that a low performer in the international department treated class-mates to expensive dinners, knowing that his parents would foot the bill. None of these students asked for their parents' permission beforehand. In fact, the idea of asking was unfathomable. After all, to the elite families in Beijing, children making purchases with cash or their parents' credit cards was a nonissue.

However, parents used elaborate expenditures on purchases that they other-wise would not have allowed as a form of emotional support. For example, Xiangzu's parents purchased an expensive membership to a private gym for him to foster better gaokao preparation. Notably, this took place at the beginning of twelfth grade, not in his earlier years of high school. Yulang's mother had not agreed to Yulang's earlier plea to have a dog, but within days the mother bought her a Maltese puppy to comfort her after she suffered an unexpected defeat in the Olympiad. Parents also promised elaborate celebrations after children com-pleted their college applications. Alex went on three ski trips in two months after the college admission deadline. Robert traveled to Thailand and Taiwan with friends and extended family members after being admitted to George Washington University. Julie reported doing celebratory shopping after taking the SAT in Singapore, to the point where she had to text her parents to ignore the alerts they received about unusual overseas activities.

Importantly, the parents in this study consciously provided emotional sup-port to their twelfth graders. Claire's mother described her main role as provid-ing emotional support to Claire during the college application process. The mother expressed in our interview, "I heard that [children] are under great pres-sure during the application season. So, I observed [Claire]." I asked the mother to elaborate what she meant. She explained, "If [Claire] was in a bad mood, I'd let her relax a bit, do something to make her feel relaxed, or chat with her. Sometimes this happened at an especially bad time, [such as] when she was working at night. Then I would sit behind her in silence, to be with her. Some-times when she complained about things, I made sure I listened patiently."

Claire's mother reported supporting her applications by listening to her, helping her alleviate anxiety, and comforting her. The mother's narrative sug-gests that these were decisions made to support Claire's college applications ("I made sure," "patiently"). By pointing out that Claire's mood swings some-times occurred at a "bad time," Claire's mother implied that she likely would not have done the same if Claire were not in twelfth grade. This example and others suggest that while parents generally cared for and helped their children, they raised their levels of emotional support when the child was preparing for college.

Shiying's mother acted similarly to Claire's parents. In the spring of twelfth grade, Shiying unexpectedly failed the additional test for extra points for THU. Seeing that Shiying was upset, the mother made sure to deemphasize the significance of this failure. I walked with Mrs. Liu to a parent-teacher meeting one afternoon a few days after the additional test results were publicized. On the way, I asked her if Shiying was alright. Mrs. Liu shrugged. She smiled and replied with a theatrically cheerful tone, "I said to her, it's okay. We have other types of extra points. We don't need to have this one anyway. Really, it's okay."

Shiying quickly recovered from the setback, but the additional test became a taboo topic. She never talked about it, and the family refrained from mentioning the experience in my subsequent visits. While the mother claimed the defeat was manageable to soothe Shiying, as I show in the next chapter, Mrs. Liu's level of parental involvement drastically increased after the test failure, suggesting that she did not take the defeat lightly. These examples show that parents' emotional support of their children was part of the conscious effort that parents demonstrated at home.

In addition to lending an ear and providing verbal encouragements, parents refrained from arguing with their twelfth grader. This was especially clear when the child's behavior led to parents' visible displeasure. A typical parent-child interaction took place at the front gate of Omega, with a student I call Ping. As part of trying to help their child focus on college preparation, parents would pick up their child after school and carry the child's book bags on the way home every day. These parents often stood beside their illegally parked cars that blocked the road and anxiously waited for their child. Ping's parents, a middle-aged couple, joined other parents in parking at the side of the road. The father stood at the closed door of the driver's seat with one arm resting on the shiny black Audi. The mother, a petite woman, got out of the front seat and opened the door to the passenger seat. She stood a few steps in front of the car toward the school gate, stretching her neck at the students walking out. She soon spotted Ping, a tall boy, and hurried toward him. Without a word, Ping shoved his book bag, his lunch bag, and two paper bags filled with test papers and books at his mother, who scrambled to catch it all. Walking in front of the mother, Ping headed straight toward the car without slowing down and slammed the car door with a stony face. Seeing this, the father looked annoyed and walked over to the passenger seat. He reached for the door, seemingly wanting to say something to the son, but the mother made a gesture that stopped him. She told him to open the trunk for her and then put the four heavy-looking bags into the trunk. The couple entered the car and drove off.

Parents did not always approve of their children's behaviors. Ping behaved in an entitled manner: he was rude to his parents and treated his mother as his own personal porter. Seeing his behavior, the father was ready to admonish him (looking annoyed, walking toward him). Yet the mother accepted the assigned role and refused to let the father defend her (making a gesture to stop him). While parents could exercise authority to correct their children, most did not. Instead, the parents swallowed their anger and allowed children to be rude to them in public.

In short, elite parents in China typically took care of many daily chores and put much effort into helping their children prepare for college. Raising a twelfth grade child included providing for elaborate consumption, withdrawing from the labor force, and changing the family's residence. The parents in this study had good reason to indulge their test-taking child. They saw twelfth grade as a special year during which children's stress levels skyrocketed and their future was at stake. However, while both were true to a certain degree, parents bowing down to their children's wishes carried unintended consequences. Through these routine parent-child interactions, the elite students came to expect parental sacrifices. They learned to judge parental support instrumentally and decide whether a parent was "useful" or "useless." They could behave rudely to parents; they expected their parents would respond to their demands upon request. These parental practices, which were intended to create the ideal college-focused environment, fostered children's strong sense of elite entitlement toward their parents.

High Performers Handle Their Parents

The elite students I came to know generally grew up in warm, loving, and supportive families. Parents provided for their children to the best of their ability; children worked hard to shoulder the family's expectations. Nonetheless, parent-child interactions systematically differed by children's test scores. Parents granted favors to the high performers who were study gods and studyholics, allowing them to behave in strikingly disrespectful manners that went beyond the general levels of elite entitlement. These behaviors include snapping angrily at their parents, dismissing parental reprimands, and demanding parents to accommodate their desires.

Enduring Children's Rage: Huating Blames
Her Mother for a Mistake

Family focus on college preparation led the children to take their privileged treatment for granted. The children considered it normal for their parents to take care of everything. Many of the top-performing students in this study had a particularly strong sense of entitlement against their parents. Huating, an energetic high performer at Pinnacle, shared an incident of her being upset with her parents at the end of high school. I met Huating at a bustling ice cream shop near Pinnacle a few days after she received her gaokao scores. She told me that she had scored 676 on the gaokao, just three points below the cutoff score (or one multiple-choice question away) for her dream school. Huating shared how she had spent the past few days anguishing about her college placement. She saw her second choice (a technological university in central China) as beneath her, and the family decided to immediately apply for universities in Hong Kong.

After summarizing her decisions, Huating switched topics by mentioning that she had a particularly tense relationship with her mother in the past few days. She took a sip of her drink and complained, "[My] mom is an idiot. I thought I shouldn't be unhappy in twelfth grade . . . but I was even unhappier at home, facing an idiotic mom every day." She sighed and added, "[She's] such an idiot."

I asked her why. Huating stuck her spoon in the ice cream and sat up straight, evidently prepared to tell a long story. "Other than being an accountant, my mom can't do anything." Huating said with a frown, "I was going to apply for [universities in] Hong Kong myself. She applied to the business school for me without even asking. She just told me that the business school would have a lower cutoff score, so I'd get in. I said [to her], 'Are you crazy?'" Huating raised her voice and angrily continued, "One day I went home after spending a day outside. I took a nap at six o'clock. When I woke up at eight, my mom came in and told me, 'I did the applications for you.'" Sinking against the back of her chair, Huating said tiredly, "I was too tired to talk about this with an idiot, and she, she just applied for me."

Huating accused her mother of messing up her college list and hindering her chances of going to her dream school in Hong Kong. Huating never told her mother that her gaokao score was not high enough to apply for the business school in the targeted university in Hong Kong. Nor did Huating inform her mother that she planned to apply to the engineering school, which had a lower cutoff score, and then double major in business. Despite her withholding critical information from the mother, Huating nonetheless insisted that her mother was fully responsible for the mistake.

"[My application] got hijacked." Huating said tiredly, "I cried yesterday, I cried so hard. And my mom was, at that time, standing aside and trembling. She was crying, I was crying. My sister called her stupid.[8] She walked away. Every time these things happen . . . I feel that my parents, other than knowing how to make money, [are] useless."

In a later conversation, Huating commented that her "biggest mistake" in high school was to let her mother do the applications to Hong Kong universities for her. Huating's opinion of her mother was not a secret, as the mother agreed with the daughter. I interviewed Huating's mother, Mrs. Xue, ten days after my ice cream outing with Huating. As soon as Mrs. Xue greeted me at the front door of her office, she warned me that I might find the interview unhelpful because she had "failed as a parent." In our interview, I asked Mrs. Xue to talk about how she took over Huating's Hong Kong application list. Mrs. Xue defended her actions but willingly took the blame.

"[Huating] always wanted to study business," Mrs. Xue answered, and then explained nervously, "She always told me, 'I don't know what to study in college, but I'm interested in business. Nothing else matters, [I'm] not interested in anything else.' So that's how we did her applications, we focused on what she liked." The mother then explained that she tried to make amends. She called the university, but it was not possible to withdraw or change the application.

I then asked why she had taken over Huating's applications. Mrs. Xue stuttered a little as she recalled the incident. "When we talked about applications, she kept saying, 'Say something else. Stop bugging me.' . . . So when she blamed me, blamed me, then I, I told her, but this is what parents, this is what parents should do, what parents should do. And as parents, and I, I told you the moment we met that I had failed as a parent. Why? Because I screwed up her college list." Mrs. Xue sighed, "It's right for her to blame me. I'm very stupid, like she told you, I'm very stupid."

In this example, Huating's mother tried to help, but the daughter felt devastated by the mother's involvement. Huating was a single child from a wealthy background. Yet, more importantly, she was a high-performing student in the top-performing class at Pinnacle. Huating felt entitled to better treatment from her parents, especially her mother. Her parents yielded to her demands and did not "bug" or "distract" her. Significantly, Huating's mother showed signs of being afraid of her daughter when faced with Huating's fury (trembling, standing aside, crying, and walking away). Huating later attended the Chinese University of Hong Kong. However, seeing the school as having unsatisfactory status, she transferred to Oxford the following year. In our text exchanges, Huating said that her parents were overwhelmed with joy at her achievement. When I inquired about the additional expenses associated (estimated $56,000 each year), she responded that the costs of higher education in the United Kingdom were "not that high." She later brushed the topic aside by claiming that her parents never expressed any concern about the expense and that the prestige was what mattered most.

Failed Reprimand: Fei Stays Online

The elite parents in this study tried to instill discipline into their child, especially regarding schoolwork. One example was by regulating the child's access to the internet, which many parents saw as a distraction from studying. However, the effectiveness of these disciplinary attempts depended on the child's test performance. Fei was a top performer at Pinnacle who received guaranteed admission to THU by landing in the top tier of the Olympiad in physics. In my third and last home observation with his family, in the late afternoon, at four thirty-six, Fei stretched with a yawn and informed me that he needed to help a neighbor with a test question. Fei turned on his desktop, put on his yellow headphones, picked up his math test, and held it up to the sunshine that shone through the window beside his desk. A few seconds later, his friend also logged on. As the two discussed questions, Fei opened a web page to read the news, checked online social networking sites, and texted on his phone. A few minutes later, Fei's father (Mr. Li) walked into the room without making a sound.

Mr. Li stood with a straight back behind Fei and looked at what Fei was doing for a few seconds, and then he quietly walked out. The father then checked on Fei six more times in the next hour and a half. Fei could have seen his father out of the corner of his eye, but he did not close the computer windows. At six thirty, Fei was still talking with his friend, texting, and skimming websites. Mr. Li walked in and was clearly annoyed. He took a few steps toward Fei and furiously yelled, "That's enough! Haven't you talked enough? [You're] talking endlessly! I think you're just chatting!" Fei immediately turned his head toward his father and shot him a nasty look, with furrowed eyebrows, a scrunched-up nose, and bared teeth. Mr. Li stood there and glared at Fei, who kept talking with his back facing his father. A few seconds later, Mr. Li walked away.

In this example, Fei's father was upset with Fei. The father thought he was slacking off by surfing the internet and demanded that Fei focus on his studies. Yet despite the father's rage, Fei persisted and ended his conversation only when it was time for dinner. As I joined the family at the dinner table to enjoy Mrs. Li's home-cooked meal, the father attempted to scold Fei for wasting time online. However, Fei rolled his eyes as his father said, "You were going online . . ." and dug into his bowl of rice. Seeing Fei's reaction, the father looked down at the dishes on the table and did not finish the sentence. This episode ended with the parent yielding to the child and walking away. The parental reprimand became a one-sentence complaint that the high-performing child could freely ignore.

Yielding to Children's Demands: Tracy Wants Duck for Dinner

High-status students felt free to push through their demands in the face of their parents' refusal. Tracy, a studyholic, insisted that her parents immediately fulfill her meal requests. On a hot summer day, I joined Tracy and her classmate Tony for lunch. We decided to go off campus but had trouble deciding which restaurant to dine at. As we stood outside the school gate, Tony named about five moderately priced restaurants that were Chinese, Korean, or fast food (comparable to Chipotle, Subway, and Panda Express in the United States). Trying to decide, Tony murmured, "Hmm, let's see, which one [do I] feel like having?" But before Tony made up his mind, Tracy suddenly tapped our arms and asked, "Hey! Can we get Peking duck at Dadong?" Tony and I looked at each other incredulously. The restaurant she suggested was not particularly far away, but we may not have had enough time. In addition, students typically did not eat at Dadong, a high-end restaurant that cost about ten times more than the restaurants Tony had suggested. Tony winked and signaled me to reject Tracy's proposal.

I hesitantly said, "Um, I don't think that's a good idea." Tony immediately nodded.

"Why not?" Tracy frowned and raised her voice. "I want to have Peking duck!"

"Are you sure?" Tony asked timidly.

"Well, yeah!" Tracy replied without hesitation. She then said a third time, "I really want to have Peking duck! Let's get that!"

"Um, well. . . ." Tony looked at Tracy and then turned to look at me.

Sensing that Tony wanted me chime in and knowing that cost was not an issue for both students, I scrambled for an excuse and suggested there would be too much food for the three of us. However, Tracy frowned at my excuse. "What are you talking about?" She shouted, "There are three of us; that's just about right for a duck." She looked at me as if I was talking nonsense.

"Well, um. . . ." Avoiding Tracy's gaze, Tony awkwardly asked again, "You sure?"

Seeing that both of us were reluctant to go to Dadong, Tracy pouted and rolled her eyes at us. Without saying another word, she took out her phone and called her mother. She demanded, in short sentences, "Hey, mom? I wanna have Peking duck. Can we have it tonight? . . . Why not!? [raises voice] . . . Well, go and make the arrangements. That's it for now. *Un.*" After hanging up, Tracy smiled broadly at us and announced that she would have duck with her parents that night. She then agreed to go to one of the restaurants Tony had suggested.

On a brief phone call with her mother at work, Tracy insisted that her mother fulfill her wishes immediately. Although the mother initially refused ("Why not!?"), Tracy demanded that her mother make the necessary arrangements and topped off the demand with a sentence-final particle ("Un"), a nasal sound commonly added to the end of directives. Tracy exercised her entitlement in two ways in this incident. She first demonstrated entitlement in her freedom of access to luxurious consumption by seeing an expensive restaurant as a suitable place for lunch. Second, she demanded to go to dinner at the restaurant of her choice regardless of her parents' schedule. As Tracy expected, her parents surrendered and took her out to eat.

In sum, elite parents indulged the study gods and studyholics. These high performers subjected their parents to their whims and expected full parental compliance despite their anger or disapproval. As the elite parents routinely compromised, the elite teenagers learned to not make any when dealing with their parents. Parents of high performers anointed their children as the elite among elites and allowed them to demonstrate a very strong sense of entitlement at home. As I show later in this chapter, having learned that high test scores legitimize otherwise disallowed behavior, study gods and studyholics continued to handle their parents in a similar manner many years after high school graduation.

Low Performers Obey Parents' Orders

Elite teenagers' levels of rudeness toward their parents and their degree of freedom in imposing demands on their parents varied by test performance. While the high performers forced their parents to cave in to their demands, the low performers relented to parental pressure. Study gods and studyholics like Julie and Huating felt free to terrorize their parents (especially mothers) with outbursts of rage, but underachievers and losers held back their anger against parents. Study gods and studyholics could force parents to change course, such as in cuisine choice; underachievers and losers had difficulty obtaining the academic assistance they needed. Finally, study gods and studyholics were able to effortlessly brush off their parents' reprimands and carry on with their activities, but underachievers and losers refrained from annoying their parents and carried out their decisions.

Public Humiliation by Parents: Wanru Is Body-Shamed

While high performers could call their parents "idiots" and have them agree, low performers were on the receiving end of such remarks. One example is Wanru, a girl with low status at Capital. When I met Wanru during the last month of high school, she had been hanging out with Lili on a daily basis. Wanru was a slightly plump girl with a short ponytail who had a cheerful and sarcastically humorous personality. Lili told me that Wanru had been a toned athlete who aspired to get additional points through her gymnastic excellence. Wanru never talked about what had happened, but according to her friends she suffered a serious hip injury in eleventh grade. Wanru had been low-performing because she spent most of her time training. Her low status in school was firmly established after obtaining the desperately needed extra points was impossible because she could no longer train.

On graduation day, Wanru's mother, Mrs. Deng, arrived on campus and enthusiastically took pictures for Wanru and her friends in the stadium. After the ceremony, I walked around, congratulating the students I knew and taking pictures with them. When Wanru and I caught sight of each other, she cried out, "Ahhh!" She ran toward me, grabbed my arm, and dragged me toward her mom, a middle-aged woman with neatly permed hair in a black-and-silver dress. Wanru asked her mother to take a picture of us. We stood still, with Wanru smiling broadly at my right. As we posed, her mom put down the camera and said loudly, "Step back, Wanru! Your face is too big!" Hearing her mother, Wanru lowered her head and took a small step back, looking stone-faced. I patted Wanru's shoulder and said that she looked fine. Wanru shook her head and replied in a low voice, "No, my face is too big." As she stepped back again emotionlessly, Mrs. Deng agreed loudly, with one hand holding the camera and the other making shoving gestures, "Ai, right, you're too fat!" A few girls came by and stood beside Mrs. Deng, waiting to take pictures with Wanru. Hearing the mother's comments, the girls awkwardly peered at the mother and Wanru and then looked at each other as the mother kept directing Wanru to "step back a bit so your face looks smaller." Wanru stepped back a bit more, but her mother kept telling her to move back. Finally, Wanru gave up and moved completely to my left, ultimately using my body to block half of hers. Wanru faked a smile as she looked at the camera. By the time we took the picture, the other girls had left. Wanru quickly moved to the opposite side of the stadium and disappeared into the crowd with her mother.

While it may be more acceptable to comment on other people's figure in China than in the United States, the elite Chinese parents in this study usually did so in private. For example, Shiying's mother also made similar comments about Shiying's body. However, the mother spoke to her daughter at home and sought to draw the child's attention away from her imperfect body by telling Shiying, who was a study god, "It's okay to be fat, just focus on maintaining your brain power." Compared to that of Shiying's mother, Wanru's mother's behavior was unusual. Throughout fieldwork, I did not observe other occasions when elite parents body-shamed their children in public, less to say in a volume and manner with hand gestures that attracted other people's attention. Other students' reactions also suggested that they felt uneasy hearing the mother's remarks toward Wanru (awkward glance, looking at each other).

This parent-child interaction between low performer Wanru and her mother was in contrast to that between high performers and their parents. Unlike Huating's mother, Wanru's mother was not at all scared of her daughter. Mrs. Deng felt free to body-shame the daughter in public and demanded multiple times that the daughter stand in the back of her own graduation photo. Although these behaviors clearly upset Wanru (stony face, fake smile), the mother paid no mind. Simultaneously, while study gods and studyholics such as Fei interrupted and rejected their parents' criticisms, Wanru responded in an opposite manner. Wanru posed no objection to the body-shaming comments and agreed with her mother ("my face is too large," stepping back multiple times). Wanru later attended a provincial university in northeast China, which was what her parents had expected.

Demanding Obedience: Jiaqi's Phone Is Confiscated

Low performers did not enjoy as great a degree of entitlement vis-à-vis their parents as did high performers. Jiaqi, an underachiever, cared greatly about the goods he possessed, especially his cell phone. Students could not use their cell phones at school, and Capital teachers could confiscate students' phones for seventy-two hours. Jiaqi's teacher, Mr. Long, kept all the confiscated cell phones in a locked drawer in his desk. One day Mr. Long pulled out the drawer and showed me the half-dozen phones inside. He said in a slightly amused tone that he was often stuck with a bunch of unclaimed phones each semester because students forgot about their phones at the end of the three-day period, and certainly none cared enough to argue with him. None, that is, except for Jiaqi. I observed Jiaqi going to great lengths to talk Mr. Long out of confiscating his cell phone after being caught using it in the classroom.

However, Jiaqi was unable to hold on to his phone. Around the end of twelfth grade, a few months before the exam, Jiaqi's mother took his high-end phone because she thought it was distracting him from focusing on the exam. I ran into Jiaqi one afternoon in the hallway when I was shadowing another student. Seeing me, Jiaqi walked over to say hello with a pleasant smile. I jokingly asked if he was too busy studying to respond to my messages on WeChat (an online messaging system in China). Jiaqi's face dropped.

"I couldn't respond because I didn't see them!" He almost yelled in despair in the hallway. "My mom took away my phone, and she handed me an old piece of crap!" He angrily reached one hand into his pocket to pull out something that might have been his current phone. But he stopped halfway and decided to just describe the phone instead. "You know, those old phones that wouldn't break even if you dropped them on the ground? Those that you can only call and text, but can't do anything else with?"

"Why did your mom do that?" I asked.

"Because she thought I was getting distracted by it!" Jiaqi frowned. "In her mind, I wasn't getting high test scores because I spent too much time [going online] on the phone." He smirked in disagreement, "If I were truly distracted by the internet, who would she be stopping by taking away a cell phone? We have computers in our classrooms." He let his shoulders droop, looking distressed, "But she wouldn't listen. She took it away and wouldn't give it back to me."

Jiaqi stayed offline until June 8, the last day of the gaokao. I joined Jiaqi and his parents in a car ride to a celebration dinner at a Russian restaurant. On our way to the restaurant, Jiaqi spoke with his extended family using a rugged-looking silver Nokia that was about his age. The phone did not feature internet, a camera, or a color screen. As Jiaqi said, it performed only calls and texts. After we arrived at the restaurant, in the thirty minutes that we waited, Jiaqi asked for his mother's smartphone, which she took out from her purse and handed to him right away. Jiaqi started multiple conversations with his friends and scheduled summer plans with a smile across his face.

Despite his strong resistance, Jiaqi surrendered his beloved phone to his parents. Jiaqi's mother was not alone in seeing the internet as a distraction from test preparation. Many elite parents took issue with their children's internet use, but parents of low performers exercised control to a degree that was unimaginable to parents of high performers. Jiaqi and Fei (the high performer in a previous example) both went online for a long period of time, and the parents of both tried to reprimand their children. However, the father of the high performer Fei was immediately dismissed and could not even finish his sentence at the dinner table. By comparison, the mother of the low performer Jiaqi not only demonstrated successful parental control in scolding Jiaqi ("She wouldn't listen") but also disciplined Jiaqi by confiscating his phone. While high performers like Fei did not worry at all about the father confiscating their computers or phones, low performers like Jiaqi were careful about whether their parents considered their treasured possessions to be distractions and wearily held on to what their parents allowed them to use.

Enforcing Parental Decisions: Brandon Files College Applications Independently

While high performers expected their parents to satisfy their demands, low performers learned that their parents would not provide them with everything they requested. I invited Brandon for a follow-up interview a few weeks after he received admission to UCLA. We met at a park near his apartment, where thousands of cherry blossoms were in full bloom. After two hours of circling the over-three-hundred-acre park with rowdy tourists, I grabbed an unoccupied stone bench and sat down to rest. Brandon joined me, the athletic boy showing no sign of weariness. The interview, conducted on the bench, was short. Brandon seemed to have put the applications behind and was looking forward to his next chapter in the United States. He kept his sentences short, using minimal words to answer each question, until I asked if his parents helped him in the application process.

Brandon paused and took a breath. He slowly said that his parents were "very helpful" by offering emotional support, which "kept my spirits up." However, he saw their support as insufficient. Brandon described his application as a process through which "you did everything yourself, [but] you still needed someone for help. There are a lot of things you wouldn't know unless you got a [college application] agent. You just had to ask someone about these things."

Hiring college admission agents to help with the application process was a common practice in China.[9] I asked Brandon why he had not done so. Brandon slumped and put his hands together. He spoke with suppressed anger, "Because my dad thought I shouldn't. My parents thought that college applications were a training opportunity [for me]."

Brandon's story was validated five days later by his father, Mr. Wu, a middle-aged man with a moderate temper who was a Tsinghua alumnus. As we talked at an empty coffee shop, the father brought up the issue of college application agents at length without probing. Mr. Wu expressed strong disapproval of other elite families' employment of these agents, who would "write essays for the applicant for 1,000 RMB." He believed that independence was a virtue and hence insisted that Brandon complete all his applications personally and without external assistance. Brandon protested and was angry at the father, shouting (many times) that "I'm just as busy as [my classmates]!" and "Why can't I hire an agent to deal with trivial things like them? I also have a full plate!" Yet despite the conflict between the father and son, Mr. Wu remained steadfast.

Mr. Wu also revealed that, as a first-time applicant, Brandon made a mistake by submitting his first name and surname in reverse order. Since Capital uploaded supporting documents in the proper order, none of the universities received Brandon's full materials. Brandon found out about his mistake close to the application deadline and was immediately thrown into a panic. Mr. Wu recalled Brandon being "extremely worried" and "at a loss." As Brandon's amount of anxiety and distress escalated in the subsequent days, the father finally stepped in and resolved the issue by ordering Brandon to email an apology to the universities addressing the issue. Toward the end of our interview, I asked Mr. Wu if he had any regrets about Brandon's college preparation process. He blinked a few times and said unsurely, "I probably should have hired an agent," explaining that this was not worth the conflict and anxiety in the family. However, seeing that Brandon had "adjusted well" (i.e., learned how to fill out forms), the father concluded that he was satisfied with his original decision.

Compared to Tracy and other high performers who could successfully challenge parental decisions on the spot, Brandon's experience was clearly different. Dining and hiring application agents both reflected students' perceived needs, with the latter being directly related to college outcomes. However, while parents yielded to their high-performing children's wishes, from buying a cup or changing personal schedules to taking them to a fancy restaurant, low performers did not receive identical treatment from parents and succumbed to parental decisions ("adjusted well"). These students failed to receive the resources and assistance they saw as necessary, even if the request was an academic one, and even with prolonged conflict and heated arguments with parents. Mr. Wu's decision to provide Brandon with the opportunity to learn to be independent was well intended, considering that Brandon never made the same mistake again.[10] In the years to come, Brandon would apply for graduate school and internships by himself without repeating the error.[11] However, Brandon considered himself at a serious disadvantage compared to his peers, whose parents hired agents to assist them with their college applications. Despite the son's protest and anger, the father pushed through with his decision.

Taken together, these examples show that test scores shaped the interaction patterns between adolescent children and their parents to no small degree. Underachievers and losers did not speak ill of their parents but were disciplined by them. These students could not force their parents to fulfill their desires. Instead, they obeyed and carried out their parents' demands. When they made requests of their parents, they were often denied the resources or assistance they perceived that they needed. These dispositions acquired in adolescence were demonstrated later in young adulthood. While parental influence diminished as the children aged, the high performers continued to make purchases with little or no parental supervision and continued to act entitled.[12] The low performers warily held on to what their parents allowed and complied with their decisions.

Parent Perspectives of Family Interactions

While parent-child interactions varied by test scores in my observations and interviews, neither parents nor children acknowledged these differences. Parents formed networks with other parents in school to exchange information about test scores and colleges,[13] but refrained from commenting on each other's family life.[14] When asked about their perceptions of parent-child interactions at home, most parents reported that they wished they could do more for their children. These parents denied playing any important role in the application or exam preparations and framed college outcomes as a purely individual achievement. On the other hand, a small minority of parents perceived themselves as the invisible hands who led their children along certain directions and pathways. They indicated that their children enjoyed considerable freedom if they stayed on the "right track," but the same would not have been true if they had deviated from the planned trajectories.

Students did not acknowledge the differences in parent-child interactions either. Being singletons, they had no siblings to compare parental treatment with, and peers' interactions with their parents were not part of daily conversation. Instead, teenagers adopted their parents' narratives and learned to perceive college outcomes as individual achievements. Many treaded the path that parents approved of, often unaware of the parental guidance behind the scene. Consequently, as the elite teenagers in this study shouldered high levels of family expectations, they simultaneously became the anointed youth used to unwavering parental support.

Insufficient Parental Effort: Claire's Mother "Did Nothing"

Elite parents were eager to alleviate the child's academic burden in twelfth grade. However, by being audiences and not the gladiators fighting for top university placements, most found their efforts insufficient.[15] Claire's mother, Mrs. Chen, was one of these parents. I met Mrs. Chen, a military physician, in her office after Claire's graduation. Mrs. Chen signaled for me to sit down on the soft leather sofa. She quickly stepped out of the room to give her team of assistants a few instructions and then joined me on the sofa as a quick break. In the middle of the interview, I asked how she had supported Claire in the past year. Mrs. Chen responded apologetically that she in fact had not. Instead, she was distressed about her meager role in the college application process.

"I really didn't do much for [Claire]. She did everything herself." The mother looked me in the eye, making sure that I knew she was seriousness. She then continued, "Helping Claire is something I'm upset about. The last phase of the applications was really tough. If I had helped her a bit more, if I had gotten into my role sooner, helped her sooner, and not acted like an outsider . . . because most of the time I just asked about things, but I did nothing for her. This is the truth."

However, after Mrs. Chen claimed to have done nothing for Claire, she followed up by listing all the tasks she had completed to help her daughter apply for college. "After Claire discussed her college list with her school counselor, she'd tell me about it. I would go online to do a bit of research myself, and she'd analyze these choices for me. I agreed, and then we decided on the list. This was my role."

While this sounded as if Mrs. Chen had a supervisory role, the mother nonetheless labeled herself as insignificant in the process. Mrs. Chen elaborated on her role in the process by saying, "I did nothing, really. If Claire needed anything, she knew I was there. Including her going to Hong Kong to take the

SAT, getting tutors, going on trips, I did all these external things for her. Things she didn't have time to do. Including gathering information, or when she wrote her application essays, we discussed them, and I gave her advice on what to write. I think this is all. She basically did everything herself."

Ironically, while Mrs. Chen claimed to have "done nothing," she in fact offered much support to Claire. Mrs. Chen gathered college information, gave advice, discussed essays, sent Claire on SAT trips, and searched for tutors. Even so, the mother concluded that her actions were insignificant and implied that she should have done more (being upset, "if I had gotten into my role sooner"). Like Claire's mother, many parents were anxious about college applications. Being unable to share in the children's burden, they blamed themselves for not helping as much as they could. These parents often concluded that they "did a terrible job" or "did nothing," and that their children "did everything [by themselves]." However, these claims could not be further from the truth, as the same parents reported having "provided everything [the child] needed," such as "loading the child's bike with text books needed for classes every morning," "gathering university information," or "performing test reviews at home."

There were at least three reasons for parents denying their own contribution. One was that the tasks parents carried out were too numerous to remember. For example, Huating's mother reported doing "a bunch of things for her all day long." But since she "couldn't remember anything that I did in the past year," the mother concluded that she "did nothing for [Huating]." Another reason was that children rejected parental assistance. For instance, Julie's mother hired an application agent to help Julie. However, Julie fired the agent by their second meeting, claiming that the agent was incompetent, had "poor English," and would have "completely sabotaged my applications." Third, parents considered anything not directly related to college placements as "external" and hence unhelpful, as illustrated by Mrs. Chen's narrative. Regardless of the reasons, parents' perceptions of offering insufficient contributions and self-denial of parental effort were common themes that characterized parental understanding of their interactions with their children.

With few exceptions, students also denied parents' role in college applications.[16] A few months before I interviewed Mrs. Chen, I had asked Claire if her parents had helped her with college applications. At the time, Claire had just accepted Yale's admission. She responded that parents had contributed very little in the process other than "paying a considerable amount of tuition for high school." When I probed further, she smiled forgivingly and said, "My parents definitely wanted to help. My dad wanted to give me more information whenever he could, such as by asking his colleagues who had sent their child abroad. If this even counted. But it wasn't very useful. Basically, they barely helped." Claire brushed her long hair aside and explained, "Applications are personal, after all. Your parents can't help you do anything; it's mostly up to yourself."

Claire was not ungrateful. Quite the contrary, she was among the few who mentioned parental provision (such as tuition and emotional support). Yet Claire nonetheless considered her parents to have provided minimal assistance. She shrugged off her father's efforts in gathering information through the family network ("if that even counted," "wasn't very useful"). She brushed away her mother's actions with a simple statement that "parents can't help" and rendered the myriad tasks her mother undertook as trivial. Because Claire's understanding of parental assistance mirrored her mother's, she became oblivious to the amount or existence of parental effort and claimed all the credit for her personal, gloriously successful college outcome.

Unspoken Guidance: Robert Did "Exactly What the Father Wanted"

Not all elite parents perceived themselves as noncontributors. Some reported ensuring their children followed the "correct pathways" on which parents had set their minds, while strategically framing each decision as the children's individual choice to solicit children's compliance. Robert's father was unusually outspoken about how his parental guidance worked in practice. Mr. Guo was a gentle, soft-spoken man in his mid-forties whom Robert's teachers described as "an extremely kind man whom Robert takes advantage of." Like many other parents, Mr. Guo was a top student in the 1980s—he scored among the top fifty out of over four hundred thousand gaokao participants in the populous province that year. Having ranked in the 99.99th percentile, yet being the father of an underachiever, Mr. Guo admitted that Robert would "have considerable difficulty" filling the shoes of his legacy of exam success.

Mr. Guo decided early on that foreign education was imperative to mold children into a creative learner and a global citizen. After he expressed his skepticism of exam selection and the importance of receiving a foreign education, I asked him, "When did the family decide to send Robert abroad?" Mr. Guo noticed my word choice, "family," and quickly corrected me. He said gently but firmly, "Robert chose to go to college in the U.S. by himself. I didn't force him or ask him to do that."

It turned out that the decision to go abroad, which was apparently an independent decision that Robert made, was inescapably related to Mr. Guo's tactful guidance. Mr. Guo went on to explain, "Still, we directed him. At first, we didn't give him any advice on whether to go abroad. None at all. He went on an exchange trip to the U.S. in eighth grade, [which] took kids from the east to west coast. They visited some universities over fifteen days. He had a good impression of the U.S. This is how he started to want to go to the U.S. for college." The father concluded proudly, "Even though it didn't seem so on the surface, this was exactly what I wanted."

"What would you have done if Robert had decided to take the gaokao after the trip?" I asked.

Mr. Guo answered without hesitation, "If he had chosen to take the gaokao, I probably would have given him more guidance." He nodded slightly as he spoke, giving off a sense of determination and confidence.

In this example, Mr. Guo planned ahead and purposefully guided Robert to arrive at the same set of educational decisions as himself. He wanted Robert to go abroad, thus he had sent Robert on a summer visiting trip designed to introduce students to American college campuses in eighth grade. In our conversation, Mr. Guo also revealed that he wanted Robert to perceive these predetermined choices as a teenager's independent decisions, thus he strategically disagreed when Robert first mentioned the possibility of applying for American universities ("didn't seem so on the surface"). In the event that Robert did not follow his unspoken directions, the father was willing to deploy more strategies to achieve his goal ("would have given him more guidance"). Mr. Guo's strategies worked as planned. He was pleased that Robert "had his heart set on going to the U.S." since the summer of eighth grade and never deviated from this path.

Importantly, Mr. Guo's response also explained why parents had different parent-child interactions based on children's test scores. Children were given considerable freedom to do what they wanted, provided that they followed the trajectories that parents had decided for them. By virtue of having gone to university, the elite parents in this study were within the 98th to 99th percentile in educational attainment in the country. Many even ranked within the 99.99th percentile in their respective provinces for the gaokao. These parents hoped that their children would do better, or at least as well as they had, in higher education. These expectations, in turn, meant that study gods and studyholics fulfilled parents' expectations by being high-performing and thus enjoyed considerable freedom in the family, with parents tolerating their entitlement. However, by being low-performing, the underachievers and losers failed to do so, and thus parents gave more "guidance" in their efforts to redirect the children toward having high performance.

Robert did as his father had planned. He reported that going abroad was his "own choice" and his parents agreed with his decision. He applied to college in the United States, worked with the agent his father hired, and applied to universities that his father deemed satisfactory. By the end of high school, Robert remained unaware of parental influence, an impression his father skillfully directed him toward. Robert never realized that his father had spoon-fed him the ideas about going abroad and becoming a global citizen; the possibility of being under strong parental influence had not crossed his mind.

Beyond High School: Growing into Autonomous Young Adults

In 2019, the teenagers had become young adults whose number of years since high school equaled the number of years since they left home. Instead of living together and sharing meals with their parents every day, they now visited their parents on the weekends or over the summer. Whereas they used to have face-to-face conversations with parents, many of them now primarily talked online. Family life was no longer customized to fit their schedules. Some children found their bedrooms converted into storage spaces; a few no longer had a room since parents leased out the apartment or moved away. Of the twenty-eight students in this study, twenty-five left the country for school or work. The few elite parents who spoke fluent English visited their children around the world, but the majority, who did not, waited for their children to visit them at home. The parents in this study were experts in navigating the domestic job market but had limited understanding of school and work in a foreign land. They could arrange jobs with a phone call to large corporations and state-owned companies in China, but when it came to positions in countries such as the United States, United Kingdom, Singapore, France, or Japan, they had few strings to pull and none were as effective.

The limitations of parental influence implied that parents were further removed from their children's lives and became truly hands-off in their parent-child interactions. This also suggested that the elite who hailed from China became autonomous in their pursuit of global elite status. The young adults indeed perceived status competition as based on personal ability and took pride in being independent from their parents. Selena, a high performer at Capital, said that she had "tried to distance herself from parental influence" since college and refused to take up the positions her parents offered. She went through the job-hunting process in the United States and landed in a position in New York City. Huating similarly refused to accept parental assistance after moving to the United Kingdom. She stayed in London after graduation and found a position at the branch office of an American technological and social media company. Like Selena and Huating, most of the students in this study perceived no need of parental assistance.

Yet despite the increased independence, the elite young adults' parent-child interaction patterns resembled those observed in high school. The study gods and studyholics continued to summon their parents for unwavering support and felt free to act entitled when interacting with them. The underachievers and losers did not think parental resources would be immediately available upon request. In other words, while high performers still perceived parental support to be at the children's discretion, low performers were wary of being denied parental support.

Study god Julie remained as rude to her mother and entitled to parental sacrifices in 2013 as in the next six years. I visited Julie in 2014, when she returned home for the summer from Bryn Mawr College. In our meeting at the food court of the local department store, she said that her mother went back to work soon after she left for the States. Julie had serious health issues and took sick leave for a semester the following year.[17] During that time she returned home and her mother dropped out of the labor force again. In our text exchanges, Julie said that her mother had done so partially to take care of her but primarily because "she disliked her job." I visited Julie in Beijing in 2019, a year after she graduated college. We met at a Starbucks on an extremely windy day. I arrived to see Julie wearing slightly gothic-style makeup, reading journal articles about neuroscience on her laptop at the bar table. As I sorted the knots and tangles in my hair, Julie told me she still identified as a study god but that she spent more time preparing graduate school applications. She said with a shudder, "I'm becoming a studyholic these days!" Julie thought about getting a PhD in neuroscience but did not want to go into academia "because academia is too easy, it's not challenging at all." Instead, she aspired to start her own company, saying in a dreamy voice, "I want to create something with my own hands." Being an academic, I shot back by asking, "Have you thought about knitting?" Julie laughed so hard that she tilted her chair. Trying to control her laughter, she lightly tapped my shoulder with one hand, "You're toxic!"

Our lighthearted conversation, however, turned serious when I asked about her parents. "I had a fight with my mom in early April," she said succinctly. "I can't tell you what it was about, it's too complicated. But I couldn't take it. I just couldn't." I nodded, noting that this argument had lasted a month and a half already.

"I love my mom. Seriously, I do." Julie said, looking into my eyes with sincerity. "But I couldn't take what she did. I'm still angry at her until now. My mom apologized, but I'm not ready to forgive her." She waved her hand in circles between us. "I told her, don't do anything for me from now on. Don't cook for me, don't do anything." Julie paused and took in a breath, "I'm even using the money I saved [to support myself]!" She stared at me, making sure that I knew the seriousness of this incident. Julie declared with a proud smile that narrowed her eyes, "I haven't asked her for money ever since then. I've been using the allowances she previously gave me."

I reminded her, "But that money still came from your mom."

"No, it's different; it's a matter of principle!" Julie said with determination, "I haven't eaten anything she cooked. Until yesterday." However, she immediately added a disclaimer, "But I'm not going home for dinner today. She needs to understand that she irritated me. Before she does, I'm not going to talk to her, eat with her, I won't take allowances from her, and I refuse to acknowledge her presence even though we live together. She needs to learn a lesson."

Julie's relationship with her mother had not changed. She still attributed her mother's withdrawal from the labor force as a personal choice ("she didn't like her job"). However, the fact that the mother became a full-time homemaker only when Julie needed special care (first for her college application year and then during her sick leave) suggests that the mother had done so to take care of her daughter. Julie continued to dominate interactions with her mother. Just as the mother had expressed fearing Julie and succumbing to Julie's wishes six years ago, she apologized to the daughter again. Instead of the parent instructing the child on appropriate behavior, the daughter instructed the mother ("she needs to learn a lesson") and punished the mother by stripping her of her perceived maternal duty (cooking, eating together, giving allowances, or doing anything for the child).

Low performers had a clearly different experience when interacting with their parents. Recall how Robert's father skillfully guided his son to choose the path he had in mind. Jiaqi reported something similar, but with more overt parental guidance. In 2014, just two months before the gaokao, Jiaqi's parents informed him of their decision to ship him to France because his test scores were too low for top universities in China. The mother recalled that Jiaqi "was shocked to tears, but he soon accepted" the parents' decision.

Jiaqi continued to follow his parents' orders with a similar level of obedience in college. Like Brandon, who failed to receive the assistance he deemed necessary, Jiaqi was forced into independence in college. I met with him in 2015 in a vacant study lounge at Capital, a year after he enrolled in the Université de Technologie de Compiègne. Jiaqi arrived in his high school jacket to avoid being questioned by security at the school gate. He had grown a short beard and was a few inches taller, but he maintained his signature chubby cheeks. He informed me the minute he sat down across the table that he had received an expulsion letter due to his poor performance. I was shocked as I listened to his story. Jiaqi said he immediately called his parents, requesting that they speak to his academic advisor. However, his parents refused.

"They basically hung up on me." Jiaqi sat in a hunchback position and spoke in a low voice, "They told me they couldn't do anything. My mom said she had done everything she could already, sending me to France. She told me that I was in France now, I was on my own, and I had to deal with anything that happened." Jiaqi put his hands on the table between us. He took in a breath, "I was like, 'Oh my god, what should I do?' I was terrified. I mean, this was serious! If I got expelled, what would I do? I wouldn't have a BA degree. What would I do without that degree? My life would be over!"

"What happened then? You're still in school, right?" I asked hastily.

"I called my academic advisor," Jiaqi answered calmly. "At first he said there's nothing he could do. But I kept talking to him. I almost cried, I pleaded with him to give me a second chance. [After] two hours of me begging, he said, 'Fine, Fine. I'll talk to [the higher-ups] about this. Don't you dare fail any course again, ever!' Of course, I swore that I wouldn't. That's how I stayed."

Jiaqi's parents constantly held considerable authority in parent-child interactions. They could dominate his trajectory or become uninvolved at their convenience. In twelfth grade, Jiaqi and his mother both acknowledged that the family meeting about sending him to France was not a discussion but an announcement, which he ultimately accepted. In college, Jiaqi accepted his parents' refusal to help. He did not argue with them, nor did he engage in prolonged negotiations ("they basically hung up on me"). He did not demand that his mother do as he asked (talk to his advisor) but instead obediently negotiated for school completion alone. Jiaqi's mother might have been involved without telling him. Alternatively, she might have been decidedly uninvolved in order to cultivate Jiaqi's personal sense of responsibility at the risk of him flunking out of college. Yet regardless of what the mother may or may not have done, Jiaqi followed his parents' orders in college, as he had done in high school.

In sum, having abundant family resources at their disposal, elite young adults such as Julie and Jiaqi were generally entitled to pursue their dreams. Elite Chinese parents indeed willingly provided for their children, but differences in parental efforts in high school were strikingly similar to those in young adulthood. High performers, who had high chances of succeeding in status competition, seemed to enjoy unlimited family resources and parental support. Low performers, who had relatively low chances of succeeding in global competition, accepted their parents' withholding of necessary assistance and parental claims about developing their independence. In some cases, the latter parents' efforts seemed to bring forth a positive turn in children's outcomes. Although he took a detour, Jiaqi was back in the competition for elite status reproduction. When I last visited him in Beijing in 2019, he had become a hardworking student with high levels of academic anxiety. He took me to dinner in Beijing and proudly announced that he would be the first Chinese national to graduate from the program. Furthermore, realizing that his less-than-top credentials excluded him from the best, high-paying jobs, he switched from competing for income to prestige. Jiaqi focused on getting the most prestigious position in his field and made plans to become an engineer at Mercedes, one of the top two race car producers in the world. "Mercedes!" He shouted with excitement in the busy restaurant, "The best race cars in the world! *Nothing* beats the prestige of working there!"

Summary

Armed with unlimited resources and undying support from wealthy parents, elite students enjoyed a distinct advantage in pursuing their goals and realizing their ambitions. However, while their parents willingly sacrificed themselves to support their college-bound children, parents treated their children based on their test scores. Parents routinely refrained from irritating their children when they were on track to go to top universities around the world. On the other hand, parents of low performers engaged in close parental supervision and did not tolerate their entitlement at home. By yielding to high-performing children's demands, the parents of high performers turned them into the so-called little emperors whom scholars and media portray as entitled, spoiled teenagers who routinely disrespected their parents, while the low performers did not demonstrate such behavior.

As key adults who shape students' everyday experiences, parents convey to their children the value of test scores in everyday life outside of school. Because test scores and school status are inseparable in adolescent society, parent-child interactions based on test scores are indistinguishable from status-based treatment. In fact, parents systematically extending differential treatment from school to home sustains elite youths' engagement in status competition in multiple ways: it drives home the importance of status, validates students' status system, and signals approval from the adult world about the rules that govern status competition in school. Considering that parent-child relationships often continue to be related to students' status outcomes, parents play a crucial role in supporting the students' status system that goes beyond resource provision and school involvement. As the young adults competing for global elite status become entitled to parental devotion, parents enable them to compete with peers around the world without worries. The race toward global elite status thus involves not only a generation of globally oriented young adults but their elite parents as well.

6

Saving the Day

On my first day at Capital, Mr. Long, the eleventh grade headmaster and debonair math teacher in his mid-forties, greeted me in a meeting room. He informed me that he was going to introduce me to four students, and I could start from there. I asked if he could also introduce me to a few parents. Mr. Long asked, flabbergasted, "Why on earth would parents have anything to do with students' performance?" A year and a half later, I met with Mr. Long to bid him farewell. We occupied a study booth outside the meeting room where we had first met. He brought up my earlier request and said, "You were right. Parents really did play a role. Students who had better communication with their parents did better on the gaokao."

CONCEPTUALIZING ELITE status reproduction as a competition, elite children are a group of predicted winners. They go to top high schools, study with the most qualified teachers, and have abundant family resources at their disposal. Importantly, they know how to play the game. They are exceptionally familiar with its rules, know what to expect given their positions, and have the support of key adults who either are experts or were winners themselves. Because all the chips are in place, it seems hard for them to lose. The elite parents in this study knew this as well. These parents perceived no need to utilize every bit of affluence or the family's various forms of capital. Parental efforts were directed at enhancing children's well-being at home. Parental activities, from providing a college-focused environment to offering emotional support to the stressed-out child, took place outside the school. They saw all preparations that took place on campus as the teachers' responsibilities. Tasks directly related to college attainment, such as exam preparation and creating the perfect application packages, were taken care of by schoolteachers and counselors.

While most teachers welcomed and upheld the norm of no communication, some American counselors strongly preferred to meet with parents.

Chris, Tom, and other counselors at Capital estimated that "less than one-third of the students were able to make their own decisions as to which schools and majors to apply." Given parents' strong hand in students' college application choices, counselors considered these meetings highly important and necessary. However, few parents responded to these requests. When they did, the parent-counselor meetings did not go as expected. Chris summarized his interactions with parents with a sigh: "We meet with very few parents. When we do, the parents don't say much. Most of the time it's us talking to the students." Tom, another American counselor at Capital, also experienced great difficulty communicating with parents due to language and cultural barriers. To make matters worse, he found out that the translator (the student) sometimes "purposefully mistranslated what we said to the parents" to "get their parents on their side."

From elite parents' perspectives, there was no need for them to interfere with school under ordinary circumstances. However, status reproduction does not always progress as planned. Just as even the most skillful contestants sometimes find themselves on the verge of losing, elite parents sometimes find their children at risk of failing. Not every move progresses the family toward the end goal, and things simply do not always go well in the gaokao preparations and application process. It was in these moments of crises that the parents in this study showed their cards. Trying to save the day, they crossed into what was perceived as the teachers' domain. Specifically, they imposed plan B, contingency plans that they had formulated long ago.

Throughout the fifteen months of fieldwork, I observed two incidents of parents visiting the school outside of parent-teacher meetings. One occurred at Capital, when I was shadowing Jiaqi. Students had just finished their last class. The hallway was filled with chattering, and the atmosphere was quite relaxed as students clustered in twos and threes. All of a sudden, two anxious-looking parents passed through the hallway in a brisk manner. Voices in the hallway immediately died down as they passed through. The students looked warily at the parents, and all turned their heads toward the direction where the couple were headed. No one talked until the parents entered the elevator and were out of sight.

"What happened?" I asked Jiaqi.

Seemingly reluctant, he replied in a hushed tone, "Parents. Something probably went wrong."

"How do you know?" I probed.

Jiaqi rolled his eyes as if I had asked a stupid question. "Look," he explained patiently. "Why do you think parents are here? Something must have gone wrong. Probably terribly wrong. Now it's just a question of whose parents those were." Jiaqi tried to eavesdrop on others about the incident but was soon distracted.

In this incident, student reactions (quieting down and looking at the parents) suggested that it was rare for parents to visit schools. Student comments further showed that parents were not to appear on campus unless absolutely necessary, such as when something went "terribly wrong." The infrequency of parents' unannounced visits suggested very few students were troublemakers in top high schools. Additionally, it was likely that elite parents were able to identify risks early on and change the course before things went so badly that they were summoned to school. Mr. Long's newfound understanding of the benefits of parent-child communication supported the second possibility.[1] For the elite parents, university placement was a crucial step that largely determined future status. They refused to let their children fall behind in the race toward elite status and reacted quickly when things did not go as planned. Given that parents rarely contacted teachers, parents sensing the possibility of failure largely depended on smooth parent-child communication.

The ability to turn the tables before things went sour was undoubtedly an elite advantage. These actions were possible only for parents with the insider knowledge and means to put their children back on track.[2] As I show below, in many but not all instances, these actions made a difference and gave the children an edge as they competed for top university enrollment. The seemingly losing children were kept in the race, and the seemingly winning children performed even better in each round of competition. With these bursts of parent backup at critical moments, the teenagers were set on track to win the grand prize—future global elite status.

Parents' Contingency Planning

Elite parents understand that higher educational attainment is a crucial step in status reproduction. The families in this study were no exception. The idea of going to college was so fundamental to the parents that asking if they'd let children not go to college was like asking if elephants could fly. Many shuddered at the idea that their single child might fail to get into any university. The main issue for them, however, was which exact school the child would attend. The parents saw intense competition for top universities in China and abroad as a corridor of uncertainty. Those in the domestic department understood that failing to pass a certain cutoff score on a certain test might shatter the child's dream of entering a top university in China, and along with it his or her future status. Those in the international department envisioned that a mishandled situation in the American college application process might derail the child, leading to potentially disastrous outcomes. Consequently, regardless of children's test scores, these elite parents prepared for contingency in children's college preparations.

Didn't Do Well on the Gaokao? Go Abroad Immediately, or Retake the Exam

Most students in the domestic departments in the top high schools never thought about not passing the gaokao. My hypothetical question of what they would do or how they would feel if they did not get into any university always seemed to shock the twelfth grade students. Fei, a study god at Pinnacle, was one of the more confident ones. When I asked what he would do if he did not get into any university in China, Fei responded immediately, "The only way out was to repeat [twelfth] grade. There's no other option for students in China." Fei then tried to change the hypothetical scenario into a more probable one: "A more likely situation is if I failed to get into Tsinghua or Peking universities. In that case, I'd just go to my second-choice university. There are two or three very good universities that allow students to put them as a second choice. I'd accept those." Fei then revisited my question: "But you meant if I didn't get into any university. I'd need to stop and think about life. First, I'd tell myself this is not the end of the world. I would then figure out the problem and what my options were. This has honestly never crossed my mind." He then added with unclear grammar, "This brain dysfunction knows what this problem was. No, I mean."[3]

The idea of not getting into any college was so shocking that Fei had trouble speaking well. It was understandable that Fei, being a study god, perceived this as impossible ("never crossed my mind"). Yet even the underachievers and losers felt far removed from such a possibility. For the elite Beijingers in top high schools, the question was *which* university they would attend, not *whether* they would go to college.

Although students in the domestic departments at top high schools perceived having no choice but to pass the gaokao, parents prepared exit plans without informing the child. Recall from chapter 5 that Jiaqi was suddenly informed that he was to move to France due to his low test scores. Recall also that Huating was instructed to pursue transfers after she failed to enter Tsinghua. Something similar would have happened to Fei if he performed poorly in the exam. I interviewed Fei's mother, Mrs. Li, at their apartment a few days after Fei took the gaokao. I asked her what she would do or think if Fei did not pass the Olympiad and also did not do well on the gaokao. Mrs. Li responded as if she had been prepared for this possibility all along: "If he didn't pass the Olympiad, it would all depend on his exact gaokao scores. If he could go to a good university, then he'd go to that one first, and then try to go to a university abroad. Repeating a grade was too burdensome; we never seriously considered that. In the case that he wasn't himself and did poorly on the gaokao, only then would we consider retaking the gaokao." I asked what universities she had considered. Mrs. Li answered, "We first thought of Hong Kong University as an option. But if he could go to Tsinghua or Peking universities, then we wouldn't consider HKU." Mrs. Li also made clear that those plans never materialized, and the family "never looked for foreign universities or anything, because [Fei] passed the Olympiad early on" and was accepted to the family's top choice, Tsinghua.

Compared to Fei, who felt challenged by the question, Mrs. Li showed no signs of surprise. She seemed prepared for contingencies surrounding the gaokao. The mother acknowledged the likelihood of her son doing extremely poorly on the gaokao, expressing that the chance of this happening was low but not impossible (if "he wasn't himself"). She considered at least three contingency plans and was prepared to enact them if necessary. First, if Fei scored slightly lower than his average performance, the mother would send him to Hong Kong University. Hong Kong was not the only possibility. Later in the interview, Mrs. Lis revealed that Fei's uncle had experiences working abroad and that he could provide more information on foreign universities and majors. Alternatively, if Fei did extremely poorly, she would let him take a gap year to retake the gaokao. Mrs. Li listed a third option, which was to repeat a grade, but rejected it outright ("too burdensome"). Interestingly, Fei thought that this option, which meant going through twelfth grade again, studying in a classroom for fifteen hours every day including weekends for another entire year, was the only solution. Mrs. Li might have strategically allowed Fei to perceive the worst-case scenario as the only outcome should he fail the gaokao. Alternatively, the mother might have simply withheld the information so that Fei could devote himself to the gaokao. Regardless of the mother's reasons, it was clear that Mrs. Li made multiple backup plans for Fei without his knowledge.

In the end, the mother's ideas remained strings of thoughts. Things went well for the family, and Mrs. Li filed away her contingency plans. Fei received guaranteed admission by winning the Olympiad, took the gaokao to boost Pinnacle's average, and later went to Tsinghua University and majored in electrical engineering. However, the mother was aware that no matter how low the possibility, lightning sometimes strikes. Until Fei signed the contract with Tsinghua, she was prepared to jump into action to provide her son a way out at a moment's notice.

Didn't Get into an American University? Move Down the U.S. News Rankings

Compared to students in the domestic departments, those in the international department were sometimes worried about not being accepted to any American university. Claire, who later went to Yale, had been haunted by this idea because she applied only to top-ranked universities. Student anxiety over the possibility of reapplying the next year was uncommon but real. I ran into Chris outside of Capital's counseling center in May. Chris was a tall, middle-aged American counselor whom students called "the English gentlemen."[4] He told me that he was scheduled to meet with a student who had not yet received any acceptance letter.

"Oh, none yet? That's quite late." I commented.

"It is," Chris sighed. "She's worried that she might not have been admitted by any. She's very anxious, which I understand."

"I thought everyone had a placement!" I asked with utter surprise.

"Eventually every student will," Chris explained with his usual smile. "But there are a few who get their results very late each year. Two or three girls haven't heard back from all of the schools. I wouldn't worry, but she wanted to meet. We'll see what we can do." He then walked into the center.

For Chris, the students had nothing to worry about, and all of them would be accepted by at least one university ("eventually every student will"). However, despite the counselor's assuredness, the idea of failing loomed large in the mind of students. The very fact that a few students didn't receive their placements until the very end of the semester was sufficient to cause group anxiety among the applicants, who were concerned until they received an acceptance letter in their inbox.

Compared to the assured counselors, parents shared the anxiety of their children. However, while the parents in domestic departments made concrete exit plans for their child should anything go wrong with the gaokao, parents in the international department had none in mind. They widely rejected the idea of switching back to preparing for the gaokao, citing that their children would be at a significant disadvantage compared to peers who had spent all of their high school years preparing for the exam. Having their backs against the wall, the parents prepared for contingencies by instructing the child to cast a (very) wide net in college applications.

Most counselors I spoke to suggested that students apply to ten schools at most. Some families followed this advice, but most saw ten as the minimum number of applications. Alex and his family belonged to the latter group. In fact, he submitted so many applications that he could not remember the universities he had applied to.[5] I asked Alex twice to share with me the universities he applied to. He came up with two overlapping but different lists. When I pointed out that they were not the same, he laughed and said, "Really? I can't remember. I applied to so many universities. Some twenty of them!" Alex suggested that I combine the two versions for a full list of his submitted applications. However, even the combined list had missing information: it did not include Boston College, which Alex later attended.

I asked Alex's mother about his applications. The mother admitted to going way beyond the amount advised by Alex's school counselor, Tom, and laughingly described the number of applications as "huge [*juduo*]." She explained that the decision was due to parental anxiety. "You see," she said as she clutched her purse, "we were a bit nervous. Alex applied via [early action] to three universities,[6] but none of them took him. [We] got nervous, and in the end, Alex thought that applying for more universities might give him more chances. As parents, we had no experience in these things. We were anxious. We thought, 'What if he didn't get into any school?' Like that. That's how he applied to so many universities." She then smiled and folded her arms, adding, "Actually, in hindsight, this anxiety was completely unnecessary, right? Those universities ranked in the forties and fifties? They were nonproblems [definitely going to admit Alex]. It was totally unnecessary to be anxious."

Like many other parents in the international department, Alex's parents had no experience with the American application system. To combat the feeling of uncertainty, these parents encouraged or directed their children to apply to a myriad of universities as a contingency plan. Alex's mother directly attributed this behavior to parental anxiety ("we were anxious"), fearing that Alex might not have any college placement ("What if he didn't get into any school?"). The family cast a net wider than necessary, resulting in Alex applying to not ten but over twenty universities in one application season. Like with other families, the additional applications were sent to universities that ranked below the targeted tier ("universities ranked in the forties and fifties" that were "nonproblems"). In Alex's case, he was unwilling to miss his chance of getting into one of his dream schools, thus some of the additional applications went to universities that his counselor suggested were beyond his reach. Alex's mother ultimately concluded that her strategy of applying to a "huge" number of universities was "unnecessary." Nonetheless, her plan served its purpose: to provide a buffer for Alex against potential failure in the college application process.

In sum, elite parents assumed responsibility as children's ultimate safety net. They were determined to catch their children if they fell. The anxiety surrounding college placements prompted parents to invest in contingency plans. Those in the domestic department drew from personal experiences with the gaokao and prioritized certain alternatives while rejecting others. Parents could plan ahead for their children even without firsthand experience, as lacking the knowledge of the application processes in the United States did not stop the parents in international departments from securing a college placement. They improvised based on the school counselors' suggestions and their rational calculation, ultimately deciding to cast a wide net for universities at the expense of potentially crowding out other applicants who aimed at those institutions. Not all parents enacted these strategies, especially the parents of study gods and other high performers. However, the fact that even parents of study gods were prepared revealed the parental determination to help their children successfully reproduce elite status.

Parents of High Performers Have a Winning Game Plan

Studies often portray elite students' college entrance as a seamless process.[7] About half of the students in this study indeed smoothly transitioned to top universities in China, the United States, or the United Kingdom. However, elite students could encounter unforeseen issues that turned the tables. Just as a player on a winning streak might suddenly suffer a losing spell, even the study gods and studyholics could suddenly find themselves at a serious disadvantage after failing a certain test. In these moments of difficulty, elite parents acted quickly and saved the day. The parents in this study knew about the struggle for status by heart. They had won these intense competitions themselves. Armed with an intricate understanding of the status system, these parents effectively pushed their child to succeed while staying within the structure and rules. Their elite family background thus entailed more than resource advantage, also bringing into play parents' knowledge and ability to buffer children from setbacks in the application process.

Audience Behaviors: Tony's Mother Has Nothing to Worry About

Parents of consistently top-performing children relied on the school for college preparation. Examples of these students include Fei, Mingjia, Ashley, and Tony, all of whom smoothly transitioned to Tsinghua University, Cambridge, and Cornell. In our interview, Fei's mother denied helping Fei with college preparation: "No, I didn't do [much]. I just paid the fees." Mingjia's mother reported providing minimal help. When I asked about the proudest thing she did for Mingjia when preparing for college, the mother thought for a moment and replied: "The proudest thing. Let me think, the proudest thing. Hmm. The proudest thing I've done, is, I think, is that, that I helped [Mingjia] organize her notes. I stapled them together." Stapling notes, however, was a low level of assistance, and in a separate interview Mingjia did not recall her mother doing so. Similarly, Ashley's mother reported little involvement and even infrequent attendance at parent-teacher meetings: "If I'm free, I'd go to parent-teacher meetings once in a while. Basically, I don't go."

Parents of study gods and studyholics often expected their children to transition smoothly to elite universities and perceived no need to invoke backup plans. Among these parents was Tony's mother, Mrs. Cao, a short-haired teacher and businesswoman who spoke very fast but clearly. I met her at a coffee shop near the school she taught. She set the tone and tempo of the interview with an air of confidence. Mrs. Cao described Tony as "a child whom adults did not worry about." When asked about whether and how she helped Tony with college applications, she made clear that she had not. She explained, "[The applications] depended on [Tony]. He could get an agent, or get someone to guide him at Capital. He could do these things. I might help him a bit with language issues if [he had trouble], but he dealt with those things in private by himself. After all, children don't think the way adults do."

In Mrs. Cao's mind, there was nothing for her to do in Tony's application process. She had prepared Tony for Western higher education from an early age. She took Tony to the United Kingdom when she was studying there as a graduate student and later cultivated his study habits. As Mrs. Cao proudly shared in the interview, she had instilled in Tony her motto: "Never stop studying, never stop improving." Having set Tony on track, she perceived no need to plan for contingencies during high school. Tony was consistently a study god at Capital. With Tony's high performance, the mother was able to help ("might help him a bit with language"), but ultimately decided not to because Tony could take full responsibility for his studies ("he dealt with things himself").

Mrs. Cao was certain that her son would enter a top university in the States. Wondering whether she had made a backup plan, I asked what she would do or say if Tony could not go to his dream school. Mrs. Cao brushed aside this question with a confident smile and waved her hand in the air: "I didn't think it would matter at all. All American universities ranked in the top thirty are similar. I thought he wouldn't land at a school outside the top thirty. Judging from his ability, he's the type who wouldn't have any problem. Maybe a school in the top twenty would be a bit different from one in the top thirty. But the difference wouldn't be significant, you see."

Having a son who had a top GPA and very high SAT scores, Mrs. Cao perceived that Tony was doing well and would reproduce her high status. Believing that Tony was destined to go to a top university ("judging from his ability," "wouldn't have any problem"), she neither enacted contingency plans nor seriously entertained the idea of making them. Like other parents in the international department, the only contingency planning Mrs. Cao performed was to let Tony cast a wide net. However, Tony's additional applications did not carry the same purpose as those of other students. While Alex's safety schools were much below his original targeted universities, Tony's were not. Mrs. Cao reported that the lower ranked schools (institutions ranked between twenty-one and thirty by *U.S. News & World Report*) were "not significantly different" from those that Tony aimed for (institutions ranked in the top twenty). This showed that the mother had a very high sense of security, so much so that the safety net no longer served its usual purpose of catching the child should he fall because such a possibility did not exist. Rather, these added applications became additional targets.

The mother's high level of confidence even led her to refuse to help Tony in instances where he could have needed parental guidance. One such instance was when Tony wanted to drop a project and focus on preparing for the SAT, as described in chapter 4. He was in conflict with his teacher, who was a potential letter writer. However, the mother was unconcerned throughout the incident. When I asked her about it, she commented with a chuckle, "If you thought about it, it was really a nonissue. I could have told him how to deal with [his teacher] and make things go away. He was anxious, but the anxiety was completely unnecessary." Another moment was when Tony had trouble finding a student in the next cohort to succeed him in his position as chair of the social science club, without which the school would shut down the club. If this happened, he would be on record for a lack of leadership, and his applications would be negatively affected. Yet his mother remained unworried. I followed up by asking about the reasons for her withdrawal from these potentially harmful events. Mrs. Cao seemed tired of my probing and responded with a cavalier sigh, "I'd say, there's got to be a mechanism. Things would adjust by themselves. You didn't need to worry, you see." Then, she concluded the series of questions by saying, "I didn't go into the details. Tony took care of things himself."

Mrs. Cao could have helped her son but did not. She acknowledged that Tony was not without potential problems in his application process. He had questions about the applications, annoyed a letter writer, and had been on the verge of being officially punished by the school. Yet throughout the interview it was clear that the mother did not see any of these as reasons for parental involvement. To Mrs. Cao, these issues posed no threat to Tony's college applications and his future. She could rest assured that Tony was on track for a top university, and he would have a solid foundation for elite status competition. Knowing this, the mother claimed that these risks were insufficient to throw Tony off track, and even Tony himself should not have been bothered in the slightest ("anxiety was completely unnecessary").

Tony transitioned smoothly to college. As his mother predicted, Tony found a student in the next cohort to take over as chair of the social science club. Feeling relieved, he gleefully withdrew from all club activities. In twelfth grade, he scored 2320 on the SAT and gained acceptance to Cornell University, which was ranked in the top twenty of American universities.[8] His family was pleased with the outcome. Having complete confidence in Tony, the mother continued to take a hands-off approach, believing that he could handle anything, not just in high school but also in college and as he entered adult society.

Bolts of Assistance: Shiying's Mother Coaches Her Daughter

While some parents felt relaxed about their children's applications, others saw the need to come to their children's rescue. The parents of study gods and studyholics occasionally provided bolts of parental assistance when they sensed that top college placement and hence future elite status were at risk. One such example was Shiying, the top performer at Capital. Shiying's mother, Mrs. Liu, was an alumna of Tsinghua University and professor of Chinese literature. In the fall of twelfth grade, Mrs. Liu reported being minimally involved in Shiying's schoolwork. During my four-day stay at their apartment, I observed no conversation about the gaokao or college. Parent-child communication consisted almost entirely of Mrs. Liu's succinct reminders, such as "it's gonna rain tomorrow," "time for bed," or "remember your lunchbox." At the time, Capital teachers, parents, and Shiying herself all thought that she was destined to go to THU and major in a field of her choice. At this time, Mrs. Liu acted similar to Tony's mother and took a backseat in Shiying's college preparation.

The turning point was when Shiying unexpectedly failed the additional test for THU. As soon as Mrs. Liu learned that Shiying did not do well on the test, she began to coach her daughter in a previously unobserved way. On the morning of the additional test, Mrs. Liu and I waited for Shiying outside the test location. As we took a short walk around the neighborhood, she stated again that she didn't coach Shiying on anything, even though she could, by virtue of her being a professor. Three hours later, around noon, we joined a group of parents waiting outside the exam building. Shiying briskly walked toward us in a pink down jacket with her ponytail dangling at the back of her head.

"How was it?" Mrs. Liu hastily asked.

"Oh, exams," Shiying sighed with a girlish cavalier. Meeting her mother's eyes, she switched to a more serious tone and said, "I didn't have time to finish math. Chinese was easier, although some questions were hard to answer."

Seemingly worried, Mrs. Liu, who had just told me while waiting outside that she never talked to Shiying about exam details, initiated a discussion of the harder Chinese questions as we walked to the car. One question that bothered Shiying was completing the couplet for "cars lost their way in fog-locked Beijing." Conversation around this topic continued during the car ride.

"Tell me what you wrote," Mrs. Liu asked.

"I wrote," Shiying replied, hesitantly, "People lost their homes in ice-closed New York."

After a moment of consideration, Mrs. Liu said in a firm tone with her eyes locked on the road, "Hmm, I think I'd write 'people lost their homes in water-flooded Nancheng.' If it were the case, I would definitely contrast water and flood. That would be the right way to answer it, because then it'll both be about the weather and disasters in the country."

"Beijing to [Nancheng], that's good." Shiying agreed at first but then defended her answer, "I'd contrast Beijing with New York. Didn't New York have a snow storm a couple of years ago?"

"You used Beijing to New York, but I'd use Beijing against another capital." Mrs. Liu suggested, "Also, New York is a translated term, Beijing is not. Nancheng is a better choice. This would also be contrasting north [*bei*] and south [*nan*]."

Shiying seemed tired of discussing this question and tried to divert attention by saying, "This is already too much time spent on one question; I had other questions to answer." But Mrs. Liu pressed on. Conversation over this couplet continued for over half an hour and did not end until we arrived at a restaurant for lunch.

The mother's efforts did not end there. Two weeks later, Shiying texted me that she had failed the additional test. She had aspired to accrue thirty additional points for THU but instead got none. Although Shiying had twenty additional points from being an exemplary student, Mrs. Liu felt that Shiying was at a disadvantage compared to other students who had obtained more extra points. Mrs. Liu then became heavily involved in Shiying's college preparation. One major change was that Mrs. Liu started contacting Shiying's teachers.

About a month after the additional test, I ran into Mrs. Liu on campus as I was heading home from a daylong observation. I greeted Mrs. Liu and asked what had brought her to school. She said she had just come back from a parent-teacher meeting. She wanted to raise Shiying's test scores, so she approached Mrs. Nie, Shiying's homeroom teacher, after the meeting.

"It was my first time to go to her!" Mrs. Liu said, looking slightly amused. "I said to her, 'About Shiying's Chinese composition . . .' and then, Mrs. Nie immediately said to me, 'I didn't teach her well. I'm sorry.'" Mrs. Liu laughed, "I wasn't trying to blame her or anything, I was just thinking about what to say!"

To my surprise, I ran into Mrs. Liu on campus again in the same month, when it was an ordinary day with no parent-teacher meetings. I again asked what had brought her to school.

"There was a college choice consultation going on. I thought I'd drop by to ask for suggestions. Honestly I didn't know what to ask." She chuckled, "But I thought I should come. I talked to the Tsinghua admission officer. The officer suggested that Shiying should put down [a particular] major in THU." Mrs. Liu shrugged, "I guess now we'll think about it."

In this example, the mother changed and adjusted her parenting involvement according to how events unfolded.[9] Mrs. Liu was a potential exam reviewer by virtue of her academic position in Chinese literature. She could have discussed exam prompts with her daughter on a regular basis. The mother knew what to do, how to prepare for the exam, and whom to approach concerning Shiying's performance. Yet she never coached her daughter, never approached teachers, and never visited school until Shiying unexpectedly failed the additional test. Having gone through gaokao selection in China, Mrs. Liu understood the significance of obtaining additional points as well as the possible consequences of losing them. As soon as the mother realized that a problem existed, she took matters into her own hands and activated all the plans she had that could salvage the situation.

Notably, the mother tried to save the day while abiding by the norms. She did not attempt to switch tracks, such as by giving up the gaokao or going abroad, nor did she make moves that were against the rules, such as drawing on professional networks to solicit possible exam questions. Instead, she began to instruct Shiying with alternative answers that she thought would have received higher scores. Even though Shiying tried to change the topic, she pressed on and made sure that her daughter would be able to give a better answer on a future exam. Mrs. Liu also approached Shiying's schoolteachers possibly for the first time over Shiying's entire twelve years of schooling ("my first time to go to her"). Finally, the mother consulted admission officers and was willing to consider a major that was not on her radar.

Shiying later performed well on the gaokao as expected, but the mother's role was not static over time. The mother was able to assist her daughter by using her status-based knowledge.[10] Shiying's gaokao score put her within the top sixteen in the city. She was admitted to Tsinghua and majored in her top choice, the one recommended by the admission officer. In short, the mother provided timely assistance to her daughter and the daughter was well situated to reproduce elite status.

Invoking Special Rules: Yulang's Mother Pesters the Coach

Saving the day also involved invoking special rules that few players knew about. Yulang, a high performer at Capital, was interested in math and aspired to be placed in the first tier of the national high school tournament to enter Tsinghua University. Her mother, an alumna of Tsinghua University and editor of a government newspaper, found that Capital offered high-quality training in the Olympiad and transferred Yulang there. At Capital, Yulang devoted herself to preparing for the Olympiad to the point of giving up on additional tests and other channels to obtain extra points. However, to Capital's and Yulang's great dismay, Yulang did not compete successfully. This unexpected defeat led her to take a leave from school for a month. Yulang's mother bought a puppy to comfort her. More importantly, she started calling Yulang's Olympiad coach, Mr. Sun, at the same time. Mr. Sun did not appreciate the mother suddenly initiating frequent communication. In our conversation on campus, Mr. Sun complained that he was frustrated by the process. Initially, he was reluctant to help because he felt that the family was utilitarian. He said with a frown, "Yulang [or her mother] was a utilitarian. She only wanted to attend the Olympiad because it guaranteed admission to THU. Now that the policy changed and it no longer guaranteed admission, Yulang wasn't motivated anymore. That's why she lost in the competition."

Yet Mr. Sun was pressed to help and hence told the mother a little-known fact—that Peking University held a winter camp for unsuccessful Olympiad participants that might grant extra points for the gaokao. Yulang's mother immediately expressed that they would give up Tsinghua for Peking University. She then requested that Mr. Sun recommend and enroll Yulang for that camp. Yulang did not pass the end-of-camp exam and hence did not gain extra points through her participation. Seeing that her daughter was still without extra points and at a serious disadvantage, the mother contacted Mr. Sun again. This time, Mr. Sun revealed that Tsinghua also held a camp for unsuccessful Olympiad participants two weeks later. Unsurprisingly, Mrs. Liu demanded that the teacher enroll Yulang in that camp as well. To Mr. Sun and the family's relief, Yulang passed the end-of-camp test this time and accrued sixty extra points. After Yulang received the extra points, her mother left Mr. Sun alone.

Yulang's mother helped Yulang not just once but twice in gaining ground in status reproduction. Recognizing that top university attendance was a first step to future success, the mother first transferred Yulang to Capital to maximize her chances of winning the Olympiad. Although Yulang reported suffering from social isolation in school for about a year, the mother perceived things were going well and refused to make changes. As soon as Yulang was at risk of failing to get into a top university, the mother reemerged as a rescuer. Like other elite parents, Yulang's mother knew which criterion was key: test scores were of ultimate significance. She focused on gaining extra points for Yulang.

However, Yulang's mother went one step above and beyond what Shiying's mother and most other parents had done. While Shiying's mother behaved similarly with most elite families, Yulang's mother played a wild card with the help of the coach. More accurately, the mother made use of a special rule that was unknown to other players. Across my interviews, no other respondent had heard about the winter camps. The teachers, including Mr. Hu, my key informant and the Olympiad coach at Pinnacle, never revealed such information. Other students, such as Xiangzu, who also failed to pass the Olympiad, would have greatly benefited from this information. Other parents, including Kaifeng's and Fei's mothers, would have been less anxious if they had known about this backup route. Given the secrecy involved, earning extra points through winter camps was akin to a special rule of the game.

The example of Yulang's mother showed not simply that elite parents could lend a helping hand at key moments but that they were able to do so in ways that others often could not have imagined. Yulang's mother correctly identified Capital's star Olympiad coach as someone who might hold insider information that others did not. She was not afraid to pester the coach and insist that he help out despite his reluctance. With these actions, Yulang's mother helped the daughter overcome unexpected setbacks in their pursuit of top university admissions. The mother's support proved critical. Yulang scored just below the cutoff score for Tsinghua University but was admitted after adding the extra points to her original score. Obtaining top university credentials, Yulang was able to continue as a contestant in elite status reproduction.

Parents of Low Performers Fight an Uphill Battle

Parents of underachievers and losers also made backup plans. However, these parents encountered a different problem than their counterparts with high-performing children. While parents of low performers were just as willing to help their children gain footage, their children lacked the crucial chip: test scores. Parents focused attention on improving children's test scores, but these efforts were not always successful. Sometimes a parent marshaled all the available resources but remained powerless to change the child's outcome. Other times a parent who had personal experiences succeeding in status competitions simply remained a passive bystander. In the former case, the rules of the game once again proved to be a decisive factor that powerfully shaped individual outcomes regardless of parental efforts and family resources. In the latter situation, the parents did not perceive how parental assistance would make any difference given the child's test scores. Instead of trying to change course like high performers' parents, low performers' parents took responsibility for their children's unsatisfactory results and swallowed their disappointment.

Supervisor Roles: Robert's Father Handles the Situation

Parents understood that test scores determined college outcomes, which in turn were related to children's future status. With this knowledge, parents of low performers typically focused on raising their children's test scores on the gaokao or the SAT as high as possible. Robert's father adjusted his level of guidance to improve Robert's test scores. I interviewed Robert at the beginning of eleventh grade, when his SAT scores hovered around the 1800s. When

I asked whether and how his parents helped him prepare for college applications, Robert replied in a straightforward manner, "They were probably more of a supervisory role." He followed with a few examples, saying, "They stopped me from going out, and they talked to other parents in the [international] department about stuff, such as what might take place, or what classes [in tutoring institutions] to take. Like that."

However, Robert had a completely different perception of his parents' role by the end of twelfth grade, after he raised his SAT by two hundred points. When I asked him the same question, he replied smoothly, "We, over here, rely on ourselves as far as academics is concerned. My parents saw that I didn't do well on the SAT the first few times, but they didn't do anything. They let me do the work, and maybe sometimes checked if I memorized the vocabulary. They didn't do anything." Surprised, I probed further. Robert patiently explained, "My dad took charge of my studies; my mom had no need to supervise me. She sometimes told me to work more efficiently on essays. I spoke to my dad about college choices. Yeah. Such as the directions of my applied majors. They couldn't do much. Right." He then ended our conversation on the topic by concluding, "They didn't help much at all."

The two interviews showed that his parents had different levels of parental involvement. The parents were highly involved with his schoolwork in eleventh grade (parents had "supervisory roles") but became unhelpful adults in twelfth grade ("can't do much," "didn't help much"). Robert did not provide any explanation for the differences, but a number of factors might have contributed to the change. For example, it could be that Robert's parents switched approaches after perceiving there was nothing they could do. In our interview, Robert even used his low SAT scores in eleventh grade as evidence of his parents' lack of guidance, claiming that they "didn't do anything." While Robert's explanation reflected his point of view, a key difference that Robert had neglected was that, between the two interviews, he had significantly improved his SAT scores. Robert's teacher, Mrs. Hua, revealed that the parents helped Robert turn the tide on his test scores.

In our interview in a vacant classroom at Capital, Mrs. Hua reported that Robert's parents had once called her around the end of eleventh grade. Robert had scored in the 1800s the second time he took the SAT, making him among the lowest academic performers in Capital. It was also clear for the parents that children with such low scores could not attend a top U.S. university but were more likely to attend public universities that were unknown to many in China. Robert's father contacted her after identifying his low SAT score as a serious setback. In Mrs. Hua's words, the father expressed that they were "extremely concerned" and were determined to "take care of the situation." He then asked her to make sure that Robert stayed emotionally uplifted at school. Mrs. Hua interpreted this as the parents announcing that they would step in and handle the situation.

Robert's example of parents granting him a lot of freedom attested to his father's tactful approach of adjusting levels of parental involvement to increase test scores. The father, having done extremely well on the gaokao, saw test scores as key to entering college. After all, he was able to become a Beijinger due to his exam success. The father thus implemented heightened degrees of parental control when Robert had very low levels of performance (stopped him from going out, networked with other parents, checked if Robert memorized the vocabulary). By the same logic, he granted Robert more freedom and performed hands-off parenting after Robert's test scores improved. Robert later scored 2050 on the SAT and enrolled at George Washington University, which Mr. Guo considered satisfactory. Near the end of our interview, the father concluded, "Overall, Robert is doing well. Although there was a time when he suffered, overall he had a smooth process."

Alternative Strategies: Luohao's Father Works around the System

Not all parents tried to improve their children's test scores. In fact, some felt that their children's test scores were unimprovable and saw the low test scores as a given. Instead of trying to raise their children's scores, these parents found other ways to assist. In the Beijing context, this took the form of preparing for another source of contingency, which was the "guessing system" that characterized college choice submissions.[11] One of the parents who did so was Luohao's father. Luohao was a student with poor test scores whom I did not know personally. I met his father, Mr. Deng, through other parents. Mr. Deng was a gray-haired, middle-aged mathematician with gold-rimmed professorial glasses. I heard him talk to other parents about making up a college list for his son. The father complained loudly, "I did three months of statistics for my son and stayed up until one or two [AM] every day for three months. I took out all of [my son's] test scores in high school, put them in front of me on my desk, and calculated his possible score in the college entrance exam. His test scores fluctuated a lot, so I needed to know the standard deviations to determine his possible exam score and where he might end up." Other parents looked at him and nodded, approving his hard work.

I later approached him to further inquire about the example he had shared. Mr. Deng showed intense seriousness with the furrowing of his eyebrows and spoke grimly about the importance of the gaokao and the complications of strategizing over the most beneficial college choice list. He began by acknowledging that top universities were out of the question because "my son's test scores weren't there." He then placed his hands separately on the table as if pressing on two invisible piles of paper. He pressed his right hand, "If he scored this much, he could get into this university." He then pressed his left hand, "If he scored that much, he might be able to get into that university, but it's not a safe choice, so he'd better put down another school. But if he missed the other school narrowly and didn't get in, he'd be bumped down to his second choice. Not all schools allowed students to put them as a second choice, so I needed to know which schools accepted [being placed as second choice] and which ones didn't. Then, if his second choice had a cutoff score too close to his first choice, he'd be bumped to his third choice, and typically third choices are bad universities. But you don't want to list a school with cutoff scores too low for him as a second choice, because he'd be missing all the other schools he could've gotten into."

Mr. Deng utilized his professional skills to prepare for contingencies in Luohao's exam preparations. Yet while other parents focused on raising their children's test scores, Mr. Deng instead focused on the uncertainties embedded in making college choices. The decision did not mean that the father was oblivious to the importance of test scores. Quite the opposite; Mr. Deng was all too well aware of it. Reporting that he attended a top university by doing extremely well on the gaokao, the father knew how test scores determined college placements. His immediate reaction toward questions about his son's college outcomes also implied that he was first and foremost focused on children's test scores ("his test scores weren't there"). Finally, Mr. Deng was not only a faculty member in the math department at a university in Beijing but also a committee member who helped design the high school math curriculum in the city. Given these experiences and positions, the father likely recognized his son's predicted scores as a lost cause for top university placement precisely due to having intricate knowledge of the system. In other words, it was familiarity with status competition that led the father to direct his efforts to problems that he perceived to be salvageable. The father did not work on his son's low test scores but chose to work around them. He drew heavily on his occupational skills and planned ahead for contingencies to secure the best possible outcome for Luohao.

I later learned that Luohao received a low score on the gaokao and failed to get into his top-choice university. In a sense, Mr. Deng's strategy worked. His thoughtful college choice helped Luohao land his second choice, which was a provincial university outside of Beijing. However, the fact remains that despite the father's effort, Luohao did not enter a top university. Although his father heavily strategized and was involved to the point of being sleep deprived, the son was not admitted to a top university due to his unsatisfactory performance on the gaokao. The fact that parental assistance could not compensate for a low exam score showed that the benefits accrued by parents' involvement and support could be limited by features of the status system. In particular, even the most thoughtful preparation against contingencies was insufficient to compensate for a child's low exam score.

Following the Rules: Jianmin's Mother Stays on the Sidelines

While most elite parents enacted some sort of contingency plan when their children's test scores were disappointing, or at least carefully planned out their children's college choices, a handful did not. One of these rare cases was Jianmin, whose parents had not perceived any problems until it was too late. Jianmin came from a cross-class marriage: his father was a high school graduate worker, his mother a literature magazine editor who dropped out of college.[12] When I met Jianmin in twelfth grade, he was an above-average student in the top classroom at Pinnacle who was confident about being admitted to Peking University. Jianmin reported taking the lead in his education, which his mother, Mrs. Wu, affirmed in our interview: "Really, I'm quite at ease about Jianmin. I've never told him to pay more attention in class, get work done, or stop playing, or like that. He took care of things himself."

Like Shiying, Jianmin unexpectedly failed the additional test for Peking University. However, unlike Shiying's mother, Jianmin's mother did not perceive the risk of failure. She did not talk to teachers, did not coach Jianmin, and did not visit the school to ask about Jianmin's college choices. Jianmin performed poorly on the exam. His score was not high enough to enroll at Peking University. His second-choice university raised its cutoff score by twenty points, which disqualified Jianmin. His third choice did not allow students to list it as third, and his last two choices raised their cutoff scores too high. Underperforming and with poor college choices, Jianmin was without a university placement despite scoring in the 93rd percentile in Beijing. Jianmin's family scrambled for him to apply to universities in Hong Kong. However, his mother continued to adopt a hands-off approach and let Jianmin apply on his own. Jianmin failed to gain admission; instead, he landed at a provincial-level university outside of Mainland China and one that he had not previously considered. When talking about Jianmin's college path, Mrs. Wu regretted her lack of involvement. She said sorrowfully in our interview, "If, I think, if [I] had done my homework, if I had been a bit more diligent, I could've figured out if some schools took students who set them as later choices. It's entirely possible that his third choice didn't accept being placed as third. [But] I wasn't too mindful of that information. Now all of this has passed, but I didn't do my job."

Mrs. Wu was the only college-educated parent in this study who did not prepare for unforeseen setbacks. She had gone through the application process and had attended college. She considered herself able to help Jianmin by reading the application guidelines, strategizing over college choices, or talking to teachers. Coming from a family of college-educated elite parents herself, the mother clearly knew how to compete for status reproduction through educational success. Yet she allowed her familiarity and knowledge of the system to remain unutilized. It is unclear why Jianmin's mother neglected all signals that other parents did not and failed to offer assistance when needed. One possibility is that, being downwardly mobile herself, she was ambivalent toward higher education and elite status competition in China.[13] Indeed, the mother reported intergenerational conflict between herself and her parents, both of whom were college educated. However, the mother cared deeply about her son's college outcomes and was almost in tears as she reflected on her lack of involvement.

Another, more likely explanation was that the mother felt the structure of the status systems was clear and let the system guide her every move. Analyzing Jianmin's mother's response showed that she understood the setup of status competition. She was able to feel "at ease" precisely because she understood that test scores were what mattered most for college admission. Moreover, she felt no need to worry because Jianmin completed school assignments and showed effort (he was "[paying] attention in class, [getting] work done, [and was] not playing"). Since Jianmin's predicted scores were high enough to attend Peking University, she did not see the need for extra points. Also because Jianmin was on track to attend his first choice, the later choices seemed superfluous and even unnecessary. The mother's confidence might have stemmed from the family's educational history. While other students had uneducated grandparents, Jianmin was the third generation in the family to take the gaokao. Knowledge of the rules of status reproduction (succeeding on the gaokao) and the family's track history in exam success, along with the son's high school record, likely led to the mother's overconfidence. In turn, this multigeneration familiarity blinded her to the need to prepare for contingencies.

The mother's lack of involvement seemed to carry consequences for Jianmin not only at the academic level but also emotionally. I visited Jianmin two months after college started. He reported having lost touch with almost all of his high school classmates, half of whom attended Peking or Tsinghua. Before I bid farewell to him at the bus station, Jianmin said sadly, "I've left home, so my neighbors and friends and family can't point fingers [at me]. But my parents probably had to explain to everyone else why their son went to Pinnacle but failed to get into a top university."

Beyond High School: Parental Involvement over Time

Elite status reproduction does not end when elite children pass through the gates of top universities. Securing job offers or graduate school admission is the next step that must be navigated with equal care. After their children were admitted to college, the elite parents in this study were able to intervene in the transition in helpful ways. Simultaneously, having successfully obtained elite status, the parents were able to spot the potential hurdles and setbacks in their children's planned trajectories. They identified risks before their children did and acted to facilitate their children's continued participation. Of course not all parents reacted to bumps in the road. In college as in high school, some parents perceived no need to become involved. While these parents simply watched as things progressed, others found their efforts rejected by children and were forced into noninvolvement.

Parents whose children transitioned smoothly to the labor force stayed on the sidelines. They did not seriously prepare for contingency plans; even if they did, they had no need to enact them. Fei majored in electrical engineering at Tsinghua University. After four years of college, he smoothly transitioned to a doctoral program at UC Berkeley, where his field is ranked in the top three in the world. Likewise, Tony transitioned to his current job in New York City after graduating from Cornell. To land his ideal job, Tony crashed with his high school friend in the city during summers so he would socialize with "the right people" and have a New York City address on his job applications.[14] Throughout the process, Tony discovered the niches and did all of the work himself. His mother perceived no need to help out, in college as in high school.

Other parents reacted to risks in children's transitions. These parents were able to provide their children with insight and in doing so set them on the highway to success. After college graduation, Shiying debated between going to graduate school and joining an NGO for a year to work with ethnic minorities on animal conservation. She obtained the opportunity to join a group of conservationists in western China but also received offers from top universities in Europe and the United States. Seeing that her daughter was excited about both opportunities but uncertain of which to choose, Mrs. Liu instructed Shiying to ask for deferrals immediately. Shiying was disappointed when she found out that none of the programs allowed her to defer for a year. Her mother, by comparison, was not the slightest bit concerned. Being confident that Shiying would be admitted to the same (and better) programs if she applied later, Mrs. Liu encouraged her to obtain hands-on experience and apply again a few years later. Heartened by her mother's confidence, Shiying turned down the offers and moved to a mountainous area in Qinghai province. Mrs. Liu's prediction proved true. Shiying reapplied the following year and was accepted to the same master's program at Cambridge, except this time she was awarded a prestigious full scholarship from the U.K. government given to only eight international students each year. With her mother's supervision and timely instructions, Shiying is steadfastly pursuing her dream job working in wildlife conservation and plans to work in Switzerland after graduation.

Sometimes parents' contributions at critical moments buffered children from failure and helped them gain footing. In summer 2019 I met with Wenbin at a Starbucks near his parents' apartment at the south of the city. Wenbin was a tall and frail-looking study god at Pinnacle who graduated from Tsinghua University. He updated me about his past five years over coffee, beginning with "I've always wanted to get a PhD." To pursue this goal, he willingly spent his college summers preparing for the GRE and TOEFL. He received a near-perfect score on the GRE and was recruited to be a part-time GRE instructor at the largest cram school in the city. He also worked at a lab during his study-abroad trip at UC Santa Barbara to gain research experience. Wenbin beamed with joy as he talked about research. He recalled the responsibilities of each member in the lab and described how the results came together with great enthusiasm. However, despite these efforts and genuine interest in the field, his applications were unsuccessful. Determined to pursue his goal, Wenbin worked as a research assistant for his professor and reapplied the following year. This time, to his surprise, his father suddenly adopted a hands-on parenting approach with his applications.

"I wanted to apply only for doctoral programs, but my dad told me to apply for a few master's programs. He even said that if I still didn't get in, I should primarily apply for master's programs next year. Initially, I wasn't very happy with this suggestion." Then, Wenbin suddenly lifted his head and looked me in the eye. He said loudly with widened eyes, "But I got into two out of the three MS programs I applied for. The thing is, I *only* got into MS programs!"

"Hah, how do you feel about your dad's suggestion now?" I smirked.

Wenbin smiled bashfully, "It was a wonderful suggestion. He was totally right. He saved the day."

Wenbin gave me a tour of the neighborhood after coffee. We ran into his mother, who enthusiastically invited me into their two-bedroom apartment. She showed me pictures of Wenbin's childhood as the three of us sat on the redwood couch in the living room. The mother expressed that she and Wenbin's father, as well as extended relatives, were thrilled that Wenbin would be studying in the States the coming fall. However, the process was not a smooth one, and the parents had been concerned about Wenbin's applications. "We were worried. After all, he didn't get into any program last time. And to be honest, his materials haven't changed that much. We were worried sick that he wouldn't be accepted for a second time." Wenbin looked down between his feet in awkward silence. His mother explained, "That's why his father told him to apply for master's programs as backups. Wenbin thought he didn't need them. But his father talked to him until he agreed." The mother glanced at him, "Thank goodness he did!"

Wenbin's father was a manager at a state newspaper who had no experience abroad. Yet he was able to make contingency plans for his son. He saw the lack of backup schools as a problem that Wenbin had overlooked. He then made sure that Wenbin applied for those programs even though Wenbin had not considered them. Furthermore, the father's larger plan included a third round of applications, which would target the programs that Wenbin considered beneath him. With these actions, the father not only found Wenbin a placement but also brought home the importance of planning for contingencies ("he saved the day"). Wenbin attended a program ranked in the top fifteen in the world. His parents took care of the expenses needed for the two-year master's program, estimated at about $120,000. The family was confident that Wenbin would get into a top PhD program after completing the master's program.[15]

Finally, parents who intended to help out sometimes found their assistance rejected. Jianmin's mother was one of the unwillingly uninvolved parents whose contingency plans were brushed aside. I last met Jianmin in 2016, when he visited Taiwan with college friends. His already soft voice diminished and his shoulders drooped as if he were bearing the weight of the world. At some point during lunch he flipped out his phone, downloaded his transcript, and proudly flaunted his 3.85 GPA, which he claimed was "highest in the cohort." We kept in touch through WeChat in subsequent years. In his junior year, Jianmin reported having no plans after graduation. He signed up for an exchange trip to Japan to buy time and afterward decided to stay there for work. Building a career in Tokyo was hard; doing so with no network and as a foreigner was even harder. Applying with a degree from a provincial university in China, he received no job offer nor graduate school admission by the end of his senior year. His high academic performance gave him no advantage over other applicants. Yet, determined to land a job in Tokyo, where he felt his major had the highest value, Jianmin delayed graduation to extend his visa and worked part-time to support himself.

Seeing that the risk of failure loomed large, Mrs. Wu was ready to take action this time and had a backup plan ready at hand. In our text exchanges, Jianmin said, "My mom said she got me a position in Beijing." However, he immediately turned down his mother's suggestion because he had no interest in the position his mother offered and possibly saw it as beneath him.[16] Transitioning to the labor force proved more difficult than Jianmin imagined. He made two more rounds of unsuccessful job hunting, until one day in 2019 he texted me with excitement: "I got a full-time job at a company in Japan!" Although the search took longer than planned, he felt as if he was back on track to pursue global elite status along with his peers.

Instead of making the same mistake as a few years back, Mrs. Wu intended to become hands-on about Jianmin's career. Mrs. Wu prepared a position for Jianmin because he was struggling to compete for elite status—he had received no graduate school or job offer even though he was in one of his strongest years as an applicant, having been fresh out of college. Yet the future

Jianmin intended to build was not the same as what his mother had to offer. Mrs. Wu's plan provided a buffer of economic security, but Jianmin perceived working in Tokyo as being much more glorious than working in Beijing, so much so that he was willing to endure years of part-time work with a meager income to have a shot at his dream.[17] Because Jianmin refused to go along with his mother's plans, she unwillingly remained hands-off about his future.

Summary

As the elite youth in China prepare for and engage in global competition, their parents assert their position as their strongest allies. This is particularly true among the Beijing families I observed. The parents almost never visited school, rarely talked to teachers, and seemed to be hands-off with children's high school education. Yet their remaining on the sidelines did not mean that they were resting. Quite the opposite; these parents kept watch of events that might put their children at a disadvantage and were immediately responsive to them, prepared should contingencies strike. From the beginning, parents were able to discern threatening from nonthreatening events. Annoying a teacher, for example, was considered as nonserious. Failing a test, however, required immediate correction. The parents also knew how to correct the problem they identified. They could subtly pressure teachers into paying more attention to maintaining a study god's academic performance; they understood that it took more than calling the teacher to significantly boost an underachiever's test scores. Much like coaches giving orders to players on the field, these parents knew when to let the child handle things alone but also when to insist that the child agree to their contingency plans. With parents' timely assistance, failure was not a setback for the new generation of elites from China but was conceptualized as an opportunity for improvement. In other words, the children were given chances to recover from failure.

Clearly, not all parents possess the ability to do as the elite parents did in this study. Elite parents' ability to intervene reflected their deep knowledge of status competition. They focused on boosting test scores because they knew they mattered the most at the high school stage. They could predict the qualities that faculty and admission committees in the United States and United Kingdom were looking for in graduate applicants and made suggestions to children accordingly. These parents knew that elite status at the global level was worth fighting for, and the grand prize was significant enough to justify decades of devotion. And as parents, they were ready to fight alongside their children, not just by providing the best training and resources but also by saving the day when needed.

Conclusion

HOW DO ELITE Chinese students prepare for global status competition? As I have shown in the preceding chapters, they learned about the setup of status systems and were trained to strategically navigate them since high school. The adolescent status system deeply and powerfully shaped students' daily lives. Those with high status received privileges that others did not, and those with low status were treated more harshly for similar misdeeds. This message was driven home to the elite students in high school. In the schools and homes I visited, study gods were consistently at the center of attention. They were entitled to peer admiration, teacher pampering, and parental indulgence. They felt free to do as they pleased in school and at home because they fully expected others to bow to their wishes. Studyholics, who ranked second but nonetheless were in the high-status group, were also considerably entitled. They enjoyed many of the privileges shared by study gods but were more careful of preserving their hard-earned position in the status hierarchy in school. By comparison, underachievers and losers saw themselves as belonging to the other end of the status spectrum on campus. They admired the high performers, refrained from breaking rules, and were subject to the whims of teachers and parents. These systematic differences illuminated to the elite students that status led to differences in how behaviors were evaluated. As a result, through daily interactions, elite students developed a firsthand understanding of status consequences and learned that they should always strive for high status. These perspectives, expectations, and behaviors instilled in them during high school were then reaffirmed on college campuses and later enacted in the workplace.

For the students in this study, interpersonal interactions were natural and instinctive. A few were upset with teachers' differential treatment based on test scores, but most were oblivious to these patterns. They did not perceive the need to justify interaction patterns based on test scores and school status. Lili and her friends did not feel that they had been hard on Kangwei, the boy who was widely regarded as having bottom status in school. Tracy did not realize that her opinion of Kevin was fundamentally based on test scores. When presented with the hypothetical scenario that a low performer received a perfect score on an exam, most students intuitively responded by rejecting the scenario. Neither did teachers and parents acknowledge the student status system. The adults never used status terminologies and did not see their behaviors as being in any way related to students' levels of academic performance. Dehong's test scores improved, resulting in his promotion to studyholic status over the course of a year. While his mother became more lenient toward his choice of leisure activities after his test scores improved, the mother had not perceived that she interacted with him differently. Simply put, the adults scarcely noticed that their behaviors mapped onto the status system in school, nor did they see how they oriented the teenagers toward specific behaviors.

Despite the lack of deliberate acknowledgment, elite students and their families collaborated in reproducing high status. The students, who bore the stakes of the outcomes, learned valuable lessons in the seemingly natural, harmless school setting. They instilled in each other the importance of understanding the status system, in which test scores were a trump card that held greater value than all other resources or achievements any competitor could possibly possess. They practiced and validated each other's status-based strategies, providing immediate feedback on whether a player could make certain moves. Study gods and studyholics could break the rules when flashing their high test scores, but underachievers and losers had to keep a low profile or else risk rejection and ostracism. Through daily interactions, the students in this study constructed, supported, and justified their status system. Conceptualizing status reproduction as a card game, the students learned its rules, played accordingly, and saw the outcomes as legitimate.

Teenagers, however, are not the only ones involved in elite status reproduction. Adults, especially parents, play a crucial role in guiding students and ensuring that each benchmark is met. Some scholars see the adolescent world as unique and separated from the adult "real" world.[1] From their perspective, teenagers' status competition is distinctively student based and the strategies and skills that they learn have no value beyond school campuses. Yet the parents and teachers in this study were active participants and respectively granted favors to and withheld them from students of high- and low-status groups. Teachers repeatedly linked students' test scores to their future position in society on a daily basis. Parents emphasized that college outcomes were life-defining. By doing so, they sent clear signals to the students that adolescent society was tightly connected with the adult world. Furthermore, the adults oversaw the competition process, interrupted it when perceived as necessary, and maximized children's chances of reproducing elite status. They upheld the same rules as the adolescents and affirmed the importance of winning. With these behaviors, the adults took a seat at the table and established themselves as attentive players in elite status reproduction.

Global Elite Formation

The arrival of elite Chinese students brought changes to receiving countries in the West. These youths shaped the places they stay at with their sheer numbers, their purchasing power, and their study habits. The public and media have constructed various images in an effort to better know the students from China. Some say that these students embody and demonstrate the power of a rising China, while a few accuse them of being spies for the Chinese government. Scholars are also interested in whom these Chinese students are. Social scientists venture into China to trace out the formation of these students. Scholars argue that these youths are a generation created by the Chinese government to strengthen the country's influence in the world. They also portray them as little emperors, going as far as calling them "spoiled brats," and highlight that their families have no budget constraints in investing in their futures.[2] In a different but related manner, others emphasize the pressure these youths endure for shouldering the extended family's educational aspiration. Pitted against each other in ever-increasing levels of competition, it is understandable that these students are incredibly anxious and psychologically stressed.[3] Overall, despite the different focuses (such as wealth flaunting behavior versus adolescent well-being), scholars and the public alike believe that students from China, especially the elite ones, are a unique group who differ from their predecessors as well as from students in Western societies.

While these findings shed light on the multifaceted images of youths in contemporary China, they are often intertwined into an obscure pattern. In this book, I have shown that the wealth-flaunting stereotype does not describe all elite students, nor are the exceptionally high educational desires of their families equally burdensome to them. Rather than seeing them as a homogeneous group, I have emphasized the significance of status positions in shaping individual experiences in school and their transitions to adult society. Following American-based research on elite adolescents, I perceive schooling as a key process in preparing the future socioeconomic elite. Yet, simultaneously, I reject the analytical approach that focuses exclusively on events that take place on school campuses. Instead, I see these teenagers as actors who are embedded in the school and family, where interpersonal interactions uphold the student status system by sending coherent signals of adequate behaviors. I have shown that these daily interactions are helpful in understanding how elite Chinese students learn to appreciate and navigate the status system, not simply in China during adolescence but also outside of China in their early adulthood.

A growing body of literature examines the experiences of the elite and the processes through which these youths become entitled to their future leadership positions. This perception conveys two ideas that most would agree with. First, elite status reproduction is perceived to be a smooth process. Parental wealth flows across generations, and children inherit their parents' status through justifying mechanisms, such as education or occupation attainment. Second, this perspective implies that elite status reproduction is fundamentally a domestic process. In other words, these students are born and go to school in a country and will later obtain important positions in that country. If they go abroad, it is for family vacation or short-term adventure, such as an exchange program or a few years for graduate school, after which they inevitably return to their country of residence.[4] According to this view, despite their freedom to travel, the elite in a country rarely or never move across borders.

In this book, I have challenged both ideas. The aggregate levels of status reproduction differ by society, and there is an undeniable correlation of status across generations. However, most children do not grow up to find themselves in the exact same status as their parents.[5] The elite are no exception, and elite status reproduction is far from certain. Each of the students in this study could recall encountering formidable difficulties in school and at work. Some failed important tests, while others saw their test scores gradually diminish despite their best efforts. They made big and small mistakes, from submitting a problematic college list to entering their names wrong on applications. In these moments of potential disaster, elite status entailed important advantages. Some of their parents drew on occupation-based knowledge and resources to prevent their children from falling down the status ladder. Family resources became buffers that shielded children from failing and in many instances gave the children a second chance at success. Of course not all elite parents came to the rescue; sometimes, even the most skilled assistance could not help the child gain a foothold.

I have also challenged the idea that the elite are produced within the confinements of a nation. The elite youths from China are in fact far from restricted by geographic boundaries. They are internationally minded, globally oriented, and overwhelmingly choose to reside outside of China. They go to top universities around the world and hold credentials that have global recognition; their starting incomes put them at the top of Western, developed countries. The fact that these young adults emerge as strong competitors in the international arena points to elite status reproduction at the global level. Hitherto, most research on social inequality and status reproduction has considered them only within a country.[6] Even in the 2018 *World Inequality Report*, the extensive discussion of the influence of a society's socioeconomic elite is limited to individual countries. However, elite status reproduction takes place internationally. It is entirely possible for the new elite to be born in one country, educated in another, work in a third, and retire in a fourth. While the elite are identified as a strong force of social inequality in their home countries,[7] together they contribute to inequality on a global scale. Importantly, individuals with high status often perceive inequality as natural and hence unchangeable. Such a perception in turn shapes whether and the extent to which high-status groups support policies that tackle issues of social inequality.[8] The finding that these youths see themselves as legitimate holders of high status in China and abroad sheds light on global social inequality as well as the internationalization of an elite class.

Thus, I have stressed that elite youths are prepared to compete for elite status around the world through daily interactions. These youths construct their understanding of social order by the response they receive from key others: peers, teachers, and parents. While not all students approve of the systematic differential treatment peers receive, teenagers conform to group behaviors and follow the behaviors of high-status peers.[9] I have described the sets of interactions as a learned understanding that students use to navigate status systems. When they leave school and join the adult world, these understandings are validated by colleagues, authorities, and family. There is evidence that the elite students benefit, unknowingly and invisibly to them and their families, from such training in the schooling process. In the following sections, I acknowledge that there are limitations that obstruct these Chinese adolescents' quests for global elite status. I then highlight the ways in which education systems are critical to elite status reproduction and point out the differences between college selection in China and the United States. Finally, to the extent that attitudes and behaviors are critically shaped during adolescence and young adulthood, I discuss broadly what might be expected of the new generation of elite from China.[10]

Developments in the COVID-19 Pandemic

The lives of the elite youths in this study largely unfolded as they and their families had expected. Most of them settled in countries outside China, with only a few planning to return. They were either working at high-paying jobs or attending top-ranked graduate programs; half resided in the United States, and the other half were located across Europe and East Asia. America's tightening of work visa quotas, which was never an issue in their minds, proved unthreatening. Some felt lucky that they could pursue their dream jobs. Tony, for example, was relieved that he entered the job market the summer before the revised visa policy was implemented, after which the company he worked at no longer hired any international students. Others who did not feel the impact reasoned that the policy must have targeted a specific group that they did not belong to, such as "the Indians," or "certain fields" that few of them were interested in. Seven years after high school, these youths were on their way to asserting their status as part of the global elite. All felt free to pursue their dreams without border restrictions.

In 2020, the COVID-19 pandemic posed economic challenges that hit the labor market in the United States. Many Americans took unpaid leave, millions lost their jobs, and many more became vulnerable.[11] The youths who stayed and worked in the United States felt the impact as well. They saw their travel plans disrupted, endured lockdowns and curfews in various cities, and were annoyed by discriminatory comments toward Chinese nationals. However, they remained financially afloat. None of them were laid off, graduate students kept their funding, and most stayed on track at work and school. The companies that Claire, Kaifeng, and Tony worked for laid off a portion of the junior employees, but the three kept their positions. The PhD students were shielded from the economic impact of the pandemic. Joe, Brandon, Fei, Haochen, and Yulang continued to carry out their summer internships and research without interruption. A few of the youths in this study seemed better off during the pandemic. Huating left London for a better offer in the United States; Alex and Selena both applied for and were admitted to graduate school. They saved on tuition, as their graduate programs at Princeton charged less tuition due to courses moving online. Altogether, these students seemed unconcerned about their future job prospects. Alex, in particular, wrote in our text exchanges, "Tech companies have been encouraging people to work from home since way back. We're doing much better [than other fields]." If their futures progress as envisioned, upon graduation Alex, Selena, and others will hold similar positions with pay comparable to what they would have had if the pandemic never hit.

The graduate cohorts of 2020 and 2021 had a slightly different experience in their job outcomes. Mingjia and Lili went home after New York University canceled in-person courses in the spring of 2020. The two girls had hoped to stay in the United States but decided to work in Beijing for lack of alternative options upon graduation that summer. In our text exchanges, Mingjia wrote that she "couldn't find a suitable job" and felt compelled to accept an offer from the same company she had turned down two years previous as a college graduate. Lili's summer internship in Beijing led to a full-time position. But given that she had previously reported that the internship was a backup choice, the job was less than ideal. Determined to pursue their goals, which involved geographic mobility, both girls came up with viable backup plans. At the time of writing, Mingjia was keeping her options open and was on the lookout for other job opportunities. Lili planned to return to the United States via education; as she wrote, she would "probably go back to the U.S. by pursuing a PhD in economics after two or three years" of work. In 2021, Wenbin successfully applied for a PhD program at Brown and moved to Providence. Shiying and Stacey respectively graduated from Cambridge and Harvard the same year. Both girls had hoped to stay in the United States or Europe to embark on their dream careers but later accepted offers in Shanghai and Hong Kong.

Not all students were as reluctant to return to China. Robert, also a member of the 2020 cohort, had intended to stay in the United States. Yet his perceptions about the United States changed drastically after the pandemic outbreak. In our text correspondence, Robert described America as "a dump (*guidifang*)" and declared that Chinese people should "get the hell out of there." He gladly flew back to Beijing and passed multiple licensing tests within a few months of his return. Robert reported no plans to move back to the United States. Instead, being the laid-back young man he had been since high school, he cheerfully took his time to search for a position at a foreign enterprise that he would enjoy. Only a minority of the elite youths returned to China for other reasons. Shuhua, a social science major at Stanford, delightedly went home prior to the pandemic outbreak.[12] When I asked about her decision, she spoke at length about the bamboo ceiling and discrimination in the United States and claimed that China had better long-term career prospects. Simultaneously, Shuhua kept one foot in the global arena through employment at a European investment bank. These examples suggest that while most of the students in this study chose to stay in the West to fulfill their ambitions, returning home was not an impediment to that goal. Instead, being based in China, whether temporarily or permanently, became a part of their pursuit of global elitism.

Limits of Global Elite Formation

Despite the pandemic disrupting some of their plans, the students I came to know are doing well in school and at work overall. Yet just as not all their paths were smooth, they will likely experience barriers and hostilities in their career progression. One challenge was the exclusion of Chinese students from the social scenes on Western campuses. American higher education has a norm of socializing through partying.[13] However, elite Chinese students are not accustomed to partying and are used to making friends through study groups. Claire reported being uncomfortable with the party scene in Yale's college structure. She soon found refuge in a college that was "mostly Asian" and "selected by students who didn't want to party." Even those who ventured out later decided to cultivate international or intraethnic friendships. Ashley was one of the students who wholeheartedly embraced Western campus norms. Being excited about befriending local students, she followed her British peers in fashion, style, and taste to the best of her ability and frequently joined parties at school. Feeling that she adapted well, Ashley volunteered as a student counselor for the next cohort. However, starting her second year, Ashley's social media posts became a documentary of cultural clashes (disagreements and quarrels) with British friends. Before the end of college, Ashley found herself "being tired" of the social activities and endless partying. She retreated into her ethnic enclave, where she quietly enjoyed the company of her Chinese peers.

Racial segregation was another challenge these students faced. The students studying outside of China were not in close contact with local students. All of them lived with other Chinese students. They joined Asian student clubs and traveled with other Chinese students. Part of such ethic segregation reflects individual choices; Chinese students might share similar hobbies and choose to live with others who speak the same native language. Yet on-campus racial segregation is also an institutional practice.[14] Roommate assignments, especially among freshmen, are often determined by the university. All of the students abroad reported being assigned Chinese roommates, which suggests this pattern is the result of not individual preferences but institutional segregation. Membership in student organizations is also related to race and ethnicity. For example, Claire wanted to join a dance club and learn to dance, but since the only club that accepted beginners was labeled an Asian organization, she had no choice but to join the Asian dance club. These snippets of de facto social and residential segregation suggest that this group of elite Chinese experienced some degree of racism at school. In response, they likely confronted these challenges by limiting their contact with local students.

Although there is no correct way in which to associate with others, one must learn and adjust to interaction norms of the dominant group to successfully compete for high status. Students who are not accustomed to socialization norms on campus are often marginalized and do not build a strong friendship network with those who are adept at navigating social spaces. Culturally and racially shaped preferences over extracurricular hobbies, activities, and social behaviors carry long-term consequences. For the international students, elite and nonelite, these differences contribute to their widely reported experiences of race- and nationality-based segregation on campus.[15]

The fact that these young adults have good starting points at the entry level for elite jobs does not mean that they are free from setbacks later in their careers. They continue to report social and racial segregation at work. Reflecting on his birthday party, Tony took note of clear racial segregation. Specifically, he noticed that while some Chinese nationals tried to join the non-Chinese group(s), eventually it got "so awkward" that the Chinese and non-Chinese groups remained separated until the end of the party. Tony's company held group competitions on projects and factored the results into contract renewals. Considering this company practice, the birthday party was not simply a leisure gathering but a networking opportunity. Chinese youths' exclusion and segregation in social gatherings translate into hindered networks, which might have detrimental effects on future career opportunities.

Racial hostility and anti-Asian racism also shaped elite youths' career decisions, from location to future plans. Three of the elite youth (Shuhua, Xijun, and Robert) dealt with unfriendly racial environments by leaving the United States and Europe. That elite youth voluntarily returned to China for better career opportunities and advancement possibilities suggests that they are not naïve in their pursuit of elite status. Many envision hurdles staying in the West and withdraw from environments they sense to be potentially disastrous to career advancement. Yet other youths were forced to change course since the pandemic outbreak due to ethnic and racial hostilities.[16] In 2021, Shiying, the only student who stayed a study god throughout this study, reluctantly returned to China and started working in Shanghai. When asked about the reason she left Europe, she frankly attributed her decision to the U.S. government's crackdown on research led by Chinese nationals: her husband, a PhD graduate from Yale, had his lab suddenly shut down and was ordered to stop all research activities. He took the family back to China, where he set up a tech company. When asked if she still hoped to move abroad, Shiying simply responded with a sigh. Other young adults who graduated in 2021 also reported feelings of forced return migration.[17] These incidents show that anti-Chinese sentiment can form an insurmountable obstacle and have lasting effects on elite youths' pursuit of high status, so much so that even the highest achieving elite Chinese students seemed powerless to overcome it.

Finally, the bamboo ceiling is another hindrance that awaits the elite Chinese youth who stay in the United States. Studies show that Asian Americans have high starting points in their careers but face limited income and career advancements during midcareer.[18] The underrepresentation of Asians in leadership and management positions has been observed across fields. Many of the young adults in this study majored in biological sciences and computer engineering, and some plan to stay in higher education. Yet despite the high proportion of Asians in these fields, racialized microaggressions against Asians remain prevalent.[19] While the elite youth who stayed in the United States see workplace discrimination as an expected challenge, they have thus far minimized the role of race. Stalled careers at midlevel remain a significant barrier to obtaining global elite membership. The elite youth are beginning to learn about their job cultures and workplace hierarchies. However, to fulfill their status ambitions, these youth must put forward a new strategy to counteract workplace discrimination.

The elite Chinese youth whom I followed over the years are at the early stages of the life course. They have just embarked on their careers, and many are still in graduate school. These young adults have achieved considerable success so far, but just as they experienced bumps along the way in high school, their journey toward global elite status is laden with difficulties and setbacks. Anti-Asian racism, hostility toward Chinese nationals, and stalled progression at midcareer are some of the obstacles that could adversely influence their status outcomes as they progress in their careers. Yet because the bumps on the road are not unforeseen, elite students often make career decisions around these expected hurdles to the best of their abilities. In my latest conversations with them, all were optimistic about the future, and most were open to returning to the West should the racial and work environment become more favorable. Whether and how ethnicity- or nationality-induced restrictions cast a shadow over their chances of becoming the future elite remains an important topic for future research.

Chinese and American Ways of Student Selection

Education is widely seen as a vehicle that distinguishes socioeconomic classes. When examining the production of a global elite class, countries do not select and groom their future elite in identical ways. Just as every society is unique, each country adopts a specific educational selection method. These differences, however, often determine the value and reward of student characteristics and affect the outcomes of global elite formation.

Historical Differences

Two common selection methods are the exam and application systems. The gaokao in China can be seen as an exemplar of the exam system, while the United States follows an application system and emphasizes students' "well-roundedness."[20] The gaokao follows the historical precedent of many centuries of imperial examinations for government positions.[21] The levels of competition in these exams were also very high since medieval dynasties. Moreover, as the Chinese population grew, the numbers of competitors expanded. The exams became longer and more difficult, and thus credential inflation and emphasis on formal exams expanded.[22] Despite these challenges, children of elite families oftentimes outcompeted those from nonelite backgrounds, and in the Qing dynasty, elite families had disproportionately high chances to pass the civil service examination. The abolition of the civil service exam in 1905 led to a temporary shift away from exam-based selection. Yet this had little effect on the preexisting elite because family background (along with physical appearances and recommendation letters) directly determined school admissions. In the Republican era, children from wealthy backgrounds had improved chances of testing into Peking University. The communist regime reacted against this in an effort toward social equality, especially during the Cultural Revolution, when proletariat children whose families were not "struggled against" had the greatest chances of obtaining recommendation letters, the sole criterion for entry to top universities.[23] During the Red Guards movement, an ultra-communist purge of elites, students were politically mobilized and formed collective school identities in their struggle.[24] However, reaction to the chaos of the movement and the shift to market-centered economic growth soon brought renewed emphasis on competitive exams. Emphasizing exam-based competition might have also carried benefits for the regime, as it keeps students focused on individual success and deters them from forming collective school identities. In response, elite children have reaped the largest educational benefits by enrolling in top universities through the gaokao.[25]

With these developments in mind, it seems understandable that Chinese educators and scholars strongly support exam-based selection. They argue that the gaokao is a fair and efficient method of student selection by minimizing family influence on exam results, and the general public support it as well.[26] Student information is condensed into a number, and colleges cannot identify student backgrounds. Because there is no legacy admission, families cannot use their resources (such as political power, economic resources, social network, etc.) to obtain admission for their children. However, although the intention is to set up a system that is the least biased, there are loopholes in which family wealth comes into play. Recognizing the systematic privileges that elite children receive, in the twenty-first century the country has introduced non-exam-based components into college selection, such as interviews and principal recommendations. Educators and experts in China seeking to lower class-based inequality in education have called for government intervention and equalization of educational resources. They implemented a series of educational reforms, primarily alternative ways of extra points and panel interviews.[27] Yet these proposed solutions seek not to abolish exam-based selection but to amend the existing system. The system thus remains focused on exam scores, and no other criterion trumps test scores in determining college placements.[28]

American colleges have valued the wholistic criteria since the late nineteenth century.[29] Initially, only the upper classes who could afford to pay attended colleges. Entry requirements were minimal, and colleges emphasized athletics. After women were admitted, fraternities and sororities set up dances and parties that served as a marriage market by which children of upper-middle-class families found class-appropriate partners.[30] Changes set in during the early twentieth century as education expanded at all levels.[31] Colleges began to draw on a national population and no longer educated only the local elite. Formal admissions and exams were then used to sort out the growing stream of applicants, but the old criteria remained alongside the new. For example, seeing that Jewish students applied in large numbers and with an intense focus on academic preparation, top universities emphasized students' class background, manifested in manners, sociability networks, and legacies.[32] Students with athletic backgrounds and extracurricular participation in religious or artistic activities were favored over those without. Parallel development soon followed in public educational institutions. Public universities imitated private universities, adopting football as well as fraternities and College Board exams.[33] While exams mattered, colleges downplayed academic achievement and emphasized public events that captured the attention of students' families and the surrounding communities. Historical events in the mid-1990s also distinguished the United States from China, most notably the civil rights movement vis-à-vis the Red Guards movement. One emphasis of the civil rights movement was to make schools more accessible to the disadvantaged, such as by reducing the amount of cultural capital required or using athletics as a prominent pathway for minority individuals to receive college admission.[34] American educators paid special attention to the exclusion of minorities and the lower classes, and these developments were generally supported by schoolteachers and administrators, who saw themselves as providing a peaceful pathway to social integration.[35]

In light of these developments, educators and scholars in the United States support the college applications system in U.S. higher education, claiming that it acknowledges multiple types of intelligence, is effort based, promotes motivation, and takes advantage of the multicultural character of American society.[36] Furthermore, they are strong critics of the exam system, asserting that standardized tests are discriminatory, provide limited information on students, do not reflect student diversity, and do not generate higher thinking.[37] Certainly, there has been a temporary boost in the significance of academic achievement.[38] Some scholars cite the increase in shadow education institutions that provide students with after-school academic training and caution that American teenagers participate in increasingly high levels of exam competition.[39] University admissions officers also try to woo the highest-performing students to maximize incoming cohorts' average SAT scores.[40] Yet the main thrust of reform in college admissions has gone in the opposite direction. An increasing number of universities have made the SAT optional, and some high schools have abolished the valedictorian honor.[41] These are some examples of the movement toward downplaying the role of exam scores in university admissions.

In short, China has a somewhat path-dependent tradition of using national exams to determine elite positions. By comparison, U.S. schools focused on athletics, social gatherings, Greek life, and the marriage market in the late nineteenth century. No educational selection method is perfect, as each has its strengths and weaknesses. The outcome of these selections, however, is largely the same: they distinguish the future elite and prepare them for elite status. Regardless of political regimes, and despite temporal changes in admissions criteria, family background has remained key to children's educational outcomes. Throughout these developments and reforms, the elite in both countries have powerfully shaped the field of education and set up the rules that govern student selection into higher education. Considering the changes within each system, it is unsurprising that the elite have remained considerably advantaged over time across the two countries.

Valuing Elite Characteristics

High schools in each country emphasize the same kinds of activities as the colleges. Chinese and American students going through two different educational systems and selection methods are expected to set up distinct status systems and prepare for elite competition in the global arena in unique ways. In China, top public high schools have a single focus on doing everything possible to help students excel in the exams. The mutual emphasis on test scores in Beijing is likely a necessary condition for the students to navigate the status system with a singular focus and like-mindedness. In the United States, private prep schools funneling upper class students into elite colleges provided training in exam, but also a mix of cultural repertoire, athletics, and formal dances.[42] Public high schools also had series of reforms that emphasized social integration through shared activities such as dances and games.[43] These multiple criteria downplayed academic achievement by supplementing or overriding the exams. Since test scores do not dominate student attention in the United States, American students are not likely to emphasize individual academic performance as much as their Chinese counterparts in the student status system.[44]

The value of elite characteristics is context dependent, as each country instills into pupils the specific knowledge and behaviors that are rewarded in that specific society. Because the valued characteristics in one country are not equivalently rewarded in others, certain norms in China may not be as beneficial to the country's elite youth in global competition. One such example is the lack of extracurricular participation in Chinese education, a hallmark of student life that fosters students' academic success.[45] Elite Chinese students' focus on academic performance to the point of forfeiting extracurricular talents is rewarded in educational settings, and seems manageable at one's career entry. Yet, nonacademic interests and experiences will later provide institutional benefits to children in the American context, from landing lucrative job offers to gaining promotions.[46] Leaving children's nonacademic abilities unnurtured may be a norm in China, but not in the United States, where parents in the middle class and above actively cultivate children's extracurricular abilities from a young age.[47] The characteristics that are highly rewarded in each country, however, are the outcomes of long-term family cultivation. Consequently, elite Chinese students who lack the valued traits in American society would be unable to obtain these skills within a brief period of time.

While American and Chinese students have irreconcilable differences, elite Chinese students' being admitted to top American universities raises the question about what traits these students are valued for in the U.S. context. One possibility is that their stellar test scores align with admission officers' goal of increasing average test scores in each incoming cohort.[48] By admitting these top-scoring students, universities boost the SAT and GPA numbers of an incoming cohort. This suggests that the admission criteria for international students differ from those for the domestic applicants. In other words, while admission officers emphasize diversity and well-roundedness when selecting American students, they do not see the Chinese applicant as holistic individuals but evaluate Chinese applicants primarily by a number (test score). Being stereotyped as intrinsically un-holistic, however, carries more harm than benefits for these students. In the *Students for Fair Admissions v. Harvard College* lawsuit, Harvard released its application assessment criteria. These redacted legal documents, along with reports conducted on other universities, show that Asian applicants were systematically rated lower on personality traits.[49] Admission decisions in top universities are like a black box. Few have access to the decision processes, less to say study them. Considering that admission officers' preferences and evaluation criteria are considerably opaque in the United States, Chinese students who were not trained to demonstrate wholesome personalities are disadvantaged in their U.S. applications.

Alternatively, elite Chinese students might be admitted for their ability to enroll as full-tuition-paying students. Their wealth holds value even beyond graduation because top-ranked universities cultivate connections with alumni, who in return support and donate to their alma mater. By rewarding students who come from the "right" family backgrounds, top institutions grant considerable admissions advantage to elite international students not just from China, but around the world.

A third possibility also exists. It may be that regardless of the system and training, elite students around the world inevitably are alike. This explanation seems counterintuitive, considering the different training, emphasis, and

admission criteria between countries. Educators argue that exam-based selection is distinct from application-based selection in that the former overem-
phasizes rote memory, harms student motivation, alienates students from
learning, and suppresses student creativity. Yet some evidence suggests that
students in exam systems are in fact highly creative. In 2012, PISA assessed
students in creative problem solving. Singapore, South Korea, and Japan—all
exam-based selection systems—had the highest mean scores. Shanghai
(China), which the general public in China criticizes as hyper-exam-driven,[50]
also ranked among the top.[51] Importantly, as I found in this study, the adolescent elite in China are motivated learners who actively pursue knowledge
beyond what the school teaches. That Pinnacle students are known to "hang
teachers on the blackboard" suggests that elite students in top schools are
trained to become independent thinkers. The case of Dapeng, who took over
explaining test questions from his teacher, shows that at least some students
have extremely strong desires to learn and are not content with memorizing
the textbook. Together, these examples demonstrate that students in exam
systems can nonetheless be creative individuals, independent thinkers, and
motivated learners.

Societies could also move toward a different system. U.S. schools at times
have inched toward the Chinese system, and Chinese schools are gradually
moving toward the American system. Elite status in global society is related to
the hierarchy between countries, and China is increasingly seen as a powerful
global player.[52] In addition to shifts in global power, student population size
also matters. To the degree that elite students from exam systems around the
world are arriving at top American institutions in increasing numbers, elite
American students may one day find themselves competing primarily on academic achievements. In fact, American high schools, with an influx of Asians,
have already seen their racial hierarchy displaced by a status system that focuses on academic performance.[53] If this pattern continues, students in the
United States may find themselves navigating status systems that resemble the
one observed in this study. In such a situation, the experiences of elite students
in China could be a cautionary tale for American teenagers.

Finally, it should be noted that, from a global perspective, what is unique is
not China's exam system but America's emphasis on "well-rounded" students.
Although the Chinese education system may seem foreign to many, about
two-thirds of OECD countries use exams to determine educational advancement.[54] Many Western countries also emphasize academic prowess in college
selections. Canadian students compete for university admission based on their
high school GPA. In France, the *grandes écoles* rank and admit students by their
exam scores. The United Kingdom has used test scores to select children for
secondary education since 1947, based on the argument that test-based

selection provides more chances for upward mobility for children from humble backgrounds.[55] In other words, the rewarded student characteristics in exam-based selections, such as endurance or focused attention, likely carry universal value.

What about Merit?

Educational system privileges students from the elite class. The current form of higher education selection in the United States has its roots in the institutional safeguarding of elite distinction; the educational system in China consistently privileges children from elite backgrounds regardless of the social reforms,[56] suggesting that neither educational system delivers its promise of meritocratic selection. Furthermore, the strong association between elite status and top university credentials in both countries points to the role of the elite in driving social inequality.[57] When addressing issues of unfulfilled meritocracy, American researchers highlight differences between elite and nonelite students in schooling environments, in family resources, and especially in everyday experiences such as schedules, after-school activities, and cultural knowledge of the schooling system. The example of China, however, points out that a truly meritocratic educational system remains unachievable even when schedules and activities are held constant across social classes.

The issue perhaps lies within the system, namely, that the very focus on test scores turns attention away from merit and conceals the lack of merit in the exam system. When test scores are at the center of student attention and peer competition, students focus on each other's test performance. Because peers around them are doing the same things on a daily basis, elite students fail to recognize the privileges they enjoy throughout the schooling process. They do not perceive that abundant resources, highly educated and knowledgeable parents, and seemingly endless family investment in their future are all class-based advantages. However, test scores are highly dependent on class-based resources and family background, and students enter increasingly homogeneous campuses as they go through exam selections.[58] By high school, students hardly interact with peers from significantly different socioeconomic backgrounds. Pinnacle, Capital, Central, Highland, Omega, and other top high schools in Beijing had plenty of elite students, but only a handful were from the working class. In such an environment, elite students become blind to their exclusive class privileges as well as the inequalities embedded in the system.

Students' inability to spot class-based inequality further removes the subject matter from their minds. The popularity of the innate ability argument, which directly attributes one's test scores and hence status to individual ability, obscures the significance of family background. By subscribing to belief in innate ability, elite students are unable to recognize that the nonelite without comparable family advantages are less likely to get high test scores and must often work extremely hard to obtain scores similar to those of elite students.[59] This explanation places the blame for not achieving high performance on the socioeconomically disadvantaged students and suggests that distinction is natural and irreversible. Students who formulate and defend this argument thus actively sustain and justify inequality. Importantly, student attribution of test scores to innate ability not only provides a false sense of merit but also potentially exacerbates social inequality. For example, elite students who can afford Western higher education might bring back new ideas and skills to China (should they return), whereas the nonelite students who studied domestically do not. Using the innate ability explanation to justify an inherently unequal society, students thus fail to see their advantages and positions in the hierarchy as consequences of inequalities.

People change, and so do their perceptions of merit. Just as attitudes and values are not persistent over the life course, the elite's justifications for status distinction may certainly change as they age and interact with the environment.[60] Yet high school is a period when students are fixated on school status and deeply aware of the future. Adolescence is an important link that connects childhood to adulthood. It is a period that opens doors to future opportunities and critically shapes the future for young people. While behaviors and values indeed change over time, those formed during one's youth often predict adulthood habits and ideas.[61] The adolescent habit of equating innate ability with merit may persist into adulthood and shape personal behaviors at later ages.

Elite Chinese students' innate ability argument carries implications for future social and global inequalities. These students envision themselves as the future socioeconomic elite nationally and worldwide. Top students have higher starting incomes and more advantageous starts to their careers and are more likely to have access to the power elite in China. They navigate the Western job market well and secure positions even when unemployment rates are at all-time highs during economic recessions. To the extent that the elite students in this study have reasonably high chances of becoming the future elite, their perceptions of status and how they navigate social hierarchies will likely impact Chinese society and the global community. Specifically, if the future socioeconomic elite believe that the poor or less-educated masses are worse off due to innate inferiority, they are unlikely to take issue with increasing inequality around the world. They might also have limited motivation for designing and supporting effective policies for poverty relief, wealth redistribution, or other reforms aimed at narrowing inequality in general. With regard to global society, many scholars and politicians view China as a rising economic and political power. If the future elite from China consider less-developed countries as deservingly poor, international society should not rely on China to play a strong role in aiding those countries. Instead of arguing for greater equality, it would be wise to present to the Chinese alternative incentives.

That is not to say that the elite will inevitably contribute to and exacerbate global inequality. There are signs that the future of social inequality may not be as bleak as implied from the findings. Many of the elite students did extensive community work. Even if motivated by self-interest, they interacted with rural students in China, who were among the poorest in the world. Such first-hand experiences allow the elite students to learn about life at the other end of the social spectrum and may enable them to design effective solutions to help local communities. Additionally, some elite students are highly critical of their class-based privileges in an increasingly unequal society. An example is the top-scoring student in Beijing in 2017. In an interview, reporters asked about the student his secret to gaokao success. The young man attributed his high exam scores to his family background without hesitation: "I don't worry about food or clothes, my parents are both highly educated, and [I] grew up in a big city, Beijing. These exceptionally advantaged educational resources are completely exclusive to [students like me]. All top performers nowadays are rich and smart. . . . Because I had a solid foundation every step of the way, the chips naturally fell into place."[62]

This student may be an exception among the top-performing elite students by subscribing to a sociological explanation of test scores. Nonetheless, this perspective is a readily available alternative to the innate ability explanation that his peers adopted. Media broadcasting of this interview clip on national television and netizens sharing it over the internet may be analogous to dropping a pebble into water, creating ripples that, perhaps over time, will influence other elite students and introduce changes toward greater social equality.

The New Generation of Elite from China

Adolescence is a time when students learn who they are and envision what they will become. It is during this period that students acquire skills and knowledge that will help them navigate an unforeseen future. Teenagers' abilities to realize their ambitions and the available resources that help them succeed, however, are not the same. The elite, with their vast amount of parental investment and support, are given the freedom to fulfill their dreams with minimal obstacles. They move freely across borders, occupy social spaces with peers of comparable backgrounds, and are not minimally affected by failure.

Adolescents' lives unfold in unique ways. Statistically, not every elite student will assume elite status. Elite students within the same schools had vastly different experiences upon exiting campus that were related to their status in school. Jianmin (a loser) had a comeback after finding a job in Tokyo, but his achievement paled in comparison to the study gods and studyholics who were working on Wall Street. Xiaolong (an underachiever) was optimistic in applying for graduate programs as a self-funded student, but his dream school was much lower ranked compared to the top doctoral programs that the high performers joined. Students' ambitions changed over time, and their decisions of whom they will become changed as well.[63] These examples point to important differences in the processes and outcomes of elite status reproduction.

But these variations and individually unique experiences should not divert our attention from the ways that elite students obtain a competitive edge in status reproduction. In addition to the socioeconomic resources that define their status, they understand the unspoken rules that determine each other's relative position in society. In a world that operates on sets of tacit guidelines, these class-based abilities carry real benefits. Elite students reap rewards from this training because the systems and institutions that they navigate in, especially the institution of education and the job market, select members based on these traits. Top performers such as Tony, Tracy, Dapeng, and Yulang share comparable interaction styles and trajectories as they pursue their goals in life. Low performers such as Jianmin, Jiaqi, Robert, and Sarah experience important events in common. This means that, in addition to their measurable performance, interpersonal interactions in school have life-defining importance for their futures.

The Chinese, like people in other countries, tend to resist categories that signal superiority or inferiority. When asked, few elite adults acknowledge they are of high status; most identify themselves as middle or upper-middle class.[64] However, the future elite, or those who are still in the making, are acutely aware of status from a young age. Although they do not use terms such as "elitism" or "distinction" that scholars use to describe them, they readily identify status differences and directly connect status to future social positions. By accepting the status system they developed, elite students learn to support an unequal society that sorts people into different status groups. By justifying the interaction patterns associated with status everywhere they go, the elite youths learn to justify social inequality in China and around the world.

Looking at the example of elite youths from China provides a vocabulary for understanding global society. It highlights the ways in which the elite of today are a cohesive group as well as the unique ways countries prepare their affluent youths for global competition. Such cohesion connects societies in an increasingly intertwined world, where the elite of different upbringings and nationalities are tightly linked in intricate ways. An understanding of status reproduction at the global level is more accurate than examining elite forma- tion as a process that takes place within individual countries. Possessing the skills and abilities valued across countries and educational systems is critical to justifying and sustaining high status. Receiving training in these skills and abilities is a distinctive advantage. Because these processes take shape through micro-level interactions, they are invisible to the public and go largely unrec- ognized. Global society would be better off with greater awareness of the ways and mechanisms through which elite youths reproduce their parents' high status. Only then might societies acknowledge that, together, we all contribute to producing one group of what is becoming the new, global elite.

Who Are the Elite?

DEFINITIONS OF ELITE status are often contested, and there is little consensus on the best empirical measures of it. Classic studies typically define elite as those who have power and dominance over others.[1] However, others suggest that the elite are not limited to the powerholders in the economic-political sphere but exist in all fields. This line of research adopts a more general definition that acknowledges multiple types of elite. Scholars also consider the elite as those who outcompete others. These include Olympic swimmers, individuals with the most followers in digital cyberspace, and academics.[2] Another prominent approach is to define elite by high socioeconomic status, measured by a combination of income, wealth, education, or occupation. The exact cutoff for an individual to qualify as an elite differs considerably. Some focus on the top 0.1 or 1 percent in terms of wealth or the top 5 percent in household income,[3] but others have difficulty capturing enough cases in a representative sample. As a result, the definitions of elite are often exceedingly generous, such as including all in the top quintile of household incomes, which captures members of the middle or upper-middle class.[4]

The adolescent elite are just as hard to define. Research on elite education often emphasizes students' socioeconomic background, but other competing definitions exist. Elite status is commonly measured through institutional affiliation or individual academic performance. The two measures form a Venn diagram. The former considers a teenager who attends a competitive high school, such as with a 30 percent chance of Ivy League admission, as an elite adolescent. By this definition, low-performing students who have successful peers, but who themselves are not admitted by selective universities, are part of the elite. The latter definition focuses on individual students' academic performance, and thus a student from the working class is considered elite by virtue of being a top performer.[5] A third approach examines elite status by whether and how students demonstrate exclusive practices and self-distinction. This perspective draws on Bourdieu's theory of distinction and highlights the role of cultural repertoire in marking group boundaries.[6]

The criteria for elite status are also contextually specific. Studies that examine the elite in China often adopt a definition similar to that in the classic studies in the United States and focus on the group's political or economic influence.[7] Considering the substantial urban-rural disparities in China, the focus on political power to the point of forgoing the economic aspect has provided scholars with the tools to understand status and dominance in rural areas, where local leaders exert considerable influence in their communities.[8] However, while political leaders undoubtedly occupy an important aspect of research on the Chinese elite, economic influence increasingly shapes Chinese imaginations of the elite. For example, some point to additional criteria that determine whom the elite are. One criterion is having hukou, or household registration, in specific areas. Obtaining hukou in Beijing, Shanghai, Guangdong, or Shenzhen is often a prerequisite to membership in the elite strata.[9] Because hukou is tied to social security and benefits, the emphasis on hukou in fact points to a socioeconomic definition of the elite. One of the arguably most important criteria that mark elite status in China is education. Educational attainment is historically linked to political and socioeconomic power and has unwavering significance despite social upheavals and revolutions.[10] In other words, to lay claim to socioeconomically elite status (or political elite status to a certain extent) in China, one must simultaneously have a high level of educational attainment.

The contextual emphasis on educational outcomes has led studies on Chinese youth to commonly equate elite status with top academic performance, whether individually or institutionally. However, the bar for elite-level academic performance varies by region. In his study of students in Zhouping, a city famous for its textile industry in Shandong province, Kipnis considered elite students to be those at Huang Shan Middle School.[11] In 2015, the school reported sending about 26 percent of its student body to the top tier of universities in China (*yibenxian*), a rate among the highest in the province. However, this rate is considered extremely low in Beijing, where over 99 percent of the students in top high schools pass the cutoff. By comparison, the issue is somewhat easier with regard to differentiating elite from nonelite in higher education. The government announces "projects" that list specific universities that will receive concentrated government funding in upcoming years.[12] These projects offer a convenient way to identify and justify the selection of elite institutions. Since the policies are backed by the government, scholars can view all universities on the list as elite institutions.[13]

While a definition that emphasizes contextual specificities is preferable, focusing on educational performance in the definition of elite in China cannot clearly address China's role in global elite competition. Because of the significant regional disparities within the country, a common definition of elite nonetheless leads to different objective measures for "elite" high schools and "elite" adolescents across regions and studies. Elite adolescents in economically developed areas, such as Beijing or Shanghai, are likely to have dissimilar experiences than their peers in relatively disadvantaged cities, such as Zhouping. In these two regions, markers of elite status tend to differ, as do the meanings of successful elite status reproduction. Furthermore, whether elite students in less developed areas share similar behavior and insight into global competition is unclear.

In this study, I define students from families with income in the top 10 percent in the country as elite. To maintain clarity, I call students and schools with high levels of academic performance top students and top schools. This definition is fundamentally a socioeconomic one and is prominently used by existing studies on the elite. It considers China's rapid socioeconomic development in the past few decades as well as the end goal of global elite competition. Wealthy families often underreport their total income, and their "gray income" can be significant.[14] I suspect the interviewees underreported their family income by excluding gray income, which is likely many times greater than their taxed income. Nonetheless, the families in this study reported a median income that was about twice the income of a top 10 percent family of three in urban China.[15]

I compared their reported income with other indicators as well. One was that all but one parent confirmed that they could send their child to a private university in the United States for four years as a full-tuition-paying student. I also asked the teachers to validate whether student families were socioeconomically affluent. Since teachers had detailed and confidential information on student family backgrounds, their perspectives increased my confidence that the families in this study were a part of the socioeconomic elite in China.[16] I did not systematically ask about the families' wealth, but most of the families owned two or more apartments in Beijing. Some students later revealed that the parents had assets in other provinces as well.

Elite families, when defined by socioeconomic affluence, often share many other characteristics. In addition to having very high incomes, the families in this study were similar in many ways. The parents were of similar ages and achieved upward mobility through exceptionally high educational attainment.[17] The parents went to college in the late 1980s, which put them among the top 1 to 2 percent in education among the Chinese population at the time; many of them were Peking or Tsinghua alumni. Some held graduate degrees; a few even had foreign exchange experiences. Having very high income in the country also meant that the families came from similar walks of life. All but one of the twenty-eight students had at least one parent in an upper managerial or professional occupation. Some of the families' characteristics were related to my sampling pool. Two-thirds of the families were affiliated with the military or worked in the government. This is understandable, considering that the schools I studied were either close to military compounds or affiliated with top universities. Finally, my fieldwork took place in Beijing. Naturally, all of the participants in this study had a Beijing hukou, which enabled them to reside and be educated in Beijing.[18]

In short, the elite youth I followed have parents who achieved upward mobility through educational success and expect them to enter top universities as a first step toward future elite status. They are the first generation to pursue elite status not as upward mobility but as status reproduction. Simultaneously, they are among the first cohorts to grow up in an economically reformed, revolution-free China that is intricately connected to the world. As the Chinese representatives and contenders for global elite status, they thirst for such recognition at the international level.

Methodological Reflections

STUDIES OF THE elite are rare. Scholars infrequently have access to elite territories, much less the ability to wander in those spaces over time. China, additionally, is a territory difficult for non-Chinese (and nonwhite) researchers to navigate. I obtained access to the schools through family friends who negotiated varying degrees of access for me. My access primarily depended on the relationship between my "guarantor" and the school personnel. The closer the relationship, the greater the freedom I had; the higher the academic status of my guarantor, the fewer limitations I encountered. My guarantors for Capital and Pinnacle were academicians in China. One was the principal's college classmate; the other was the head math teacher's graduate school advisor. These two schools allowed me to access classrooms (conditional on homeroom teachers' consent) and granted me the freedom to talk to any student on campus. In Central and Highland, where I did not have as strong connections, I could talk to individual students but not conduct observations. Simultaneously, luck and timing mattered. Omega was under scrutiny at the time I started fieldwork and closed its doors to research activities on campus. I met Omega students through the introduction of friends and roommates, and my meetings with students took place off campus.[1]

When I entered Capital and Pinnacle in 2012, I specified my interest in studying students from wealthy, elite backgrounds. Teachers and principals introduced me to eight students, all in different classrooms, who were my key informants and through whom I became acquainted with the other students. Teachers later reported adding additional criteria when selecting the students, such as sociability and high academic performance "to maintain the school's image."[2] This meant that my key informants usually had high status in school and thus could serve as ideal representatives. Teachers also chose students who might benefit the most from research participation.[3] Because the students they introduced were indeed socioeconomically elite, I did not object to the teachers' decisions. Through shadowing these key informants, I carried out fifteen months of observations in eight classrooms in Capital and Pinnacle. I joined each classroom for up to five days, between eight and fifteen hours each day. As part of my ethnography, I also had meals and hung out with students regularly and attended school events, such as parent-teacher meetings and cohort meetings.

After establishing rapport with the students, I invited twenty-eight students with whom I was more familiar for in-depth interviews as well as follow-up interviews after high school graduation. I also asked them to introduce me to their closest teachers and primary guardian. I was able to interview thirteen teachers (of nineteen students) and nineteen parents (of eighteen students). Altogether, I conducted sixty-five interviews that averaged about ninety minutes; follow-up interviews were shorter and averaged thirty minutes. Teachers' and parents' acceptance of me was undoubtedly related to my educational background. My Ivy League affiliation helped me gain the trust of teachers and facilitated parental acceptance of their children participating in my research. Interestingly, which Ivy League school apparently did not matter. A year after I had entered Capital, the vice principal and Mrs. Nie still called me "the Columbia girl," even though I had specified that I studied at Penn. Parents of top performers allowed me to follow their child simply because their top-performing child had asked and I came from a top-ranked university. Parents of low-performing students who agreed to their children's research participation specified that they hoped I would be a "good influence" on their child. Student status also played a part in determining adult participation in the interviews. Many parents were hesitant about being interviewed. In these circumstances, the few top performers, especially those who were closer with me, helped talk their parents into accepting my interview invitations.[4]

Home observations are difficult to conduct, and those in elite homes particularly so. Such observations are intrusive, as the researcher trespasses in participants' private spheres. It is particularly difficult to carry out home observations with elite students in twelfth grade, not just because elite homes are typically guarded against outsiders, but also since twelfth grade was the height of college application and exam pressure for the students and their parents. Among the eight key informants, I was able to conduct home observations with three boys and one girl. I observed the homes of three boys two to four times each, spending about three hours per visit. Instead of making multiple short visits, the girl's mother invited me to stay over for four days with the family. The mother was unusually supportive of my research because, as she told me when we first met, "When my daughter was an exchange student [in the United States], her host family was extremely kind to her. It's my turn to return the favor to someone from the U.S." This showed that she accepted my home observation request out of luck, an exception that attested to the norm of the difficulty of observing elites.

I supplement the ethnography and interviews with information collected from media and social networking sites. College admission statistics in China, government notifications of policy changes, school admission results, and university admission results were often publicly available and contained student-identifying information. I used these resources to verify students' reported exam scores.[5] I also drew information from newspapers, education-focused magazines, and books published by these high schools. Most of these printed documents boasted of student achievement and school histories. Together, these sources provided me with information regarding how the schools presented their self-image as top in the nation as well as student narratives of school life and college preparations.

I moved out of Beijing in 2014, but I continued to visit the students as they went to college and graduate school and after they entered the labor market. Keeping in touch was easy, as we texted on WeChat (an app similar to WhatsApp) and iMessage. I sent them birthday cards and visited in person as frequently as possible. While online messaging was useful, face-to-face interactions were the foundation to maintaining our relationships. Since the students were scattered across countries, I made sure to swing by their universities or offices when I was in the area. I continued to spend most of my summers and winters in Beijing, when students returned home for vacation. Many of them visited me in Philadelphia or Taipei as well. The students I visited often willingly blocked off their schedules so we could catch up and called other students from the same high school to join the meetings. Not all visits went smoothly. One girl was considerably difficult to get hold of. For our first few scheduled meetings, I would arrive at the airport or train station just to receive an apology that she had gone on a last-minute overseas vacation. I learned to be impromptu with her and was able to meet with her when I happened to be in the same city. Over all, I met with twenty-seven of the twenty-eight students twice after high school on average. Pan was the only student no longer in touch. Yet I learned about her whereabouts on social networking sites and from her high school friends. The variation in frequency of meetings ranged from almost annually (such as with Stacey and Shiying) to just once in seven years after high school (such as Huating and Jun). I also met with students who were not part of the twenty-eight but with whom I was familiar (Xiaolong, Sinian, Samantha, Sarah, and Mark). These visits included lighthearted activities such as sleepovers, dining together, and touring the city and serious discussions that ran close to counseling sessions. Table A1 provides information about the twenty-eight students' college outcomes, gaokao or SAT scores, and positions as of 2019.

Researcher's Role

When I entered the schools, teachers introduced me to the students as "teacher Chiang," suggesting that I would be in a position of authority. However, the students quickly learned that I had neither power nor authority over them, and instead called me "big sister" (*jiejie*) almost right away. They felt comfortable talking to me about a variety of topics. They confided in me secrets not shared with teachers or parents, knowing they could trust me. Students shared with me gossip about who pursued whom, which ones dated, and who broke up for what reasons. They made sure that I abided by school regulations as they did, such as warning me not to use a cell phone in the classroom. In multiple instances the students even tried to fit me into their status system. I was close to a studyholic by virtue of being a PhD student at an Ivy League university. However, I never moved up the system, likely because I moved to Beijing for research and sat through classes with them, which counted toward demonstrated effort. I was also on the verge of downward mobility in the status system because I failed to answer most of their test questions and had typos in my English. When my performance did not match my alleged status, the students would make up excuses for me, such as "you made that mistake on purpose" and "it's been ten years since you graduated from high school." It was quite fun seeing the students struggle to sort me into a status group and then justify my underperformance.

I was familiar with students of both genders. Nonetheless, I experienced different degrees of closeness that were in line with local customs. Boys were interested in being shadowed and competed to see who had the most participation in my research, but this initial zeal dwindled by the third day. For example, Brandon asked if he could end observations earlier; Jiaqi tried to get rid of me during breaks by "going to the men's bathroom." The pattern was opposite with girls. Girls seemed uncomfortable about having a shadow at first, but by the third day they were so used to my presence that they would wait for me to join them wherever they went. As Lili put it, "It's actually kinda fun to have this one [me] following around. I thought it'd be weird, but it's kinda fun." By the end of my fieldwork, the students and I had become considerably close. Lili walked with me with locked arms so frequently that the guard let us pass into the gaokao test site without noticing. After Brandon learned that I had been "nowhere except for schools" after a year in Beijing, he scheduled follow-up interviews at local attractions. This feeling of closeness lasted well after the students went to college. When I visited Tracy at her university, we sat on a lawn to chat. Somewhere in the middle of our conversation, Tracy lay down and rested her head on my stomach as she talked about her dreams and future plans. In another visit, Xiaolong greeted me with a hug, which was rare among Chinese men. These are among the many moments that were the highlights of my extended ethnography.

I established friendly relationships with the teachers as well. To enter the schools, I had to have a teacher sign me in at the school gate. Mr. Long and Mr. Hu took me under their wings and gave me access to Capital and Pinnacle whenever they were available. Other teachers, such as Tom at Capital and Ms. Wu at Pinnacle, also helped me get past security. Not all teachers knew about my research activities. Capital and Pinnacle were exemplary high schools and often hosted groups of teachers from other provinces to observe teachers' pedagogy. My presence in the classrooms had minimal impact on how teachers behaved in the classroom, as many who did not know me took me as one of the constant stream of visitors. The higher-ups in school who did not know me thought I was a student. Capital had a new principal (Mr. Liu) after I secured access. I ran into Mr. Liu multiple times on campus. When he saw me in the domestic department, he asked about my gaokao preparation. When he saw me in the international department, he asked which American university admitted me. I explained, the first few times, that I was a researcher. Later on I simply replied, "It's going well." He would then nod, smile, and say "Good," walking away with his hands behind his back as the students walking with me hid their giggles.

Parents saw me as a member of the younger generation. When hanging out with them during family observations, parents sometimes commented that I looked like their child. Shiying's mother joked multiple times that we looked like mother and daughter, such as when we waited for Shiying outside a test location and when I accompanied her on a shopping trip. This generational relationship may have led some of the parents to refuse interview participation or to take an instructional tone. Yet this relationship also provided me a pass to visit students' homes, where I was welcomed as a friend of the student. These relationships continued after the students graduated from high school. In my later visits to Beijing, some parents joined my meetings with their children to say hello.

Challenges in the Field

High schools in China had considerably high levels of caution against outsiders due to reporter criticisms and previous terrorist attacks. Staying in the school was more difficult than I imagined. Obtaining permission to conduct observations was not identical to having institutional affiliation, thus I still needed a schoolteacher to sign me in to campus. This meant that I could enter the schools only with a teacher's physical presence. The first few months were troublesome, but then security guards began to recognize me and stopped asking for my ID and a teacher's guarantee. Personnel changes also posed some challenges because the networks that paved my entry were no longer in place. Sometimes these changes were managed by the teachers who were familiar with me. Mr. Hu, who was the head teacher of the senior cohort, extended my access at Pinnacle after the principal who granted me access was displaced. Other times, lost connections led to at least one other school withdrawing previously granted access.

To maintain relationships with the schools and families, I exerted extra caution due to my background as a Taiwanese researcher from an American institution. Before I went to Beijing, Mainland Chinese friends and scholars warned me to be wary of what I said because "government agents might pay close attention" to my research activities. I did not think that my topic was politically loaded in any way, and I did not encounter any problems with my research, my background, or myself. Infrequently, when students asked where I stood on the cross-Strait relationship, I used these as opportunities to let them know more about my family's immigration history and ethnic conflicts in Taiwan. The parents were understandably careful about associating with me. Some asked me not to let anyone know about my visits to their house for fear that it could reflect badly on their careers. Considering that Capital and Pinnacle both had relatively large proportions of families in the military, I speculate that the general caution about foreign contact among these families may be part of the reason that some parents declined research participation.

Building and maintaining relationships with elite students also required effort and care. While I observed many instances in which students demonstrated elite entitlement, it was always a challenge to be on the receiving end. One girl expected me to pay for her when we went out for meals or movies. Some students felt entitled to make suggestions about improving my taste and body image. These included harmless suggestions such as Tracy suggesting that I wear shorts, but other times the students were rather intrusive. A few weeks after I started fieldwork, Jiaqi publicly mocked my single status by shouting out loud in the classroom, "You leftover woman! You're twenty-seven and still not married, you're such a leftover woman!" I responded by tapping him on the head, a common child rearing practice in China. Jiaqi looked at me in wide-eyed disbelief (probably so did Mr. Long, who was also in the room), but then nodded in agreement when I claimed that his parents would've done the same. After that, teachers left me to defend myself. Once, in the middle of fieldwork, Dehong took me aside and gave concrete suggestions on how I should improve my bust size ("eat papaya") and ended by saying that "you should be thankful that I didn't look down on you." These instances were recurrent, but I soon learned to respond with a joke, change topics, or defend myself with academic etiquette. For example, when another boy mocked my single status in front of a classroom of students, I shouted back by quoting statistics about the low probability that he would be married by my age. I used statistics as self-defense so frequently that Shiying joked, "One good thing about knowing a sociologist is that you'll always know if you're dragging down society." Overall, because these behaviors and comments were preferable to polite but distant interactions, I interpreted them as signals of familiarity.

Readjusting to the Nonelite World

My approach to fieldwork was similar to what Matthew Desmond described in *Evicted,* an attempt to think as the informants think, feel as they feel, and walk as they walk. To do so, I immersed myself in the Chinese context by moving there. Living in China for the first time required adjustment. I rented a pantry-converted room in a shared apartment in Capital's school district, but later realized that I had underestimated the scope of Beijing when a short distance on the map turned into an hour and a half one-way commute to Capital. Even walking required adjustments. It took me three weeks to learn how to cross the streets busy with various types of motor vehicles. The triumphal moment was when a middle-aged Chinese woman came up to me at the front gate of Omega and asked, "Miss, can I follow you across the street?" I can still see the relief on her face when I agreed.

After adjusting to life in Beijing, exiting the field required another round of readjustment. Through daily interactions, I became accustomed to the students' and their families' approaches to status systems. I unintentionally sorted people around me into different status groups according to the status system that the elite students established. Phrases such as "have a life" in casual conversations started to catch my attention, as I wondered whether the recipient of that comment was given studyholic or loser status. I also adopted the students' unnecessarily strict and rank-based definition to categorize "top" universities. I understood this was a specific elite Chinese student opinion but had to remind myself that most students do not attend an Ivy League school or Peking University. Friends and colleagues relentlessly helped me readapt to the mainstream opinion through questions and comments.[6] This mindset gradually weakened, and a year later I readapted to mainstream categorization of institutional prestige.

In addition to detaching myself from the status system, I had to readjust to language use and accents outside of China. I acquired a slight northern accent when speaking Mandarin and habitually used China's terminology (for instance, "research" is *yanjiu* in Taiwan but *keyan* in China). Students did not seem to mind my Taiwanese accent, and girls sometimes amusedly mimicked my way of speaking. When Brandon said that I sounded like a Beijinger, although just for a split second, I proudly took it as a stamp of approval. Friends back home and in Hong Kong, however, had a different reaction. Some admitted to abruptly ending a conversation because they found my new accent annoying, while a few asked me to "speak normally." I was almost removed from emcee duty at a friend's wedding in Taipei. My situation of sounding like a Beijinger in Taiwan but like a Taiwanese in Beijing continued for a few years until I relocated to Taiwan.

TABLE A1. Elite Youth Demographics

	Name	High school / department	Undergraduate institution	Gaokao or SAT score[a]	Position as of 2019 (residential location)
Young women					
1.	Huating Xue	Pinnacle 2014 Domestic	University of Oxford	676	Engineer, American technology company (London)
2.	Lili Zhu	Capital 2014 Domestic	Peking University	663 + 30 (additional test)	Master's student, New York University (NY)
3.	Mingjia Song	Pinnacle 2014 Domestic	Tsinghua University	684 + 30 (additional test)	Master's student, New York University (NY)
4.	Pan Liu	Pinnacle 2014 Domestic	Tongji University	665	Master's student, Tongji University (NY)
5.	Shiying Liu	Capital 2013 Domestic	Tsinghua University	667 + 20 (exemplary)	Master's student, Cambridge University (Cambridge, UK)
6.	Shuhua Tien	Capital 2013 Domestic	Fudan University	639	Stanford alumna; strategy analyst, European investment bank (Beijing)
7.	Xijun Wu	Pinnacle 2013 Domestic	National Academy of Fine Arts	627 (art test)	Master's student, Imperial College London; self-employed film director (Beijing)
8.	Yulang Liu	Capital 2014 Domestic	Tsinghua University	678 + 60 (winter camp)	PhD student, University of California, Berkeley (CA)
9.	Ashley Fong	Pinnacle 2013 International	Cambridge University	2230	Sales, East Asian investment bank (Singapore)
10.	Claire Chen	Capital 2013 International	Yale University	2330	Consultant, American consulting firm (NY)
11.	Julie Jin	Central 2013 International	Bryn Mawr College	2170	Master's student, Columbia University (NY)
12.	Selina Su	Capital 2013 International	University of Pennsylvania	2200	Analyst, American investment bank (NY)
13.	Stacy Gao	Capital 2014 International	Claremont McKenna College	2180	Master's student, Harvard University (MA)
14.	Tracy Zhou	Capital 2014 International	Johns Hopkins University	2200	Trader, European investment bank (Hong Kong)

Young men

No.	Name	Program	University	Score	Position
15.	Dehung Ke	Capital 2014 Domestic	Fudan University	668 + 5 (ethnic minority)	Master's student, Beijing Film Academy (Beijing)
16.	Fei Li	Pinnacle 2013 Domestic	Tsinghua University	679 (Olympiad)	PhD student, University of California, Berkeley (CA)
17.	Haocheng Zhang	Pinnacle 2014 Domestic	Peking University	681 + 10 (Olympiad)	Master's student, New York University (NY)
18.	Jianmin Wu	Pinnacle 2014 Domestic	Lingnan University	641	Tax accountant, Chinese engineering and consulting company (Tokyo)
19.	Jiaqi Xu	Capital 2014 Domestic	Université de Technologie de Compiègne, France	608	Undergraduate student (Paris)
20.	Jun Liu	Capital 2013 Domestic	Peking University	672 (Olympiad)	PhD student, Peking University (Beijing)
21.	Kefeng Zhou	Highland 2013 Domestic	Peking University	648 (Olympiad)	Stanford alumnus; researcher, American trading firm (IL)
22.	Wenbin Liu	Pinnacle 2014 Domestic	Tsinghua University	691 + 40 (additional test)	Master's student, University of Washington (WA)
23.	Xiangzu Liu	Omega 2013 Domestic	Nanjing University	Above 600	PhD student, Beihang University; consultant, American automobile company (Beijing)
24.	Alex Liu	Capital 2013 International	Boston College	2150	Engineer, American technology company (MA)
25.	Brandon Wu	Capital 2013 International	University of California, Los Angeles	2140	PhD student, University of California, Los Angeles (CA)
26.	Joe Wu	Pinnacle 2013 International	Boston College	2160	PhD student, University of Texas at Austin (TX)
27.	Robert Guo	Capital 2014 International	George Washington University	2050	Master's student, Washington University in St. Louis (MO)
28.	Tony Cao	Capital 2014 International	Cornell University	2320	Consultant, British accounting firm (NY)

Note: Universities have been changed to comparable institutions. I exclude information on family and personal income, military affiliations, and government positions for anonymity. Except for Wenbin's family, all families specified they could afford sending the child to college in the United States as a self-paying student.

a. The two numbers of gaokao scores indicate students' original exam score plus added points. Channels of added points are in parentheses. The maximum score for the gaokao was 750; the SAT score maximum was 2400.

Despite the uncertainties of doing fieldwork in China and the challenges associated with studying the elite, I consider myself extremely lucky to have known and befriended this group of adolescents. I have become fond of these youths and a firm supporter of their future endeavors. Students' openness in sharing their lives never fails to amaze me. Many things changed after they became young adults. Our conversation topics changed from test scores and relationships to tax policies and the job market. I went from understanding their exam-focused mindset to being unable to understand their careers in finance. Whereas I used to treat them to meals near campus, they now treated me at pricey restaurants. Yet other things have not changed. When in high school, the students reached out when they sensed I might be in need of help.[7] Seven years after high school, they still extended similar degrees of courtesy when I visited.[8] Many continued to confide in me secrets that shall never be revealed. These elite youths' generosity in sharing a glimpse of their lives over the years is what has brought this study to life.

Introduction

1. All names are pseudonyms; university and company names have been changed to those of comparable organizations in the same country. International-bound students are given names in English, and many go by their English names in school.

2. See, for example, the elite students observed in studies by Brooks and Waters 2011; Vandrick 2011; and Waters 2006.

3. Courtois 2013; Higgins 2013.

4. Tognini 2021.

5. Heathcote 2019.

6. Nolan (2013) argues that Chinese firms have a negligible presence in Western countries, while Western firms are integrated in China. While the possibility of China's growing power in global business remains an open question, his findings provide evidence of the integration between Chinese and global economies.

7. Tan 2018.

8. Jacques 2009.

9. Lim and Bergin 2018.

10. Davis and Wei 2019.

11. Childress 2019.

12. To compete for global talent, the Changjiang Scholars Program offered a salary of approximately $150,000, which is greater than the average income U.S. faculty earn, plus over $1 million in housing allowance (Wu 2018). In 2019, universities in Beijing advertised a monthly salary of over $10,000 for visiting scholars for the duration of their stay.

13. Er-Rafia 2018; Ghuman 2018.

14. It should be noted that some argue that China "cheated" to obtain high overall PISA performances by selecting students to participate in the tests.

15. Department of Education and Training, Australia 2017; John 2016; Statistics Canada 2016; UK Council for International Student Affairs 2017.

16. The Bureau of Consular Affairs (2019) shows that the number of student visas issued has decreased at about 7 to 27 percent each year since 2015.

17. In a video clip from a news broadcast in summer 2018, a news reporter asked a few college students who wanted to study in the United States if they had other plans given the tightening F-1 visa (full-time student) quotas. The respondents reported that they did not. The participants of this study shared the same response, but with an even more confident attitude.

18. Studies on elites often limit their discussion to the group's influence within a country. For example, as the title of his book suggests, Domhoff (2017) examines the elites who rule America. Mills (1956) similarly focuses on elites in the United States. Some have turned attention to international examples. Hartmann (2006) provides examples of elites in five countries, and Milner (2015a) uses the examples of three types of elites in three historical eras to support his status theory. However, Hartmann emphasizes how each elite group is powerful within the respective countries, while Milner focuses on India, Athens, and the United States, respectively.

19. Study gods in Chinese classrooms share a few similarities with "brains," "jocks," and "popular kids" in American classrooms, but none of these groups is an exact equivalent. Study gods are comparable to "brains" in possessing academic excellence and similar to "jocks" in enjoying peer attention. Like "popular kids," they often assume leadership positions in school. However, these social categories only partially capture the elevated status that study gods enjoy and are not perceived to carry as comprehensive a sense of innate superiority.

20. Alvaredo et al. 2018; Xie and Zhou 2014.

21. Brooks (2000) gives a detailed account of general status anxiety among the middle class. Lan (2018) and Levey-Friedman (2013) also show that parental anxiety over children's uncertain future is related to high levels of involvement among the affluent and middle-class parents.

22. Brooks and Waters 2009; Mazlish and Morss 2005.

23. Armstrong and Crombie 2000; Bandura et al. 2001; Chhin et al. 2008; Dworkin et al. 2003; MacLeod 2018; Staff et al. 2010.

24. Clark and Cummins 2014; Erola and Moisio 2007.

25. Bourdieu (1976) used marriage as an example of status strategies. However, as I show in this book, education is another key factor that families use to compete for status.

26. Lareau 2011.

27. Calarco 2014.

28. Chiang 2018; Hamilton 2016.

29. For example, see Khan 2011; Hartmann 2006.

30. In *Distinction*, Bourdieu (1984) discusses the association between high culture and status. The case of models is also similar; Mears (2011) shows that in fashion modeling, the editorial circuit of models simply has higher value than the commercial ones.

31. Most would agree that education is a key vehicle for producing status outcomes. Weber (1946) argues that educational testing and selection creates a system of stratification. Turner's (1960) discussion of how elites select pupils into sponsored systems is an example of elite dominance. Findings from the Wisconsin model and research using Blau and Duncan's (1967) status attainment model also argue for the crucial role of education. Empirically, the political elites in China seem to be aware of the significance of higher education and use it both as a requisite for entry into the elite system and to boost the education level of already-elite members so that they continue to have much higher levels of education than the general population (Chen 2006; Li and Walder 2001).

32. Chen 2006; Collins 1979; Walder et al. 2000.

33. Cookson and Persell 1985; Gaztambide-Fernández 2009; Khan 2011.

34. Armstrong and Hamilton 2013; Lee and Brinton 1996.

35. Lee and Brinton 1996; Hartmann 2006; Rivera 2015.

36. Countries and educational systems often have different elite selection mechanisms (Turner 1960). Note that Gibson (2019) considers that the elites in Germany are groomed during secondary education, which would be similar to the timing in the United States.

37. Oxbridge is a portmanteau of Oxford and Cambridge, the two top universities in the United Kingdom. *Tsingbei* is a colloquial term for Tsinghua University and Peking University, the two top universities in China.

38. In addition to education, common measures of status include job acquisition and marriage. The norms regarding occupation prestige and marriage choice also differ across countries (Lin and Xie 1988; Smits et al. 1998).

39. Lucas 2001; Raftery and Hout 1993.

40. Zheng and Zhang 2018.

41. Li and Bachman 1989; Walder et al. 2000; Zang 2001.

42. Chen 2006.

43. Chiang 2018; Kipnis 2011; Xie and Zhou 2014.

44. Fong 2004.

45. Xue 2015.

46. Li and Prevatt 2008.

47. Xing et al. 2010; Zeng and LeTendre 1998.

48. See Demerath (2009) and Gaztambide-Fernández (2009) for competition among elite students. Calarco (2018) and Lareau (2011) offer many examples of teacher and parent support for children from a relatively young age.

49. All of these terms are taken from online student forums with minor changes for translation purposes.

50. This is similarly shown in Khan (2011), who finds that elite adolescents in the United States learn to associate with people from different social strata in high school.

Chapter 1: The New Elites from China

1. See Lucas (2001) for his theory on effectively maintained inequality (EMI).

2. See Raftery and Hout (1993) for their theory on maximally maintained inequality (MMI). Hao et al. (2014) examine educational inequality in China using this theory.

3. Walder et al. 2000.

4. Hannum 1999; Pepper 1996.

5. Li and Bachman 1989; Walder et al. 2000; Zang 2001.

6. This policy in 1998 led to increased college enrollment rates, jumping from 7 percent in 1998 to 24 percent in 2010 (Yeung 2013).

7. See Heckman and Li 2004; Li 2003; Wu and Xie 2003; Zhang et al. 2005 on returns to education. See also Chen 2006; Li and Bachman 1989; Walder et al. 2000; Zang 2001 for discussion on elite status acquisition.

8. Goodman 2014; National Bureau of Statistics 2017; Xie 2016; Xie and Zhou 2014.

9. Bian (2002) shows that the reform led to the emergence of new labor markets, which in turn provided grounds for occupational mobility. However, Gong et al. (2012) find that intergenerational income elasticity is as high as 0.63 in China.

10. Chiang and Lareau 2018; Hartmann 2006.

11. Peking and Tsinghua are the top two universities in China. Peking University is pronounced as Beijing Daxue, Tsinghua University as Qinghua Daxue. Students refer to the two as *Qingbei*.

12. Information gathered from Peking University Student Career Center 2014; Tsinghua Career Center 2014. See Bai 2006; Li et al. 2008; Sharma 2014 for concerns over college employment rates and discussions on overeducation.

13. *China Daily* 2014; China Education Online 2014a.

14. Alumni from the two universities occupy powerful positions in China. For example, Hu Jintao, Xi Jinping, and Li Keqiang, among others, are all PKU and THU alumni. Also see Peking University Recruitment Newsletter 2014.

15. Provinces do not share the same set of exam questions, but the exam structure and schedule are largely identical in the country. Ten provinces hold the exam over three days; all others hold the exam in two days.

16. See Davey et al. (2007) for detailed descriptions of the exam process.

17. *Sina* 2014.

18. I calculated the admission rates for PKU and THU by dividing the total number of admitted students in 2014 by the total number of test takers in the same year from a government website (China Education Online) and university admissions websites. The admission rate for the *grandes écoles* was a rough estimate taken from dividing the total number of students in the *grandes écoles* by the total number of college students in France, using information from the Ministère de l'Éducation Nationale website. The estimated admission rates for the Ivies came from dividing the number of students accepted to the Ivy League by the total number of college freshmen in the United States, using information from the National Center for Educational Statistics and Ivy League university admissions websites.

19. The Chinese government initiated Project 985, Project 211, and the Double World Class Project to strengthen the country's higher education between 1985 and 2015. The universities selected received more state funding and resources than those not on the list. The three projects selected different numbers of universities, but 20 percent of those listed were consistently in Beijing.

20. *Huawen* 2017.

21. Ye 2015; Yeung 2013.

22. Ma (2020) shows that the age of children being sent abroad is decreasing.

23. These trends concerned the government, which took measures to decrease the number of students going abroad for college. These policies had little effect, and most predicted that the number of students going abroad would continue to grow until well into the 2030s (Chen 2015).

24. Chiang and Lareau 2018; Fong 2011; Ma 2020.

25. Many of these students become the socioeconomic elite and acquire political power by building strong relationships with or by offering policy advice to the political leaders in China (Li 2006; Li et al. 2012). Others show that going abroad is not necessarily beneficial, as the foreign-educated on average earn a wage similar to that of the domestically educated, and they have low rates of return on their parents' educational investment (China Education Online 2017; Larmer 2014; Li 2006; National Bureau of Statistics 2017; *Xinhua News* 2015).

26. See Fong 2004, 2011; Rivera 2015.

27. Hao and Welch 2012; Wang et al. 2011.

28. I could not find information on admission rates for Chinese applicants to top American universities.

29. Gao 2014; Horwitz 2016; Lai 2012.

30. This information is from emails forwarded and shared by faculty at American universities.

31. DK International Education 2013.

32. China Education Online 2014b; College Board 2013.

33. Information was acquired online and from a book about the school's history. I avoided citing these materials to protect the identity of the school.

34. Almost all of the schools in this study were heavily involved in the Red Guard movement during the Cultural Revolution.

35. Very few pursue both at the same time, and even the wealthiest top performers are forced to choose one route. An exception in this study was Tracy, a high performer in Capital who made the decision only in eleventh grade.

36. One exception is Highland, which did not have an international department at the time of this study.

37. In exam-based selection, children's test scores are positively associated with family socioeconomic status. This result holds true for China, Brazil, Taiwan, and the United States (Guimarães and Sampaio 2013; Roksa and Potter 2011; Liu et al. 2005; Ye 2015).

38. Elites in Beijing are not the wealthiest in the nation, but they are known to be powerful in the country. They also have significant amounts of "gray income" that is unreported and untaxed (Wang and Woo 2011).

39. The People's Liberation Army (PLA) is traditionally seen as a powerful political group in China (Jencks 1982). Although the PLA has seen a substantial reduction in its political influence, it nonetheless remains an important political player (Kiselycznyk and Saunders 2010). During my observations, the military backing seemed to influence the school's compliance with the Beijing government. Capital has a reputation of "doing what it wants" regardless of educational policy and is a trailblazer in educational pedagogy. Pinnacle's principal is known to ignore the government's demands. For example, in 2013 the school insisted on naming a corrupt official as a prominent alumnus despite a government investigation and later conviction.

40. To curtail the number of students going abroad, the Beijing government relocated Pinnacle's international department to the outskirts of the city within two years after I exited the school.

41. A *bianzhong* is an ancient Chinese musical instrument that consists of a set of bronze bells. Most examples are on display in historical museums.

42. The perception that parents were unhelpful in Chinese classrooms contrasted with American classrooms, where affluent parents were welcomed and involved in children's college applications (Lareau 2015; McDonough 1997; Weis et al. 2014).

43. The parental norm of following the teacher is likely practiced throughout the country, as scholars suggest that the Confucian cultural heritage prompts parents to highly respect schools and teachers (Lam et al. 2002; Littrell 2005). In this cultural system, parental deference to teachers is expected and normal.

44. Bradsher 2013; Chiang and Lareau 2018; Fong 2004; Heeter 2008; Kipnis 2011.

45. Zhou 2005.

46. Beijing and Shanghai were the last two places that adopted the submission-through-guessing system (猜分填报志愿 *caifen tianbao zhiyuan*). This system was abolished in Beijing in 2015, after which Beijing students could submit their college choices after the gaokao. The same change took place in Shanghai in 2017.

47. As if college choices weren't already complicated enough, students must also simultaneously submit their choice of majors (up to five for each university).

48. I adopted these questions from a scholar who had interviewed students in top high schools in Taiwan. The fact that the same question was feasible for another group of top students in East Asia but bizarre for the best students in this study points to the importance of context when designing interview questions.

49. Another difference was that students in the tenth and eleventh grades did not have night study periods. School atmospheres in domestic departments were increasingly tense as the gaokao drew near.

50. Pinnacle scheduled an extended break of twenty-five minutes every afternoon for flag-raising ceremonies, martial arts practice, or other announcements depending on the day of the week.

51. Byun and Park (2012) show that, in Korea, affluent students often attend shadow education to prepare for their exam. However, few students in this study participated in shadow education, likely because the students spent very little time outside of school and were generally high-performing.

52. *People's Daily* 2016; *Sina* 2016.

53. Students focused on test scores before taking the SAT. Teachers often gave vague information about the classroom's aggregate performance, but sometimes showed students' detailed test results in classrooms. These instances never failed to grab student attention, to the point where students who had walked out of the classroom quickly returned to the room for more information. The ultimate form of competition in test scores, however, was the SAT.

54. Stevens 2007.

55. Student tuition for the international departments was between 90,000 and 100,000 RMB each year. By comparison, the domestic departments charged 700 RMB.

56. The numbers listed here are taken from cram school websites, student reports, and parental estimations. The exact amounts vary depending on student participation and choice of cram school or private tutoring.

57. While the schools I visited disapproved of this common practice, each had varying degrees of compromise. Capital and Pinnacle allowed students to hire agents and counselors but insisted that the students prepare application materials themselves. In practice, teachers admitted that they had control over only student transcripts and letters. Central's refusal to compromise led to conflict between the elite parents and school: some parents who were not in this study were so upset with the iron-fisted principal that they filed complaints with the city government asking that he be removed.

58. ECE stands for Educational Credential Evaluators; the organization prepares evaluation reports that translate foreign student achievements into U.S. standards.

59. Larmer 2014.

Chapter 2: Taking One's Place

1. These status markers are prominently featured in studies in American and other Western high schools. See, for example, Khan (2011) and Gaztambide-Fernández (2009).

2. Bourdieu (1976) used the card game analogy to explain marriage choice and status reproduction. I apply this analogy to examine status in high school.

3. The cutoff scores vary by year based on the difficulty of the gaokao and depending on whether students take science or humanity majors. For example, the cutoff for Peking and Tsinghua was 691 (out of 750) in 2013 and 683 in 2014 for science majors. The respective cutoff scores for humanity majors were 654 and 663.

4. The range of SATs in top Chinese high schools is quite narrow—within 8 percent of U.S. standards. The highest reported was a girl at Omega who obtained a perfect SAT score. The "lowest of all time" at Capital was a boy who scored 1980 on the SATs (1400 in the new system, 92 percent in the United States).

5. See Milner (1994, 2015b).

6. Scholars suggest that ease is a form of cultural capital that reflects an embodied social experience derived from a privileged upbringing (Bourdieu 1986; Khan 2011). However, the Chinese students in this study were generally anxious about their test scores. In this context, ease was not a component of cultural capital.

7. Not all students belonged to one of the four status groups. Milner (2015b) calls these students the "crowd," who are detached from the students who have clear status in school. However, unlike the crowd, the students who did not identify with a status group in this study nonetheless defined their positions relative to different status groups.

8. This definition also meant that an underachiever in a top high school could be a study god in a lower-ranked high school. The underachievers I talked to knew that their status in school could have changed drastically if they had been in another school, but none considered transferring to a lower-ranked school. They prioritized the prestige of the high school in which they studied and argued that top high schools offered college preparations unmatched by other high schools. While many private schools also successfully send pupils to Western universities (Young 2018), the students' decisions suggested that they were willing to exchange low status in school for the prestige of the school. Because school prestige is also evaluated by academic prowess, the students assessed each school's status in similar ways as they judged each student's status in school.

9. Robert's score of 2050 put him at 95 percent that year. This score is equivalent to 1440 in the new scoring system.

10. These include most of the universities listed in Project 211, Project 985, and the Double First Class University Plan.

11. The status system seems to also be shared among other high schools in Beijing, albeit with minor differences in the number of students in each status group. In a pilot study, I conducted classroom observations in a public high school that was not top-performing. Students in that high school shared the same status system, but they generally agreed that there were no study gods and many losers in their school. The slang-like use of these terms on online student forums also suggests the commonality of the four status groups in the country in general. In casual conversation at conferences or workshops, scholars and PhD students who conducted

school ethnographies in China also told me that the students they studied shared a similar status system in the nonelite, rural, migrant, or low-performing high schools.

12. Study gods almost never applied for universities ranked below a certain cutoff, such as the top twenty or thirty in the *U.S. News* or other international rankings. This seemed to be customary, and many study gods listed other students' top choice as backups.

13. This change was partly facilitated by his mother, who had a strong hand in determining her son's activities in high school.

14. Studies show that students often obtain prestige from participating in antischool activities, such as the drug or gang culture of being violently intimidating (Decker et al. 1996; Sánchez-Jankowski 2016). Others observe students setting up subcultural criteria for status identity (MacLeod 2018).

15. Mark soon found himself outcompeted at UBC. He reported that he worked much harder than he had in high school, to the point where he occasionally spent the entire night in the lab as an undergraduate student. His hard work eventually paid off. On social media he flaunted an A on his transcript in his senior year.

16. See, for example, Blau and Duncan 1967; Buchmann and Hannum 2001; Kao and Thompson 2003; and Shavit and Blossfeld 1993.

17. The CCP presents meritocracy as a general guideline and invokes this notion to legitimize its governance (Bell 2016; Gore 2019).

18. Herrnstein and Murray's *The Bell Curve* (1994) sparked debate with its argument that intelligence, which the authors saw as inherited, determined class status. While some scholars support this argument (Damian et al. 2015), a number of researchers oppose the innate ability argument by presenting evidence that socioeconomic background influences measured intelligence and that social inequality better explains differences in individual outcomes (Fischer et al. 1996; Kincheloe et al. 1997). The latter is the dominant view in American sociology and is shared by elite students in the United States (Gaztambide-Fernández 2009; Khan 2011). This line of research also influenced studies that argue for emphasizing individual effort, diligence, and hard work as the primary means to determine status outcomes (Arum and Roksa 2011).

19. Students agreed with the genetic explanation, although girls were gentler than boys in explaining why certain students had loser status. Boys typically used terms such as "problem with their brains," "low IQ," "pathetic," or "stupid." Girls chose their words more carefully, such as referring to the losers as being psychological "disturbed" or "ill-fated."

20. Overall, most of the study gods and studyholics in high school were no longer top performers in college. The exceptions in this study were Xijun, Yulang, and Shiying. The three girls were the top students in their respective universities.

21. This shift in the rules of the status game is likely part of urban discrimination against rural residents. When the urban elite found themselves losing the competition, they turned the rules into ones that favored them and no longer assigned high status to those who qualified for high status in the original rules. The elite students' ability to change the rules runs parallel to how elite higher-education institutions in the United States changed admission criteria when Jewish students obtained higher test scores than white elite students (Karabel 2005).

22. It is possible that Lili was tense because she was around high school friends or because she had just moved to a new country. However, others students, including Shuhua and Xiangzu, shared similar reactions upon leaving their college campus. Taken together, these examples

suggest that college in China was a curious time when the elite students switched the significance levels of the criteria that governed status hierarchy on campus.

23. The American students most likely did not agree with the same standards as the Chinese students. In fact, research shows that American college students have a different set of rules that determine status (see, for example, Armstrong and Hamilton 2013). One reason why these Chinese students perceived a similar type of hierarchy was that their social network primarily consisted of peers from China. It is possible that the hierarchy they described exists only within their ethnic enclave. However, they nonetheless used it to ascribe status to schoolmates who were not playing by the same rules. The differences in determinants of status between American and Chinese students are, perhaps, a factor that contributes to racial and ethnic segregation on college campuses.

Chapter 3: Worshipping the Gods

1. There are, certainly, many types of elites in society, and not all are elite by virtue of income or wealth (Chao 2013; Milner 2015a). The students in this study are defined as elite based on their parents' socioeconomic status. Mingjia's money analogy perhaps reflects the focus of attention among the adolescent socioeconomic elite.

2. See Eckert 1989; Gaztambide-Fernández 2009.

3. Pinnacle has over one thousand students, Highland and Central over two thousand, and Capital and Omega over four thousand. Some schools such as Pinnacle have a separate faculty cafeteria. Not all students dine at the student cafeteria, but the sheer numbers of students and teachers pouring in during meal time turned the cafeteria into a market during my many visits.

4. The prevalence of cross-status friendship patterns is likely one reason for students to refrain from naming losers in school.

5. The story is unconfirmed by Claire.

6. Bourdieu (1984) finds that members of the high status group often uphold status boundaries by excluding others from their own group. However, in the high schools I visited, social associations had very little status consequence, and status distinction was not an exclusionary practice. These examples suggest that social exclusion, which scholars perceive as crucial to status distinction in Western societies, is largely irrelevant to status outcomes in the Chinese high school context.

7. Parents shape school choices from kindergarten to college not just in China but also in the United States (Chiang 2018; Lareau et al. 2016; McDonough 1997; Wu 2013).

8. In fact, Claire expressed that a proportion of students, especially those who had poor grades and who showed off their wealth in school, were not friends with her. She reported nervously in an interview, "I'm treading dangerous waters here. But there are some who, in quality, including values, just clash with you. They clearly don't belong to the same circle as you." One example was a low performer who spent about $500 to "treat a dozen guys in our class to dinner just because he felt like it."

9. Grazian (2008) provides an example of students taking part in and celebrating each other's achievement using the case of hookups among American university students. While the ideas are similar, there is some difference between celebrating a friend's academic achievement

and congratulating a friend who got laid. One difference is that the students in this study often draw on a comparison group to highlight the individual's achievement. Another is the sense of awe given to the high achiever, which the participants in Grazian's study did not express.

10. Xijun's distance from others might be related to how she rose to stardom at Pinnacle. Xijun spent the first two years of high school working on art projects. Because these activities took time away from her exam preparation, she had low status in school and largely kept to herself. In interviews, she claimed that Pinnacle students "focused on academic achievement and were uninterested in what I do." While this understanding aligns with the rules of the status system, in which artistic talent receives no credit, landing at the top of the art school exam (in the format of multiple-choice questions on undesignated subjects) counted toward exam success. Xijun's status immediately accelerated to near the top at Pinnacle when she became the top student on a national exam.

11. This appears quite common among the high-status students. In addition to Xijun, students reported that Yulang, Jun, and Tony were loners as well.

12. The average social distance between a person and an acquaintance is less than three feet in China (Sorokowska et al. 2017). Xijun's five-foot distance is much further than the average and is beyond the confidence interval in Sorokowska et al.'s study.

13. Julie later enrolled in Bryn Mawr College with an SAT score of 2170 (equivalent to 1500 in the new system, 98th percentile by American standards). She was satisfied with her SAT score and saw no need to retake the test because her score was already high on her first attempt. However, other high performers who took the SATs multiple times in twelfth grade later achieved higher combined scores. As a result, Julie's SAT score was ranked as above average at Central. Julie was upset with her admissions outcome. In our follow-up interview, she said that her only regret in high school was that she should have studied "a bit more" for the SAT. In 2019, Julie reported to have learned from this mistake and adopted an opposite approach when taking the GRE. She studied full-time for the test and booked it twice beforehand. She received an almost perfect score on her first try and did not take it again.

14. The American college admissions system emphasizes students' well roundedness (Armstrong and Hamilton 2013; Gaztambide-Fernández 2009; Karabel 2005). Yet the fact that Brandon's extracurricular talents combined were less rewarded than Claire's academic ability raises questions about the criteria admission officers use to evaluate Chinese applicants. Whether and to what extent American universities select foreign students by their standardized exam scores remain in need of examination.

15. Serving on the student council is one of the important leadership opportunities in Chinese high schools. Each school has a set of unique rules for appointing students to these positions, but the members are typically high performers in school. Jiaqi, an underachiever, complained that he had "good administrative ability" but was denied leadership or service opportunities because "students tend to trust those who rank higher" on test scores. In general, students share a consensus that low performers do not occupy leadership positions.

16. I suspect that Ruolun joined the council through teacher sponsorship. Another possibility is that he was high-performing before or during eleventh grade, when he was chosen to join.

17. By the end of my fieldwork, I had come to adopt the elite students' interaction patterns and perspective on status hierarchies. It took me about a year after leaving the field to fully readjust to the nonelite standards of test scores and university placements. I discuss my immersion in the field and my reflections in the methodological appendix.

18. These tasks were sometimes difficult to achieve. For example, one cohort wanted to "go big" for the school anniversary. The student council was charged with this task. They obtained school consent and funding and rented a pirate ship (a swing boat about fifty to sixty feet tall) and other amusement rides on the sports field during the daylong event.

19. I asked Tracy, a studyholic, if things would have changed had Kevin gotten a full score on the SAT. Tracy replied immediately, "We'd still think he's a weirdo, but we might admire him. If he got full score on the SAT, it would feel like he shines when we see him." This suggests that, like the case of Kangwei, Kevin's primary fault was being low performing.

20. Just as affluent parents send children to extracurricular training from the time they are young (Lan 2018; Lareau 2011; Levey-Friedman 2013), many of the elite students in this study received early training in sports, arts, or music. For example, Shiying took piano starting in childhood, Shuhua did sports, Brandon played the violin, and Wanru was a gymnast. However, none of these students continued to participate in extracurricular training in high school.

21. Jina was simultaneously a graduate student, model, and e-sports streamer. However, while she was a media celebrity in China, her high school schoolmates knew about her accomplishments by following Dapeng.

22. I visited and conducted follow-up interviews with twenty-six of the twenty-eight students in college. I visited twenty-one students in 2018–19, after they graduated from college. My travel plans to visit the remaining seven were canceled due to the COVID-19 pandemic in 2020. I obtained information on their whereabouts through social media and text exchanges.

23. Interestingly, none of the elite students mentioned language difficulty or communication issues as barriers to cultivating cross-national friendships. In fact, except for the few who finished college in China had thicker accents, all the students I visited spoke fluent English. Some even were adept at using American slang.

24. Tony's birthday party struck him as de facto racial segregation. He reasoned that racial segregation was inevitable: "I didn't speak Spanish. I didn't want to get drunk, which is what the Americans were doing. I'm more comfortable playing card games with friends."

25. The price was retrieved from an online website and would be higher at a local dealer in Beijing.

26. Some studies show that professionals have low confidence in their work performance (Hirooka et al. 2014) or that professionals may be overconfident in what they do (Torngren and Montgomery 2004).

Chapter 4: Hanging Teachers on the Blackboard

1. Both the quota and schools that are given this opportunity change each year.

2. Unlike Mrs. Mao, Mr. Hu had never been "hung on the blackboard." It is also likely that he was an exception in welcoming this treatment because his students were a selected group of top performers. As the homeroom teacher of the top class at Pinnacle, over half of his students attended Peking or Tsinghua when the overall acceptance rate in Beijing was about 1 percent and, at Pinnacle, about 25 percent.

3. Liuxue (2014) provides an estimate of the total number of Chinese freshmen in top American universities.

4. Stevens (2007, 74) uses the term "have a thing going" to describe such a relationship between universities and their feeder high schools.

5. When I shadowed Lili two weeks before the gaokao, at least three teachers asked me to provide emotional support by being her companion. They hoped she would perform as expected and get into Peking University. I am almost certain that encouraging the students, especially the high performers, was one of the reasons why teachers allowed me to roam around twelfth-grade classrooms at a time when student anxiety was at its zenith.

6. A few parents also shared a similar understanding. Mrs. Xu, the mother of Jiaqi (an underachiever), reported two weeks before the gaokao that "teachers don't care about my son at all right now. He's not going to go to a top university. Why would they want to spend time on him?"

7. Xue and Wang (2016) provide information about this policy and analyze the effect of this practice in middle schools in two provinces in China. Woessmann (2011) analyzes performance-related pay and PISA test scores in twenty-eight countries. Both studies conclude that teachers' performance-related pay is positively related to student achievement. Xue and Wang further show that the increase in student test scores is greater if bonuses are administered at the school level and not by a higher-level institution. In this study, teacher bonuses were managed by the schools themselves.

8. In China, gift giving is considered a normative and primary tool of building business relationships (guanxi) and of exhibiting interpersonal strength in government sectors. The practice is so common in government and business dealings that it has become associated with corruption and bribery (Qian et al. 2007; Steidlmeier 1999; Yang and Paladino 2015). In other words, gift giving is a useful skill for students who plan to enter the business or government sectors in Chinese societies.

9. The students in this study have high purchasing power. Elizabeth Arden skincare products and Apple watches are popular birthday gifts. Gifts for teachers are elaborate and purchased by parents who are more than willing to invest in their children's education by building relationships with their teachers.

10. Many Chinese give apples for Christmas. The reason, as Shiying's mother explained, was that apples (pinguo) and Christmas Eve (pinganye) share a single rhyme (pin).

11. The students (and their parents) with instrumental motivations often hoped that teachers would grant them favors such as taking time to explain exam-related mistakes, paying special attention to them during class, and encouraging them when they failed a test.

12. Trash talking means speaking ill of a person, such as saying they know nothing or are useless.

13. See Collins (2004) for more discussion of interpersonal interactions in daily conversation.

14. Calarco (2011) offers examples from American elementary schools about class-based differences in the amount of help that children receive from teachers. In this study, however, because all students come from comparably elite backgrounds, the main driving factor seems to be test scores, which are predictors of university placements and tied to teachers' income.

15. Although 2150 represents the 97th percentile in the United States, it was average at Capital. This score translates to 1490 in the new SAT scoring system.

16. See, for example, Calarco 2011.

17. I am inclined to believe that the complaint was voiced partly due to my presence. Since the student (Jiaqi) was close with me, he likely felt more comfortable bringing up the unfair treatment to his homeroom teacher.

18. Mr. Long added the title (*tongxue*) to Yulang's full name, which can be loosely translated as "Miss Yulang." This is the only incident in which I heard a teacher refer to a student in this way. The tone that "Miss Yulang" evokes is comparable to that of a teacher calling a female student "that young lady."

19. Dapeng is now married and a consultant at the Chinese branch of one of the world's largest firms. Although he did not participate in the follow-up study, he frequently updates his social network profile with pictures of his travels around the world. His classmates estimated that his income is well above the top 5 percent in the country.

20. Studies show that initial salary and career position predict future career status and lifetime income. Blau and Duncan (1967) theorized that one's first job is directly related to one's future occupation. Oyer (2008) found that an initial position on Wall Street is highly predictive of a future Wall Street career.

Chapter 5: Grooming the New Elites

1. Cameron et al. 2013; Sun 1987.

2. Some parents do not tolerate their children's petulant behavior and instead focus on their academic outcomes during adolescence, especially when applying for college (Bin 1996; Liu et al. 2010; Mõttus et al. 2008; Zhang et al. 2001). Teenagers also complain about the high degree of parental control when preparing for the gaokao (Chen 1994). Students' suicide attempts and ideations also substantially increase at age eighteen, when students are in their last year of high school and face maximum levels of academic stress (Liu et al. 2005).

3. Information retrieved from the school website. The website additionally shows that a quarter are accepted to universities ranked in the top ten and half go to those in the top thirty. The website also provides a link to a document that lists the number of student admissions by university ranking, including many at the University of Chicago, Duke, Brown, Cornell, Rice, and so on.

4. The commonly reported parenting efforts in this study resemble what the media refer to as parents' "slavery" approach, which portrays family life as child-centered and requiring high degrees of sacrifice by the parents (Clark 2008; Xue 2015). However, this stereotype does not capture the nuances among similarly elite families, which I show in this chapter.

5. This is similar to findings on middle-class families in the United States (Lareau and Goyette 2014; Lareau et al. 2016). However, there are noticeable differences within similar patterns of parental effort. For example, both American and Chinese families make residential decisions in hopes of boosting their children's educational outcomes. However, where to raise the family is seen as a onetime decision that takes place early on in the United States, oftentimes before children begin kindergarten. Chinese parents do the same, but as I show in this chapter, families continue to move until as late as twelfth grade.

6. Affluent and middle-class parents around the world consciously direct and influence their children's emotions (Calarco 2018; Chin 2000; Ellis et al. 2014; Ramsden and Hubbard 2002). Parents' emotional coaching shapes children's educational outcomes as well as their aggressive behavior and how they cope with adverse family events.

7. Shiying, however, presented an exceptional case. She not only enjoyed financial freedom, like the other students, but also was entitled to pursue activities of her choice with no parental

supervision. During the four days I stayed with Shiying, the mother never examined what was in Shiying's book bag. Instead of studying at home, she sometimes sat in the living room and watched an hour of variety shows. Shiying did not need to report what she did at school to her parents, and her parents did not ask about her daily whereabouts. Once, during night study, she spent an hour reading news about a singer on the computer at the back of the classroom. Shiying's mother allowed her to engage in activities unrelated to gaokao preparation and even occasionally joined her in watching TV. Comparisons with other students suggest that such a high degree of freedom at home was reserved for the top performers.

8. Students in China often referred to cousins as their siblings. Shiying, for example, also called her cousin as her "sister." However, Huating was the only student in this study who had a biological sibling. Her elder sister was adopted by relatives at a young age and is officially her cousin. This family arrangement was not a secret, and the sisters grew up together.

9. The content of assistance varied, ranging from keeping track of admission progress and filling out application forms to writing application essays for the applicant. None of the elite students in this study hired agents to be their ghost writers because they believed that their English ability was far better than the agents'. However, most students requested that parents hire agents to streamline the admission process.

10. Parents would, understandably, disagree over whether to support Mr. Wu's decision against hiring an agent. Some might consider raising independent children as the most important goal; others might think the possibility of not getting accepted to college to be too great of a risk. Except for Mr. Wu, none of the parents I interviewed ever doubted their decision to hire an application agent. Many of the elite parents in this study, however, considered "filling out application forms" a simple task that required neither training nor practice. Whether the child accepted the agent's assistance, of course, was a different story.

11. Brandon's peers of high and low status also filed graduate school, internship, and job applications by themselves. Whether they made any simple mistake upon their first try, however, was unclear.

12. Parent-child relationships vary as children age. While parents might have increased or comparable levels of involvement from early childhood to early adolescence (Dearing et al. 2006), the format of parental involvement changes and its intensity often declines after children enter college (Hamilton 2016; Lareau 2011). Simultaneously, children in early adulthood are less emotionally close with their parents than at earlier ages (Harris et al. 1998).

13. Coleman's (1988) classic study points to the importance of closed parental networks. Scholars debate whether parental network closure has a positive or negative effect on students' educational outcomes (see Morgan and Sørensen 1999). I do not assess the relationship between parental network closure and college enrollment outcomes, nor do I make causal arguments about parental involvement and children's outcomes.

14. While they might have also exchanged information on parenting approaches, I did not observe them comparing or discussing family interactions on campus grounds. Only once, and during a home visit, did a study god's mother mention that another parent was "terminally ill," which was why "the daughter was extremely independent."

15. The only exception was Tracy's father, who completed the same tasks as many other parents but considered himself to be heavily involved in Tracy's applications.

16. An exception was Selena, who expressed gratitude over parents' willingness to pay for three years of tuition for the international department at Capital and four years of tuition for

an Ivy League university. Selena was so thankful to her parents that she decided not to have a celebration when she received Penn's admission offer, choosing to "save the money for tuition." However, like other students, Selena did not mention her parents providing a college-focused environment, utilizing their networks, or other nonmonetary forms of assistance.

17. At least two other young women who studied at universities on the East Coast reported having the same health issue during their freshman year. Julie was the only one who went on leave, and all had recovered a year later.

Chapter 6: Saving the Day

1. Studies show that parent-child communication is positively related to student academic achievements across countries (Park 2008).

2. Armstrong and Hamilton 2013; Lareau 2011; McDonough 1997.

3. His response in Mandarin was "Zhege naocan zhidao zheshi sheme wenti. Bushi, zhege" (这个脑残知道这是什么问题。不是，这个).

4. Chris was an American counselor who specialized in sending students to American universities. Yet perhaps due to his accent or mannerisms, his advisees firmly believed that he was British and "specialized in sending students to British universities."

5. Alex submitted a whopping twenty-two at least. It was common for students in this study to apply to more than ten universities, but more than twenty was unusual.

6. The mother's own word choice was ED (early decision). Since students are allowed to apply ED to one university, she likely made a verbal mistake.

7. Cookson and Persell 1985; Gaztambide-Fernández 2009; Khan 2011.

8. A score of 2320 is equivalent to 1,570 in the new system and the 99.67th percentile in the United States.

9. The mother's behavior became similar to that of American parents whom scholars have observed (Lareau and Horvat 1999).

10. It was unclear whether Mrs. Liu's efforts had a direct effect on Shiying's subsequent performance, and neither could the mother's efforts be translated into test scores.

11. This type of contingency planning is likely to be observed among families in Beijing and Shanghai, the two cities that adopted the "submission through guessing" system up to 2017. After the system was repealed, elite families no longer needed to prepare for contingencies by carefully planning their children's college list. Despite this change, I expect that families will continue to make backup plans in other parts of the college preparation process.

12. I kept Jianmin in the sample for multiple reasons. Although his family income was less than the top 10 percent in China, the family owned assets in Beijing. Another reason was that mothers were typically the main caregivers. Since his mother was college educated, she was able to help Jianmin in the application process. Finally, Jianmin had exceptionally elite grandparents who were college graduates. From a multigenerational perspective, his grandparents could compensate for his father's relatively low education (Jæger 2012; Zeng and Xie 2014).

13. Chiang and Park (2015) suggest that downward mobility in the parent generation, especially from educated elites, is likely related to intergenerational conflict. The example of Jianmin partially affirms this hypothesis. In the interview, she pointed to conflict between the grandparent and parent generations: "Getting into college was extremely difficult those years," but she

nonetheless dropped out "as an act of rebellion against my parents, who were college educated."

14. Armstrong and Hamilton (2013) mention the importance of having a New York City address for occupational attainment there.

15. The family's plans materialized. In 2021, Wenbin announced on social media that he was admitted to a PhD program at Brown University.

16. Jianmin did not offer details about the offered position in Beijing. Considering his family background, it might be something comparable to a position in a state-owned enterprise, which would put him in the middle or upper-middle class in the country.

17. Fong (2011) and Ma (2020) discuss the importance of going abroad as a status booster among Chinese students across socioeconomic strata.

Conclusion

1. Coleman 1961; Milner 2015b.

2. Cameron et al. 2013; Fong 2004, 2011; Sun 1987; Xue 2015.

3. Bin 1996; Chen 1994; Liu et al. 2010; Kipnis 2011; Ma 2020; Mõttus et al. 2008; Zhang et al. 2001.

4. Brooks and Waters 2009.

5. Chan and Boliver 2013; Chiang and Park 2015; Erola and Moisio 2007; Song and Mare 2019.

6. Shavit and Blossfeld 1993.

7. Khan 2011.

8. Wilson and Roscigno 2016.

9. Galak et al. 2016; Gommans et al. 2017; Haun and Tomasello 2011.

10. Bourdieu 1984; Caspi and Roberts 2001; Konty and Dunham 1997.

11. Congressional Research Service 2020; OECD 2020.

12. The other was Xijun, whose story is described in earlier chapters.

13. Armstrong and Hamilton 2013; Kim et al. 2015.

14. These experiences are not unique to elite international students. Studies show that friendship patterns are racially distinct (McCabe 2016), and Asian international students in general experience racial segregation on campus (Arcidiacono et al. 2013; Kwon et al. 2019).

15. Kwon et al. 2019; Rose-Redwood and Rose-Redwood 2013.

16. Li and Nicholson 2021.

17. Stacey graduated from Harvard Business School in 2021. She reported not being able to find a position that hired Chinese nationals despite her impeccable credentials. She did not see this outcome as related to structural racism, but her saying that "it was hard for Chinese internationals to find a job" suggests otherwise. She joined Tracy and Sarah in Hong Kong and likely gave up on her plan to work on Wall Street.

18. Chin 2020; Zhou and Lee 2017.

19. Huang 2021; Oguntoyinbo 2014; Yu 2020.

20. Such a categorization of higher education selection systems of course represents ideal types.

21. Ho 1962.

22. Chaffee 1985; Collins 1998.

23. Walder 2012; Walder and Hu 2009.

24. Walder 2012; Yang 2016.

25. Campbell 2020; Ho 1962; Liang et al. 2013.

26. Jiang 2007; Liang et al. 2013; Liu 2011; Zheng 2007.

27. This is perhaps one reason that education reforms have taken place regularly in China. Also see Yang (2012) for further discussion.

28. Chiang 2018.

29. In earlier times, the United States started with a historical model of colleges and lower schools, initially with strict discipline and a narrow religious and classical curriculum.

30. Baltzell 1987; Scott 1965a, 1965b.

31. Goldin and Katz 1999.

32. Karabel 2005.

33. Jencks and Riesman 2017; Riesman and Jencks 1962.

34. Orfield and Hillman 2018.

35. Further analysis is needed, but it seems that both countries tend to use the school system to counterbalance undesired tendencies of their society: communist leveling on one hand, capitalist widening of the social hierarchy on the other.

36. Garcia and Pearson 1991; Gardner 1993; Resnick and Hall 1998; Taylor 1994. For criticism toward the American system, see Baker et al. 1993; Burger and Burger 1994; Linn and Baker 1996; Stecher and Klein 1997.

37. Bransford et al. 1999; Supovitz and Brennan 1997.

38. Ramirez et al. (2018) show that the United States is moving toward greater conformity with other countries, but the slight resurgence of interest in high-stakes testing in the country at the time of the study in fact goes against the global trend of decreased (or similar degrees of) reliance on high-stakes tests.

39. Alon and Tienda 2007; Buchmann et al. 2010; Demerath 2009; Milner 2015b; Radford 2013; Stevens 2007.

40. Stevens's (2007) finding of the importance of test scores comes from his ethnography of a selective college.

41. The number of institutions adopting a test-optional policy grew from around three dozen in the 1980s to about 10 percent of all universities in 2015 (Furuta 2017). The COVID-19 pandemic led to a significant expansion of this policy, with over half of the universities in the United States making SAT/ACT scores optional (FairTest 2020). In this study, Julie's college was one of the institutions that adopted this policy before the pandemic's outbreak. When the news broke, she (and her schoolmates) became pessimistic alumni who were highly concerned about the future ranking and "quality" of their alma mater.

42. Cookson and Persell 1985.

43. Coleman 1961; Milner 2015b.

44. Scholars have shown that American teenagers recognize the importance of test scores and grades. But they do not equate test scores with status and thus remain less focused on test scores than the elite Chinese students in this study (Demerath 2009; Gaztambide-Fernández 2009; Milner 2015b).

45. Before senior year in high school, all of the students in this study participated in various nonacademic activities before high school. Shiying played the piano, Brandon played violin, and Joe played in a band that released its own album. Jiaqi had frequent exposure to the Spanish

language, Jina was a model, and Wanru was an aspiring gymnast. However, except for Xijun, who made a career out of her cinematic ability (and the fact that her father was in the media business), these talents went unacknowledged in the school system. The significant risks and comparatively few benefits associated with extracurricular achievements accounted for many families' decisions to forgo extracurricular activities altogether.

46. Rivera (2015) finds that, in the United States, top firms and corporations take applicants' personal extracurricular participation into consideration when making offers. Some companies, for example, prefer applicants who share a taste in classical music. These opportunities may be closed to Chinese students who have become rusty in their skills.

47. Lareau 2011; Levey-Friedman 2013.

48. Stevens 2007.

49. Card 2017; Mare 2012.

50. Tan 2017.

51. PISA tested Chinese students in Beijing, Shanghai, Jiangsu, and Guangdong in 2015. These Chinese respondents ranked much lower than the Shanghai students did in 2012. However, they remained at the average OECD level (OECD 2014, 2017).

52. European Commission 2019.

53. Jiménez and Horowitz 2013.

54. Furuta et al. 2016.

55. In Britain, Sir Godfrey Thomson started the Moray House Test, a single test used to sort eleven-year-old children into educational programs, in 1947 (Sharp 1997).

56. Buchmann et al. 2010; Byun and Kim 2010; Jencks and Phillips 1998; Ye 2015.

57. Li et al. 2013; Saez and Zucman 2016; Xie and Zhou 2014; Xie 2016.

58. Ye 2015; Yeung 2013.

59. Nonelite families do not share the same amount or type of resources and do not engage in identical types of parenting (Chen et al. 2010; Horvat et al. 2003; Lareau 2000). Additionally, considering the costs associated with sending children to Western universities, nonelite families are unlikely to pursue this route as a backup for gaokao failure.

60. Caspi and Roberts 2001; Konty and Dunham 1997.

61. Ferdinand and Verhulst 1995; Fite et al. 2010; Lubinski et al. 1996; McAdams and Olson 2010; Waterman 1982.

62. Source: https://www.youtube.com/watch?v=giM2uTH6LP8&ab_channel=%E6%88%91%E4%B8%AD%E6%96%87%E4%B8%8D%E5%A5%BD.

63. Students who have low academic performance are found to adjust their educational goals (Clark 1960; MacLeod 2018). Elite students are not immune to such a mechanism, although they enjoy ample resources that sustain them until later stages of schooling.

64. Khan 2011; Sherman 2017.

Appendix A: Who Are the Elite?

1. Domhoff 1967; Giddens 1972; Mills 1956.

2. Cao 2004; Chambliss 1989; Nilizadeh et al. 2016; Westerman et al. 2012.

3. Page et al. 2013; Sherman 2017.

4. Armstrong and Hamilton 2013; Khan 2011; Rivera 2015.

5. Radford 2013.

6. Gaztambide-Fernández 2009; Khan 2011.

7. Nee 1991; Walder et al. 2000.

8. Chen 2006.

9. Fan 2002.

10. Cao and Suttmeier 2001; Ho 1962; Li and Walder 2001; Weber 1958.

11. Kipnis 2011.

12. Examples include the 985 Project (1998), Project 211 (1995), and the Double First Class Project (2015).

13. Yeung 2013.

14. Wang and Woo 2011.

15. About half of the Chinese population is made up of rural residents. Being in the top 10 percent in urban areas can be roughly translated to being in the top 5 percent in China. It should be noted that my calculation is conservative. The participants in this study were from families of three in official records. I calculated the amount for a family of three by multiplying the per-person income of urban residents by three, using data from the National Bureau of Statistics, China (2013).

16. On one occasion I interviewed a student at his house and left with the impression that the family did not seem affluent. When I brought up this question to the homeroom teacher (Mrs. Wang), she explained that she was certain that the student was elite based on his family records. Mrs. Wang said to me, "Don't be fooled by the family situation you saw." The apparent austerity I observed, which initially also surprised Mrs. Wang in her home visit, "was an intentional choice the parents made, so [the child] wouldn't grow up spoiled." I later confirmed the family's high income with the mother's report that they had considered sending the child to an American university as a full fee-paying student should he fail to get into his dream school in China.

17. All but one student had at least one parent who attended college.

18. Except for one family who has resided in Beijing for over three generations, all others became Beijing citizens through job acquisition, which the parents attributed to their stellar educational performance and top university attainment.

Appendix B: Methodological Reflections

1. Having limited access to selected schools unintentionally turned this study into an inductive one. I arrived in Beijing in 2012 hoping to study class differences in college choices. This plan took a turn when I had difficulty finding access to a lower-ranked school that admitted large numbers of working-class students. My attention gravitated toward status systems after prolonged exposure to students' status terminology. In fact, it was only after students repeatedly explained the status system that I realized its significance.

2. In Pinnacle, Mr. Hu claimed to have "randomly" selected six students who "represented a good variety of different types of high performers." Students suspected that Mr. Hu had put much thought into their selection. Explaining the friendship circles between the six as if it were a math function, Jianmin amusedly said, "Any two of us were good friends, but no three of us were good friends."

3. Two examples were Lili and Jiaqi. When Mr. Long took me to meet Lili, he casually commented, "Having a companion would encourage [Lili] and make her more confident about the gaokao."

4. The low performers, by comparison, often could not, would not, or even dared not help persuade hesitant parents.

5. When I was gathering information on extra points, I found a widely circulated list on student forums that contained students' names, schools, and extra points obtained for Peking and Tsinghua universities. On the list, I saw that Wenbin received forty extra points for the university he later attended. However, Wenbin had neglected to mention that he received extra points in our interview, likely because his exam score was so high that he did not need them. Since his classmates reported extra points that matched the information on the list, I added the forty points to his gaokao score.

6. This was particularly clear when I labeled selective universities as "undesirable" options, just as the elite Chinese student had done. When I talked about going to UCLA as a "disastrous" outcome, which is what the students had expressed, friends immediately corrected me, saying that "UCLA is a perfectly good school." In conference presentations, American colleagues similarly asked me to clarify why going to UCLA counted as an "unsuccessful" transition to top universities.

7. Liwa texted me and offered to wire cash into my account upon hearing that I been victimized by bank fraud. Fei took me by bike wherever I needed to go on campus when I hurt my foot. Shiying organized a group trip to a theme park upon hearing that I was interested in it but never had the chance to go.

8. Brandon still ensured I toured the city by organizing day trips wherever I visited him. Kaifeng still patiently answered all the questions I had, to the point of spelling out his company's name multiple times during our meal. I flew into Beijing late at night twice, and during these two visits Xiangzu and Xijun picked me up at the airport and took me to dinner at restaurants that were still open.

REFERENCES

Alon, Sigal, and Marta Tienda. 2007. "Diversity, Opportunity, and the Shifting Meritocracy in Higher Education." *American Sociological Review* 72(4): 487–511.

Alvaredo, Facundo, Lucas Chancel, Thomas Piketty, Emmanuel Saez, and Gabriel Zucman. 2018. *World Inequality Report 2018*. Cambridge, MA: Harvard University Press.

Arcidiacono, Peter, Esteban Aucejo, Andrew Hussey, and Kenneth Spenner. 2013. "Racial Segregation Patterns in Selective Universities." *Journal of Law and Economics* 56(4): 1039–60.

Armstrong, Elizabeth A., and Laura T. Hamilton. 2013. *Paying for the Party: How College Maintains Inequality*. Cambridge, MA: Harvard University Press.

Armstrong, Patrick Ian, and Gail Crombie. 2000. "Compromises in Adolescents' Occupational Aspirations and Expectations from Grades 8 to 10." *Journal of Vocational Behavior* 56(1): 82–98.

Arum, Richard, and Josipa Roksa. 2011. *Academically Adrift: Limited Learning on College Campuses*. Chicago: University of Chicago Press.

Bai, Limin. 2006. "Graduate Unemployment: Dilemmas and Challenges in China's Move to Mass Higher Education." *China Quarterly* 185(3): 128–44.

Baker, Eva L., Harold F. O'Neil, and Robert L. Linn. 1993. "Policy and Validity Prospects for Performance-Based Assessment." *American Psychologist* 48(12): 1210–18.

Baltzell, Edward Digby. 1987. *The Protestant Establishment: Aristocracy and Caste in America*. New Haven, CT: Yale University Press.

Bandura, Albert, Claudio Barbaranelli, Gian Vittorio Caprara, and Concetta Pastorelli. 2001. "Self-Efficacy Beliefs as Shapers of Children's Aspirations and Career Trajectories." *Child Development* 72(1): 187–206.

Bell, Daniel A. 2016. *The China Model: Political Meritocracy and the Limits of Democracy*. Princeton, NJ: Princeton University Press.

Bian, Yanjie. 2002. "Chinese Social Stratification and Social Mobility." *Annual Review of Sociology* 28(1): 91–116.

Bin, Zhao. 1996. "The Little Emperors' Small Screen: Parental Control and Children's Television Viewing in China." *Media, Culture & Society* 18(4): 639–58.

Blau, Peter M., and Otis Dudley Duncan. 1967. *The American Occupational Structure*. New York: John Wiley.

Bourdieu, Pierre. 1976. "Marriage Strategies as Strategies of Social Reproduction." In *Family and Society*, edited by Robert Forster and Orest Ranum, 117–44. Baltimore: Johns Hopkins University Press.

———. 1984. *Distinction: A Social Critique of the Judgement of Taste*. Cambridge, MA: Harvard University Press.

———. 1986. "The Forms of Capital." In *Handbook of Theory and Research for the Sociology of Education*, edited by John Richardson, 241–58. Westport, CT: Greenwood.

Bradsher, Keith. 2013. "In China, Families Bet It All on a Child in College." *New York Times*, February 16. https://www.nytimes.com/2013/02/17/business/in-china-families-bet-it-all-on-a-child-in-college.html.

Bransford, John D., Ann L. Brown, and Rodney R. Cocking. 1999. *How People Learn: Brain, Mind, Experience, and School*. Washington, DC: National Academy Press.

Brooks, David. 2000. *Bobos in Paradise: The New Upper Class and How They Got There*. New York: Simon & Schuster.

Brooks, Rachel, and Johanna L. Waters. 2009. "International Higher Education and the Mobility of UK Students." *Journal of Research in International Education* 8(2): 191–209.

———. 2011. *Student Mobilities, Migration and the Internationalization of Higher Education*. London: Palgrave Macmillan.

Buchmann, Claudia, Dennis J. Condron, and Vincent J. Roscigno. 2010. "Shadow Education, American Style: Test Preparation, the SAT and College Enrollment." *Social Forces* 89(2): 435–61.

Buchmann, Claudia, and Emily Hannum. 2001. "Education and Stratification in Developing Countries: A Review of Theories and Research." *Annual Review of Sociology* 27: 77–102.

Bureau of Consular Affairs. 2019. "Nonimmigrant Visas Issued by Classification." https://travel.state.gov/content/travel/en/legal/visa-law0/visa-statistics/nonimmigrant-visa-statistics.html.

Burger, Susan E., and Donald L. Burger. 1994. "Determining the Validity of Performance-Based Assessment." *Educational Measurement: Issues and Practice* 13(1): 9–15.

Byun, Soo-yong, and Kyung-keun Kim. 2010. "Educational Inequality in South Korea: The Widening Socioeconomic Gap in Student Achievement." In *Globalization, Changing Demographics, and Educational Challenges in East Asia*, edited by Emily Hannum, Hyunjoon Park, and Yuko Goto Butler, 155–82. Bingley: Emerald.

Byun, Soo-yong, and Hyunjoon Park. 2012. "The Academic Success of East Asian American Youth: The Role of Shadow Education." *Sociology of Education* 85(1): 40–60.

Calarco, Jessica McCrory. 2011. "'I Need Help!' Social Class and Children's Help-Seeking in Elementary School." *American Sociological Review* 76(6): 862–82.

———. 2014. "Coached for the Classroom: Parents' Cultural Transmission and Children's Reproduction of Educational Inequalities." *American Sociological Review* 79(5): 1015–37.

———. 2018. *Negotiating Opportunities: How the Middle Class Secures Advantages in School*. New York: Oxford University Press,

Cameron, Lisa, Nisvan Erkal, Lata Gangadharan, and Xin Meng. 2013. "Little Emperors: Behavioral Impacts of China's One-Child Policy." *Science* 339(6122): 953–57.

Campbell, Cameron. 2020. "The Influence of the Abolition of the Examinations at the End of the Qing on the Holders of Exam Degrees" (Qingmo Keju Tingfei dui Shiren Wenguan Qunti de Yingxiang: Jiyu Weiguan Dashuju de Hongguan Xin Shijiao). *Social Science Journal* 4(249): 156–66.

Cao, Cong. 2004. *China's Scientific Elite*. New York: Routledge.

Cao, Cong, and Richard P. Suttmeier. 2001. "China's New Scientific Elite: Distinguished Young Scientists, the Research Environment and Hopes for Chinese Science." *China Quarterly* 168: 960–84.

Card, David. 2017. "Amicus Curiae Report." Projects at Harvard, December 15. https://projects .iq.harvard.edu/files/diverse-education/files/expert_report_-_2017-12-15_dr._david _card_expert_report_updated_confid_desigs_redacted.pdf.

Caspi, Avshalom, and Brent W. Roberts. 2001. "Personality Development Across the Life Course: The Argument for Change and Continuity." *Psychological Inquiry* 12(2): 49–66.

Chaffee, John H. 1985. *The Thorny Gates of Learning in Sung China: A Social History of Examinations.* Cambridge: Cambridge University Press.

Chambliss, Daniel F. 1989. "The Mundanity of Excellence: An Ethnographic Report on Stratification and Olympic Swimmers." *Sociological Theory* 7(1): 70–86.

Chan, Tak Wing, and Vikki Boliver. 2013. "The Grandparents Effect in Social Mobility: Evidence from British Birth Cohort Studies." *American Sociological Review* 78(4): 662–78.

Chao, Grace. 2013. "Elite Status in the People's Republic of China: Its Formation and Maintenance." PhD dissertation, Columbia University.

Chen, B. 1994. "A Little Emperor: One-Child Family." *Integration* 39: 27.

Chen, Chih-Jou. 2006. "Elite Mobility in Post-Reform Rural China." *Issues and Studies* 42(2): 53–83.

Chen, Te-Ping. 2015. "China Curbs Elite Education Programs: Beijing Tries to Chill Western Influence and Close a Growing Gap in Inequality." *Wall Street Journal*, December 20. https:// www.wsj.com/articles/china-curbs-elite-education-programs-1450665387.

Chen, Xinyin, Yufang Bian, Tao Xin, Li Wang, and Rainer K. Silbereisen. 2010. "Perceived Social Change and Childrearing Attitudes in China." *European Psychologist* 15(4): 260–70.

Chhin, Christina S., Martha Bleeker, and Janis E. Jacobs. 2008. "Gender-Typed Occupational Choices: The Long-Term Impact of Parents' Beliefs and Expectations." In *Gender and Occupational Outcomes: Longitudinal Assessments of Individual, Social, and Cultural Influences,* edited by Helen M. G. Watt and Jacquelynne S. Eccles, 215–34. Worcester, MA: American Psychological Association.

Chiang, Yi-Lin. 2018. "When Things Don't Go as Planned: Contingencies, Cultural Capital, and Parental Involvement for Elite University Admission in China." *Comparative Education Review* 62(4): 503–21.

Chiang, Yi-Lin, and Annette Lareau. 2018. "Elite Education in China: Insights into the Transition to Higher Education." In *Elites in Education: Major Themes in Education.* Vol. 4: *Pathways to Elite Institutions and Professions,* edited by Agnes Van Zanten, 178–94. New York: Routledge.

Chiang, Yi-Lin, and Hyunjoon Park. 2015. "Do Grandparents Matter? A Multigenerational Perspective on Educational Attainment in Taiwan." *Social Science Research* 51: 163–73.

Childress, Herb. 2019. *The Adjunct Underclass: How America's Colleges Betrayed Their Faculty, Their Students, and Their Mission.* Chicago: University of Chicago Press.

Chin, Margaret M. 2020. *Stuck: Why Asian Americans Don't Reach the Top of the Corporate Ladder.* New York: New York University Press.

Chin, Tiffani. 2000. "'Sixth Grade Madness' Parental Emotion Work in the Private High School Application Process." *Journal of Contemporary Ethnography* 29(2): 124–63.

China Daily. 2014. "Expected Salary of Graduates Hits 4-Year Low." May 28. https://www .chinadaily.com.cn/china/2014-05/28/content_17547583.htm.

China Education Online. 2014a. "Income Ranking of College Graduates: List of the Graduates from 25 Top Paid Universities" (Daxue Biyesheng Gongzi Paiming: Zhongguo Xinchou

Zuigao De 25 Suo Daxue Pandian). http://career.eol.cn/kuai_xun_4343/20140928/t20140928_1181218.shtml.

———. 2014b. "2014 Study Abroad Report" (2014 Chuguo Liuxue Qushi Baogao). https://www.eol.cn/html/lx/2014baogao/.

———. 2017. "2016 Study Abroad Report" (2016 Chuguo Liuxue Fazhan Qushi Baogao). https://www.eol.cn/html/lx/report2016/mulu.shtml.

Clark, Burton R. 1960. "The 'Cooling-Out' Function in Higher Education." *American Journal of Sociology* 65(6): 569–76.

Clark, Gregory, and Neil Cummins. 2014. "Inequality and Social Mobility in the Industrial Revolution Era." In *Cambridge Economic History of Modern Britain*, edited by Roderick Floud, Jane Humphries, and Paul Johnson, 211–36. Cambridge: Cambridge University Press.

Clark, Taylor. 2008. "Plight of the Little Emperors." *Psychology Today*, July 1. https://www.psychologytoday.com/us/articles/200807/plight-the-little-emperors.

Coleman, James Samuel. 1961. *The Adolescent Society: The Social Life of the Teenager and Its Impact on Education.* New York: Free Press.

———. 1988. "Social Capital in the Creation of Human Capital." *American Journal of Sociology* 94: 95–120.

College Board. 2013. "The 2013 SAT Report on College & Career Readiness." https://secure-media.collegeboard.org/homeOrg/content/pdf/sat-report-college-career-readiness-2013.pdf.

Collins, Randall. 1979. *The Credential Society: An Historical Sociology of Education and Stratification.* New York: Columbia University Press.

———. 1998. "Technological Displacement and Capitalist Crises: Escapes and Dead Ends." In *The Sociology of Philosophies: A Global Theory of Intellectual Change.* Cambridge, MA: Harvard University Press.

———. 2004. *Interaction Ritual Chains.* Princeton, NJ: Princeton University Press.

Congressional Research Service. 2020. "COVID-19: U.S. Economic Effects." May 13. https://sgp.fas.org/crs/row/R46270.pdf.

Cookson, Peter W., Jr., and Caroline Hodges Persell. 1985. *Preparing for Power: America's Elite Boarding Schools.* New York: Basic Books.

Courtois, Aline. 2013. "Becoming Elite: Exclusion, Excellence, and Collective Identity in Ireland's Top Fee-Paying Schools." In *The Anthropology of Elites: Power, Culture, and the Complexities of Distinction*, edited by Jon Abbink and Tijo Salverda, 163–83. New York: Palgrave Macmillan.

Damian, Rodica Ioana, Rong Su, Michael J. Shanahan, Ulrich Trautwein, and Brent W. Roberts. 2015. "Can Personality Traits and Intelligence Compensate for Background Disadvantage? Predicting Status Attainment in Adulthood." *Journal of Personality and Social Psychology* 109(3): 473–89.

Davey, Gareth, Chuan De Lian, and Louise Higgins. 2007. "The University Entrance Examination System in China." *Journal of Further and Higher Education* 31(4): 385–96.

Davis, Bob, and Lingling Wei. 2019. "China's Plan for Tech Dominance is Advancing, Business Groups Say; Critical Report on 'Made in China 2025' Issued as U.S.-China Trade Talks Are Set to Resume Next Week." *Wall Street Journal*, January 22. https://www.wsj.com/articles/u-s-business-groups-weigh-in-on-chinas-technology-push-11548153001.

Dearing, Eric, Holly Kreider, Sandra Simpkins, and Heather B. Weiss. 2006. "Family Involvement in School and Low-Income Children's Literacy: Longitudinal Associations Between and Within Families." *Journal of Educational Psychology* 98(4): 653–64.

Decker, Steve, Scott H. Decker, and Barrik Van Winkle. 1996. *Life in the Gang: Family, Friends, and Violence.* Cambridge: Cambridge University Press.

Demerath, Peter. 2009. *Producing Success: The Culture of Personal Advancement in an American High School.* Chicago: University of Chicago Press.

Department of Education and Training, Australia. 2017. "International Student Data Monthly Summary." https://internationaleducation.gov.au/research/international-student-data/Pages/default.aspx.

DK International Education. 2013. "2013 China SAT Annual Analysis Report" (2013 Nian SAT Niandu Fenxi Baogao). https://wenku.baidu.com/view/60baeac46294dd88d0d26b9d.html.

Domhoff, G. William. 1967. *Who Rules America?* Englewood Cliff, NJ: Prentice Hall.

———. 2017. *Studying the Power Elite: Fifty Years of Who Rules America?* New York: Routledge.

Dworkin, Jodi B., Reed Larson, and David Hansen. 2003. "Adolescents' Accounts of Growth Experiences in Youth Activities." *Journal of Youth and Adolescence* 32(1): 17–26.

Eckert, Penelope. 1989. *Jocks and Burnouts: Social Categories and Identity in the High School.* New York: Teachers College Press.

Ellis, B. Heidi, Eva Alisic, Amy Reiss, Tom Dishion, and Philip A. Fisher. 2014. "Emotion Regulation among Preschoolers on a Continuum of Risk: The Role of Maternal Emotion Coaching." *Journal of Child and Family Studies* 23(6): 965–74.

Erola, Jani, and Pasi Moisio. 2007. "Social Mobility over Three Generations in Finland, 1950–2000." *European Sociological Review* 23(2): 169–83.

Er-Rafia, Fatima-Zohra. 2018. "How did China Become the World's Second Economic Power?" *Rising Powers in Global Governance*, September 17. https://risingpowersproject.com/how-did-china-become-the-worlds-second-economic-power/.

European Commission and HR/VP Contribution to the European Council. 2019. "Communication: EU-China—A Strategic Outlook." March 12. https://ec.europa.eu/info/publications/eu-china-strategic-outlook-commission-contribution-european-council-21-22-march-2019_en.

FairTest. 2020. "More Than Half of All U.S. Four-Year Colleges and Universities Will Be Test-Optional for Fall 2021 Admission." Fair Test, the National Center for Fair & Open Testing, June 14. https://www.fairtest.org/more-half-all-us-fouryears-colleges-and-universiti.

Fan, C. Cindy. 2002. "The Elite, the Natives, and the Outsiders: Migration and Labor Market Segmentation in Urban China." *Annals of the Association of American Geographers* 92(1): 103–24.

Ferdinand, Robert F., and Frank C. Verhulst. 1995. "Psychopathology from Adolescence into Young Adulthood: An 8-Year Follow-Up Study." *American Journal of Psychiatry* 152(11): 1586–94.

Fischer, Claude S., Michael Hout, Martín Sánchez Jankowski, Samuel R. Lucas, Ann Swidler, and Kim Voss. 1996. *Inequality by Design: Cracking the Bell Curve Myth.* Princeton, IL: Princeton University Press.

Fite, Paula J., Adrian Raine, Magda Stouthamer-Loeber, Rolf Loeber, and Dustin A. Pardini. 2010. "Reactive and Proactive Aggression in Adolescent Males: Examining Differential Outcomes 10 Years Later in Early Adulthood." *Criminal Justice and Behavior* 37(2): 141–57.

Fong, Vanessa. 2004. *Only Hope: Coming of Age under China's One-Child Policy*. Stanford, CA: Stanford University Press.

———. 2011. *Paradise Redefined: Transnational Chinese Students and the Quest for Flexible Citizenship in the Developed World*. Stanford, CA: Stanford University Press.

Furuta, Jared. 2017. "Rationalization and Student/School Personhood in U.S. College Admissions: The Rise of Test-Optional Policies, 1987 to 2015." *Sociology of Education* 90(3): 236–54.

Furuta, Jared, Evan Schofer, and Shawn Wick. 2016. "The Effects of High Stakes Testing on Educational Outcomes, 1960–2006." Presentation at the American Sociological Association annual meeting, Seattle.

Galak, Jeff, Kurt Gray, Igor Elbert, and Nina Strohminger. 2016. "Trickle-Down Preferences: Preferential Conformity to High Status Peers in Fashion Choices." *PLOS One* 11(5): e0153448.

Gao, Helen. 2014. "(Opinion) China's Education Gap." *New York Times*, September 4. https://www.nytimes.com/2014/09/05/opinion/sunday/chinas-education-gap.html.

Garcia, Georgia Earnest, and P. David Pearson. 1991. "The Role of Assessment in a Diverse Society." In *Literacy in a Diverse Society: Perspectives, Practices, and Policies*, edited by Elfrieda H. Hiebert, 253–78. New York: Teachers College Press.

Gardner, Howard E. 1993. *Multiple Intelligence: Theory in Practice*. New York: Basic Books.

Gaztambide-Fernández, Rubén A. 2009. *The Best of the Best: Becoming Elite at an American Boarding School*. Cambridge, MA: Harvard University Press.

Ghuman, Gagandeep. 2018. "Can China Conquer the World? Yes, It Has a Plan That Works." *Global Canadian*, January 29. https://www.northshoredailypost.com/can-china-conquer-world-yes-plan-works/.

Gibson, Anja. 2019. "The (Re-)Production of Elites in Private and Public Boarding Schools: Comparative Perspectives on Elite Education in Germany." In *Elites and People: Challenges to Democracy*, edited by Fredrik Engelstad, Trygve Gulbrandsen, Marte Mangset, and Mari Teigen, 115–36. Bingley: Emerald.

Giddens, Anthony. 1972. "Elites in the British Class Structure." *Sociological Review* 20(3): 345–72.

Goldin, Claudia, and Lawrence F. Katz. 1999. "The Shaping of Higher Education: The Formative Years in the United States, 1890 to 1940." *Journal of Economic Perspectives* 13(1): 37–62.

Gommans, Rob, Marlene J. Sandstrom, Gonneke W. J. M. Stevens, Tom F. M. ter Bogt, and Antonius H. N. Cillessen. 2017. "Popularity, Likeability, and Peer Conformity: Four Field Experiments." *Journal of Experimental Social Psychology* 73: 279–89.

Gong, Honge, Andrew Leigh, and Xin Meng. 2012. "Intergenerational Income Mobility in Urban China." *Review of Income and Wealth* 58(3): 481–503.

Goodman, David SG. 2014. *Class in Contemporary China*. Hoboken, NJ: John Wiley.

Gore, Lance L. P. 2019. "The Communist Party-Dominated Governance Model of China: Legitimacy, Accountability, and Meritocracy." *Polity* 51(1): 161–94.

Grazian, David. 2008. *On the Make: The Hustle of Urban Nightlife*. Chicago: University of Chicago Press.

Guimarães, Juliana, and Breno Sampaio. 2013. "Family Background and Students' Achievement on a University Entrance Exam in Brazil." *Education Economics* 21(1): 38–59.

Hamilton, Laura T. 2016. *Parenting to a Degree: How Family Matters for College Women's Success.* Chicago: University of Chicago Press.

Hannum, Emily, 1999. "Political Change and the Urban-Rural Gap in Basic Education in China, 1949–1990." *Comparative Education Review* 43(2): 193–211.

Hao, Jie, and Anthony Welch. 2012. "A Tale of Sea Turtles: Job-Seeking Experiences of Hai Gui (High-Skilled Returnees) in China." *Higher Education Policy* 25(2): 243–60.

Hao, Lingxin, Alfred Hu, and Jamie Lo. 2014. "Two Aspects of the Rural-Urban Divide and Educational Stratification in China: A Trajectory Analysis." *Comparative Education Review* 58(3): 509–36.

Harris, Kathleen Mullan, Frank F. Furstenberg, and Jeremy K. Marmer. 1998. "Paternal Involvement with Adolescents in Intact Families: The Influence of Fathers over the Life Course." *Demography* 35(2): 201–16.

Hartmann, Michael. 2006. *The Sociology of Elites.* New York: Routledge.

Haun, Daniel B. M., and Michael Tomasello. 2011. "Conformity to Peer Pressure in Preschool Children." *Child Development* 82(6): 1759–67.

Heathcote, Andrew. 2019. "American Dominance in Tech Wealth Creation Upended by Asian Wave." *Bloomberg,* February 9. https://www.bloomberg.com/news/articles/2019-02-08/american-dominance-in-tech-wealth-creation-upended-by-asian-wave.

Heckman, James J., and Xuesong Li. 2004. "Selection Bias, Comparative Advantage and Heterogeneous Returns to Education: Evidence from China in 2000." *Pacific Economic Review* 9(3): 155–71.

Heeter, Chad. 2008. *Two Million Minutes: A Global Examination.* United States: Broken Pencil Productions.

Herrnstein, Richard J., and Charles A. Murray. 1994. *The Bell Curve: Intelligence and Class Structure in American Life.* New York: Free Press.

Higgins, Tim. 2013. "Chinese Students Major in Luxury Cars." *Bloomberg,* December 20. https://www.bloomberg.com/news/articles/2013-12-19/chinese-students-in-u-dot-s-dot-boost-luxury-car-sales.

Hirooka, Kayo, Mitsunori Miyashita, Tatsuya Morita, Takeyuki Ichikawa, Saran Yoshida, Nobuya Akizuki, Miki Akiyama, Yutaka Shirahige, and Kenji Eguchi. 2014. "Regional Medical Professionals' Confidence in Providing Palliative Care, Associated Difficulties and Availability of Specialized Palliative Care Services in Japan." *Japanese Journal of Clinical Oncology* 44(3): 249–56.

Ho, Ping-Ti. 1962. *The Ladder of Success in Imperial China: Aspects of Social Mobility, 1368–1911.* New York: Columbia University Press.

Horvat, Erin, Elliot Weininger, and Annette Lareau. 2003. "From Social Ties to Social Capital: Class Differences in the Relations between Schools and Parent Networks." *American Educational Research Journal* 40(2): 319–51.

Horwitz, Josh. 2016. "Golf Is Now Mandatory at a Chinese Elementary School." *Quartz,* March 21. https://qz.com/640572/for-one-public-school-in-shanghai-golf-is-a-mandatory-course/.

Huang, Tiffany J. 2021. "Negotiating the Workplace: Second-Generation Asian American Professionals' Early Experiences." *Journal of Ethnic and Migration Studies* 47(11): 2477–96.

Huawen. 2017. "2016 Summary of Tsinghua and Peking University Admissions in Each Province" (2016nian Tsinghua, Beida Quanguo Gesheng Zhaosheng Renshu Zonghui). May 1. https://www.cnread.news/content/2357203.html.

Jacques, Martin. 2009. *When China Rules the World: The End of the Western World and the Birth of a New Global Order*. London: Penguin.

Jæger, Mads M. 2012. "The Extended Family and Children's Educational Success." *American Sociological Review* 77(6): 903–22.

Jencks, Christopher, and Meredith Phillips. 1998. *The Black-White Test Score Gap*. Washington, DC: Brookings Institution Press.

Jencks, Christopher, and David Riesman. 2017. *The Academic Revolution*. New York: Routledge.

Jencks, Harlan W. 1982. "Defending China in 1982." *Current History* 81(479): 246–50, 274–75.

Jiang, Gang. 2007. "Equal and Fair, Promote Harmony: 30 Years after the Reestablishment of the National College Entrance Exam" (Gongping Gong Zheng, Jiangou Hexie: Jinian Guifu Gaokao Zhidu 30 Zhonian). *China Examinations* 8: 8–11.

Jiménez, Tomás R., and Adam L. Horowitz. 2013. "When White Is Just Alright: How Immigrants Redefine Achievement and Reconfigure the Ethnoracial Hierarchy." *American Sociological Review* 78(5): 849–71.

John, Tara. 2016. "International Students in U.S. Colleges and Universities Top 1 Million." *Time*, November 14. https://time.com/4569564/international-us-students/.

Kao, Grace, and Jennifer S. Thompson. 2003. "Racial and Ethnic Stratification in Educational Achievement and Attainment." *Annual Review of Sociology* 29: 417–42.

Karabel, Jerome. 2005. *The Chosen: The Hidden History of Admission and Exclusion at Harvard, Yale, and Princeton*. Boston: Mariner Books.

Khan, Shamus Rahman. 2011. *Privilege: The Making of an Adolescent Elite at St. Paul's School*. Princeton, NJ: Princeton University Press.

Kim, Young K., Julie J. Park, and Katie K. Koo. 2015. "Testing Self-Segregation: Multiple-Group Structural Modeling of College Students' Interracial Friendship by Race." *Research in Higher Education* 56(1): 57–77.

Kincheloe, Joe L., Shirley R. Steinberg, and Aaron David Gresson III, eds. 1997. *Measured Lies: The Bell Curve Examined*. New York: St. Martin's.

Kipnis, Andrew B. 2011. *Governing Educational Desire: Culture, Politics, and Schooling in China*. Chicago: University of Chicago Press.

Kiselycznyk, Michael, and Phillip C. Saunders. 2010. "Civil-Military Relations in China: Assessing the PLA's Role in Elite Politics." China Strategic Perspectives, No. 2. Washington, DC: National Defense University Press.

Konty, Mark A., and Charlotte Chorn Dunham. 1997. "Differences in Value and Attitude Change over the Life Course." *Sociological Spectrum* 17(2): 177–97.

Kwon, Soo Ah, Xavier Hernandez, and Jillian L. Moga. 2019. "Racial Segregation and the Limits of International Undergraduate Student Diversity." *Race Ethnicity and Education* 22(1): 59–72.

Lai, Alexis. 2012. "Chinese Flock to Elite U.S. Schools." *CNN*, November 26. http://www.cnn.com/2012/11/25/world/asia/china-ivy-league-admission/index.html.

Lam, Chi-Chung, Esther Sui Chu Ho, and Ngai-Ying Wong. 2002. "Parents' Beliefs and Practices in Education in Confucian Heritage Cultures: The Hong Kong Case." *Journal of Southeast Asian Education* 3(1): 99–114.

Lan, Pei-Chia. 2018. *Raising Global Families: Parenting, Immigration, and Class in Taiwan and the U.S.* Stanford, CA: Stanford University Press.

Lareau, Annette. 2000. *Home Advantage: Social Class and Parental Intervention in Elementary Education*. Washington, DC: Rowman & Littlefield.

———. 2011. *Unequal Childhoods: Class, Race, and Family Life.* Berkeley: University of California Press.

———. 2015. "Cultural Knowledge and Social Inequality." *American Sociological Review* 80(1): 1–27.

Lareau, Annette, Shani Adia Evans, and April Yee. 2016. "The Rules of the Game and the Uncertain Transmission of Advantage: Middle-Class Parents' Search for an Urban Kindergarten." *Sociology of Education* 89(4): 279–99.

Lareau, Annette, and Kimberly Goyette, eds. 2014. *Choosing Homes, Choosing Schools.* New York: Russell Sage Foundation.

Lareau, Annette, and Erin McNamara Horvat. 1999. "Moments of Social Inclusion and Exclusion Race, Class, and Cultural Capital in Family-School Relationships." *Sociology of Education* 72(1): 37–53.

Larmer, Brook. 2014. "Inside a Chinese Test-Prep Factory." *New York Times,* December 31. https://www.nytimes.com/2015/01/04/magazine/inside-a-chinese-test-prep-factory.html.

Lee, Sunhwa, and Mary C. Brinton. 1996. "Elite Education and Social Capital: The Case of South Korea." *Sociology of Education* 69(3): 177–92.

Levey-Friedman, Hilary. 2013. *Playing to Win: Raising Children in a Competitive Culture.* Berkeley: University of California Press.

Li, Bobai, and Andrew G. Walder. 2001. "Career Advancement as Party Patronage: Sponsored Mobility into the Chinese Administrative Elite, 1949–1996." *American Journal of Sociology* 106(5): 1371–1408.

Li, Cheng. 2006. "Foreign-Educated Returnees in the People's Republic of China: Increasing Political Influence with Limited Official Power." *Journal of International Migration and Integration* 7(4): 493–516.

Li, Cheng, and David Bachman. 1989. "Localism, Elitism, and Immobilism: Elite Formation and Social Change in Post-Mao China." *World Politics* 42(1): 64–94.

Li, Fengliang, John Morgan, and Xiaohao Ding. 2008. "The Expansion of Higher Education, Employment and Over-education in China." *International Journal of Educational Development* 28(6): 687–97.

Li, Haiyang, Yan Zhang, Yu Li, Li-An Zhou, and Weiying Zhang. 2012. "Returnees versus Locals: Who Perform Better in China's Technology Entrepreneurship?" *Strategic Entrepreneurship Journal* 6(3): 257–72.

Li, Haizheng. 2003. "Economic Transition and Returns to Education in China." *Economics of Education Review* 22(3): 317–28.

Li, Huijun, and Frances Prevatt. 2008. "Fears and Related Anxieties in Chinese High School Students." *School Psychology International* 29(1): 89–104.

Li, Shi, Hiroshi Sato, and Terry Sicular, eds. 2013. *Rising Inequality in China: Challenges to a Harmonious Society.* Cambridge: Cambridge University Press.

Li, Yao, and Harvey L. Nicholson Jr. 2021. "When 'Model Minorities' Become 'Yellow Peril'— Othering and the Racialization of Asian Americans in the COVID-19 Pandemic." *Sociology Compass* 15(2): e12849.

Liang, Chen, Hao Zhang, Lan Li, Danqing Ruan, Cameron Campbell, and James Lee. 2013. *Silent Revolution: The Social Origins of Peking University and Soochow University Undergraduates, 1949–2002* (Wusheng de geming: Beijing daxue, suzhou daxue de xuesheng shehui laiyuan 1949–2002). Beijing: SDX Joint Publishing.

Lim, Louisa, and Julia Bergin. 2018. "Inside China's Audacious Global Propaganda Campaign." *Guardian*, December 7. https://www.theguardian.com/news/2018/dec/07/china-plan-for -global-media-dominance-propaganda-xi-jinping.

Lin, Nan, and Wen Xie. 1988. "Occupational Prestige in Urban China." *American Journal of Sociology* 93(4): 793–832.

Linn, Robert L., and Eva L. Baker. 1996. "Can Performance-Based Assessments Be Psychometrically Sound?" In *Performance-Based Student Assessment: Challenges and Possibilities*, edited by Joan Boykoff Baron and Dennie Palmer Wolf. Chicago: University of Chicago Press.

Littrell, Romie F. 2005. "Teaching Students from Confucian Cultures." In *Business and Management Education in China: Transition, Pedagogy and Training*, edited by Ilan Alon and John R. McIntyre, 115–40. Singapore: World Scientific.

Liu, Haifeng. 2011. "The Reform of College Entrance Examination: Priority to Fairness or Efficiency" (Gaokao Gaige, Gongping Weishou Haishi Xiaolu Youxian). *Journal of Higher Education* 5(1): 1–6.

Liu, Ruth X., Wei Lin, and Zeng-Yin Chen. 2010. "School Performance, Peer Association, Psychological and Behavioral Adjustments: A Comparison between Chinese Adolescents With and Without Siblings." *Journal of Adolescence* 33(3): 411–17.

Liu, Xianchen, Jenn-Yun Tein, Zhongtang Zhao, and Irwin N. Sandler. 2005. "Suicidality and Correlates among Rural Adolescents of China." *Journal of Adolescent Health* 37(6): 443–51.

Liuxue. 2014. "Rankings of the Numbers of Chinese Students Admitted to American Elite Universities: Duke University Is Top" (Meiguo Mingxiao Luqu Zhongguo Xuesheng Renshu Paihang: Duke University Ju Sho). April 18. http://l.gol.edu.cn/school_3324/20140418 /t20140418_1100881_3.shtml.

Lubinski, David, David B. Schmidt, and Camilla Persson Benbow. 1996. "A 20-Year Stability Analysis of the Study of Values for Intellectually Gifted Individuals from Adolescence to Adulthood." *Journal of Applied Psychology* 81(4): 443–51.

Lucas, Samuel R. 2001. "Effectively Maintained Inequality: Education Transitions, Track Mobility, and Social Background Effects." *American Journal of Sociology* 106(6): 1642–90.

Ma, Yingyi. 2020. *Ambitious and Anxious: How Chinese College Students Succeed and Struggle in American Higher Education*. New York: Columbia University Press.

MacLeod, Jay. 2018. *Ain't No Makin' It: Aspirations and Attainment in a Low-Income Neighborhood*. Boulder, CO: Westview.

Mare, Robert D. 2012. "Holistic Review in Freshman Admissions at UCLA." Los Angeles: University of California, Los Angeles. http://uclaunfair.org/pdf/marereport.pdf.

Mazlish, Bruce, and Elliot R. Morss. 2005. "A Global Elite?" In *Leviathans: Multinational Corporations and the New Global History*, edited by Alfred D. Chandler and Bruce Mazlish, 167–87. Cambridge: Cambridge University Press.

McAdams, Dan P., and Bradley D. Olson. 2010. "Personality Development: Continuity and Change over the Life Course." *Annual Review of Psychology* 61: 517–42.

McCabe, Janice M. 2016. *Connecting in College: How Friendship Networks Matter for Academic and Social Success*. Chicago: University of Chicago Press.

McDonough, Patricia M. 1997. *Choosing Colleges: How Social Class and Schools Structure Opportunity*. Albany: State University of New York Press.

Mears, Ashley. 2011. *Pricing Beauty: The Making of a Fashion Model*. Berkeley: University of California Press.

Mills, C. Wright. 1956. *The Power Elite*. New York: Oxford University Press.

Milner, Murray. 1994. *Status and Sacredness: A General Theory of Status Relations and an Analysis of Indian Culture*. New York: Oxford University Press.

———. 2015a. *Elites: A General Model*. Cambridge, MA: Polity.

———. 2015b. *Freaks, Geeks, and Cool Kids: Teenagers in an Era of Consumerism, Standardized Tests, and Social Media*. New York: Routledge.

Morgan, Stephen L., and Aage B. Sørensen. 1999. "Parental Networks, Social Closure, and Mathematics Learning: A Test of Coleman's Social Capital Explanation of School Effects." *American Sociological Review* 64(5): 661–81.

Mõttus, René, Kristjan Indus, and Jüri Allik. 2008. "Accuracy of Only Children Stereotype." *Journal of Research in Personality* 42(4): 1047–52.

National Bureau of Statistics. 2013. "Average Annual Income of Urban Residents" (Chengzhen Jumin Pingjun Meiren Quanbu Nianshouru)." Beijing: China Statistics Press.

———. 2017. "China Statistics Year Book." Beijing: China Statistics Press.

Nee, Victor. 1991. "Social Inequalities in Reforming State Socialism: Between Redistribution and Markets in China." *American Sociological Review* 56(3): 267–82.

Nilizadeh, Shirin, Anne Groggel, Peter Lista, Srijita Das, Yong-Yeol Ahn, Apu Kapadia, and Fabio Rojas. 2016. "Twitter's Glass Ceiling: The Effect of Perceived Gender on Online Visibility." In *International AAAI Conference on Web and Social Media*, 289–98. Palo Alto, CA: Association for the Advancement of Artificial Intelligence.

Nolan, Peter. 2013. *Is China Buying the World?* Cambridge, MA: Polity.

OECD. 2014. *PISA 2012 Results: Creative Problem Solving: Students' Skills in Tackling Real-Life Problems*. Vol. 5. Paris: PISA, OECD Publishing.

———. 2017. *PISA 2015 Results: Collaborative Problem Solving*. Vol. 5. Paris: PISA, OECD Publishing.

———. 2020. *OECD Employment Outlook 2020: Worker Security and the Covid-19 Crisis*. Paris: OECD Publishing.

Oguntoyinbo, Lekan. 2014. "Breaking through the Bamboo Ceiling." *Diverse Issues in Higher Education* 31(7): 10–11.

Orfield, Gary, and Nicholas Hillman. 2018. *Accountability and Opportunity in Higher Education: The Civil Rights Dimension*. Cambridge, MA: Harvard Education Press.

Oyer, Paul. 2008. "The Making of an Investment Banker: Stock Market Shocks, Career Choice, and Lifetime Income." *Journal of Finance* 63(6): 2601–28.

Page, Benjamin, Larry M. Bartels, and Jason Seawright. 2013. "Democracy and the Policy Preferences of Wealthy Americans." *Perspectives on Politics* 11(1): 51–73.

Park, Hyunjoon. 2008. "The Varied Educational Effects of Parent-Child Communication: A Comparative Study of Fourteen Countries." *Comparative Education Review* 52(2): 219–43.

Peking University Recruitment Newsletter. 2014. "2014 Chart of Successful Alumni in Chinese Universities." *Gaokao Special Issue* 24: 6.

Peking University Student Career Center. 2014. "Annual Report of the Employment Quality of Graduates from Peking University" (Peking University 2014nian Biyesheng Jiuye Zhiliang Niandu Baogao). Beijing: Peking University.

People's Daily. 2016. "Worries over the Fairness of Different Beneficiary Groups in the 'American National College Entrance Exam'" (Meiguo Gaokao Luqu Gongping Kanyou, Huoyi Qunti Gebuxiangtong). January 28. http://edu.people.com.cn/n1/2016/0128/c1053-28092530.html.

Pepper, Suzanne. 1996. *Radicalism and Education Reform in 20th-Century China: The Search for an Ideal Development Model.* Cambridge: Cambridge University Press.

Qian, Wang, Mohammed Abdur Razzaque, and Kau Ah Keng. 2007. "Chinese Cultural Values and Gift-Giving Behavior." *Journal of Consumer Marketing* 24(4): 214–28.

Radford, Alexandria Walton. 2013. *Top Student, Top School? How Social Class Shapes Where Valedictorians Go to College.* Chicago: University of Chicago Press.

Raftery, Adrian E., and Michael Hout. 1993. "Maximally Maintained Inequality: Expansion, Reform, and Opportunity in Irish Education, 1921–75." *Sociology of Education* 66 (1): 41–62.

Ramirez, Francisco O., Evan Schofer, and John W. Meyer. 2018. "International Tests, National Assessments, and Educational Development (1970–2012)." *Comparative Education Review* 62(3): 344–64.

Ramsden, Sally R., and Julie A. Hubbard. 2002. "Family Expressiveness and Parental Emotion Coaching: Their Role in Children's Emotion Regulation and Aggression." *Journal of Abnormal Child Psychology* 30 (6): 657–67.

Resnick, Lauren B., and Megan Williams Hall. 1998. "Learning Organizations for Sustainable Education Reform." *Daedalus* 127(4): 89–118.

Riesman, David, and Christopher Jencks. 1962. "The Viability of the American College." In *The American College: A Psychological and Social Interpretation of the Higher Learning,* edited by Nevitt Sanford, 74–192. New York: John Wiley.

Rivera, Lauren A. 2015. *Pedigree: How Elite Students Get Elite Jobs.* Princeton, NJ: Princeton University Press.

Roksa, Josipa, and Daniel Potter. 2011. "Parenting and Academic Achievement: Intergenerational Transmission of Educational Advantage." *Sociology of Education* 84 (4): 299–321.

Rose-Redwood, CindyAnn R., and Reuben S. Rose-Redwood. 2013. "Self-Segregation or Global Mixing? Social Interactions and the International Student Experience." *Journal of College Student Development* 54(4): 413–29.

Saez, Emmanuel, and Gabriel Zucman. 2016. "Wealth Inequality in the United States since 1913: Evidence from Capitalized Income Tax Data." *Quarterly Journal of Economics* 131(2): 519–78.

Sánchez-Jankowski, Martín. 2016. *Burning Dislike: Ethnic Violence in High Schools.* Berkeley: University of California Press.

Scott, John Finley. 1965a. "Sororities and the Husband Game." *Trans-action* 2(6): 10–14.

———. 1965b. "The American College Sorority: Its Role in Class and Ethnic Endogamy." *American Sociological Review* 30(4): 514–27.

Sharma, Yojana. 2014. "What Do You Do with Millions of Extra Graduates?" *BBC,* July 1. https://www.bbc.com/news/business-28062071.

Sharp, Stephen. 1997. "'Much More at Home with 3.999 Pupils Than with Four': The Contributions to Psychometrics of Sir Godfrey Thomson." *British Journal of Mathematical and Statistical Psychology* 50(2): 163–74.

Shavit, Yossi, and Hans-Peter Blossfeld, eds. 1993. *Persistent Inequality: Changing Educational Attainment in Thirteen Countries.* Boulder, CO: Westview.

Sherman, Rachel. 2017. *Uneasy Street: The Anxieties of Affluence.* Princeton, NJ: Princeton University Press.

Sina. 2014. "2014 Acceptance Rate in Gaokao Is 74.33%, University Admission Rates Are 38.7%" (2014 Gaokao Luqulu yue 74.33%, Benke Luqulu 38.7%). June 7. http://edu.sina.com.cn /gaokao/2014-06-07/0734422104.shtml.

——. 2016. "Must Read by International Students: Changes in the American National College Entrance Exam SAT" (Guojixuexiao Xuesheng Bidu: Meiguo Gaokao SAT Gaige you he Bianhua). January 11. http://edu.sina.com.cn/ischool/2016-01-11/doc-ifxnkkuv4340046 .shtml.

Smits, Jeroen, Wout Ultee, and Jan Lammers. 1998. "Educational Homogamy in 65 Countries: An Explanation of Differences in Openness Using Country-Level Explanatory Variables." *American Sociological Review* 63(2): 264–85.

Song, Xi, and Robert D. Mare. 2019. "Shared Lifetimes, Multigenerational Exposure, and Educational Mobility." *Demography* 56(3): 891–916.

Sorokowska, Agnieszka, Piotr Sorokowski, Peter Hilpert, Katarzyna Cantarero, Tomasz Frackowiak, Khodabakhsh Ahmadi, Ahmad M. Alghraibeh, et al. 2017. "Preferred Interpersonal Distances: A Global Comparison." *Journal of Cross-Cultural Psychology* 48(4): 577–92.

Staff, Jeremy, John E. Schulenberg, and Jerald G. Bachman. 2010. "Adolescent Work Intensity, School Performance, and Academic Engagement." *Sociology of Education* 83(3): 183–200.

Statistics Canada. 2016. "International Students in Canadian Universities, 2004/2005 to 2013/2014." http://www.statcan.gc.ca/pub/81-599-x/81-599-x2016011-eng.htm.

Stecher, Brian M., and Stephen P. Klein. 1997. "The Cost of Science Performance Assessments in Large-Scale Testing Programs." *Educational Evaluation and Policy Analysis* 19(1): 1–14.

Steidlmeier, Paul. 1999. "Gift Giving, Bribery and Corruption: Ethical Management of Business Relationships in China." *Journal of Business Ethics* 20(2): 121–32.

Stevens, Mitchell L. 2007. *Creating a Class: College Admissions and the Education of Elites.* Cambridge, MA: Harvard University Press.

Sun, Lena. 1987. "The Spoiled Brats of China." *Washington Post*, July 26. https://www .washingtonpost.com/archive/politics/1987/07/26/the-spoiled-brats-of-china/10a39312 -9a46-4f0a-9e9a-a7f884469be6/.

Supovitz, Jonathan, and Robert Brennan. 1997. "Mirror, Mirror on the Wall, Which Is the Fairest Test of All? An Examination of the Equitability of Portfolio Assessment Relative to Standardized Tests." *Harvard Educational Review* 67(3): 472–507.

Tan, Charlene. 2017. "Chinese responses to Shanghai's Performance in PISA." *Comparative Education* 53(2): 209–23.

Tan, Huileng. 2018. "Political Resistance Isn't Stopping Chinese Investors from Snapping Up Property around the World." *CNBC*, September 6. https://sports.yahoo.com/political -resistance-isn-apos-t-014400697.html.

Taylor, Catherine. 1994. "Assessment for Measurement or Standards: The Peril and Promise of Large-Scale Assessment Reform." *American Educational Research Journal* 31(2): 231–62.

Tognini, Giacomo. 2021. "The Countries with the Most Billionaires 2021." *Forbes*, April 6. https://www.forbes.com/sites/giacomotognini/2021/04/06/the-countries-with-the-most -billionaires-2021/?sh=7176f6f6379b.

Torngren, Gustaf, and Henry Montgomery. 2004. "Worse Than Chance? Performance and Confidence among Professionals and Laypeople in the Stock Market." *Journal of Behavioral Finance* 5(3): 148–53.

Tsinghua Career Center. 2014. "Annual Report of the Employment Quality of Graduates from Tsinghua University" (Tsinghua Daxue 2014nian Biyesheng Jiuye Zhiliang Niandu Baogao). Beijing: Tsinghua University.

Turner, Ralph H. 1960. "Sponsored and Contest Mobility and the School System." *American Sociological Review* 25(6): 855–67.

UK Council for International Student Affairs. 2017. "International Student Statistics: UK Higher Education." April 10. https://institutions.ukcisa.org.uk/Info-for-universities-colleges- -schools/Policy-research--statistics/Research--statistics/International-students-in-UK-HE/#.

Vandrick, Stephanie. 2011. "Students of the New Global Elite." *TESOL Quarterly* 45(1): 160–69.

Walder, Andrew G. 2012. *Fractured Rebellion: The Beijing Red Guard Movement*. Cambridge, MA: Harvard University Press.

Walder, Andrew G., and Songhua Hu. 2009. "Revolution, Reform, and Status Inheritance: Urban China, 1949–1996." *American Journal of Sociology* 114(5): 1395–1427.

Walder, Andrew G., Bobai Li, and Donald J. Treiman. 2000. "Politics and Life Chances in a State Socialist Regime: Dual Career Paths into the Urban Chinese Elite, 1949 to 1996." *American Sociological Review* 65(2): 191–209.

Wang, Huiyao, David Zweig, and Xiaohua Lin. 2011. "Returnee Entrepreneurs: Impact on China's Globalization Process." *Journal of Contemporary China* 20(70): 413–31.

Wang, Xiaolu, and Wing Thye Woo. 2011. "The Size and Distribution of Hidden Household Income in China." *Asian Economic Papers* 10(1): 1–26.

Waterman, Alan S. 1982. "Identity Development from Adolescence to Adulthood: An Extension of Theory and a Review of Research." *Developmental Psychology* 18(3): 341–58.

Waters, Johanna L. 2006. "Geographies of Cultural Capital: Education, International Migration and Family Strategies between Hong Kong and Canada." *Transactions of the Institute of British Geographers* 31(2): 179–92.

Weber, Max. 1946. *From Max Weber*. New York: Oxford University Press.

———. 1958. "The Chinese Literati." In *Max Weber: Essays in Sociology*, 416–44. New York: Oxford University Press.

Weis, Lois, Kristin Cipollone, and Heather Jenkins. 2014. *Class Warfare: Class, Race, and College Admissions in Top-Tier Secondary Schools*. Chicago: University of Chicago Press.

Westerman, David, Patric R. Spence, and Brandon Van Der Heide. 2012. "A Social Network as Information: The Effect of System Generated Reports of Connectedness on Credibility on Twitter." *Computers in Human Behavior* 28(1): 199–206.

Wilson, George, and Vincent J. Roscigno. 2016. "Job Authority and Stratification Beliefs." *Research in the Sociology of Work* 29: 75–97.

Woessmann, Ludger. 2011. "Cross-Country Evidence on Teacher Performance Pay." *Economics of Education Review* 30(3): 404–18.

Wo Zhongwen Bu Hao. 2017. "2017 College Entrance Examination Champion: It is Important that Rich in Family" (2017 Gaokao Zhuangyuan: Jiali You Qian Hen Zhongyao). YouTube, June 25. https://www.youtube.com/watch?v=giM2uTH6LP8&ab_channel=%E6%88%91 %E4%B8%AD%E6%96%87%E4%B8%8D%E5%A5%BD.

Wu, Xiaogang, and Yu Xie. 2003. "Does the Market Pay Off? Earnings Returns to Education in Urban China." *American Sociological Review* 68(3): 425–42.

Wu, Xiaoxin. 2013. *School Choice in China: A Different Tale?* New York: Routledge.

Wu, Yuting. 2018. "8 Million Housing Supplement + Million Annual Salary! Behind the Soaring 'Worth' of Yangtze River Scholars: The Battle for Talents in Universities Has Started!" (800 Wan Fang Bu +Bai Wan NiAnxin! Changjiang Xuezhe "Shenjia" Biao Zhang Beihou: Gaoxiao Rencai Zhengduo Zhan Daxiang!). *Economic Observer* (Jingji Guancha Bao), January 16. https://mp.weixin.qq.co/s/GQjJ9tySOSbwBeGTN-IvbA.

Xie, Yu. 2016. "Understanding Inequality in China." *Chinese Journal of Sociology* 2(3): 327–47.

Xie, Yu, and Xiang Zhou. 2014. "Income Inequality in Today's China." *Proceedings of the National Academy of Sciences* 111(19): 6928–33.

Xing, Xiu-Ya, Tao Fang-Biao, Wan Yu-Hui, Xing Chao, Qi Xiu-Yu, Hao Jia-Hu, Su Pu-Yu, Pan Hai-Feng, and Huang Lei. 2010. "Family Factors Associated with Suicide Attempts among Chinese Adolescent Students: A National Cross-Sectional Survey." *Journal of Adolescent Health* 46(6): 592–99.

Xinhua News. 2015. "Return Students Will Reach 666 Thousand in 2017. 'Foreign Returnees' Might Become 'Foreign Leftovers'" (Liuxue Guiguo Renshu 2017 jiang da 66.6wan, Haigui Youlu cheng Haisheng). June 29. http://news.xinhuanet.com/finance/2015-06/29/c _127961858.htm.

Xue, Hai-Ping, and Rong Wang. 2016. "Compulsory Education Teacher Performance Bonus, Teacher Motivation and Student Achievement" (Yiwu Jiaoyu Jiaoshi Jixiao Jiangjin, Jiaoshi Jjili Yu Xuesheng Chengji). *Educational Research* (Jiaoyu Yanjiu) 5: 21–33.

Xue, Xinran. 2015. *Buy Me the Sky: The Remarkable Truth of China's One-Child Generations.* London: Ebury Digital.

Yang, Dan-Yu. 2012. "Family Background and Admission Chances to Higher Education" (Jiating Beijing Yu Gaodeng Jiaoyu Ruxue Jihui Jundenghua de Shizheng Kaocha). *Higher Education Exploration* 2012(5): 140–43.

Yang, Guobin. 2016. *The Red Guard Generation and Political Activism in China.* New York: Columbia University Press.

Yang, Ye, and Angela Paladino. 2015. "The Case of Wine: Understanding Chinese Gift-Giving Behavior." *Marketing Letters* 26(3): 335–61.

Ye, Hua. 2015. "Key-Point Schools and Entry into Tertiary Education in China." *Chinese Sociological Review* 47(2): 128–53.

Yeung, Wei-Jun Jean. 2013. "Higher Education Expansion and Social Stratification in China." *Chinese Sociological Review* 45(4): 54–80.

Young, Natalie A. E. 2018. "Departing from the Beaten Path: International Schools in China as Response to Discrimination and Academic Failure in the Chinese Educational System." *Comparative Education* 54(2): 159–80.

Yu, Helen H. 2020. "Revisiting the Bamboo Ceiling: Perceptions from Asian Americans on Experiencing Workplace Discrimination." *Asian American Journal of Psychology* 11(3): 158–67.

Zang, Xiaowei. 2001. "University Education, Party Seniority, and Elite Recruitment in China." *Social Science Research* 30(1): 62–75.

Zeng, Kangmin, and Gerald K. LeTendre. 1998. "Adolescent Suicide and Academic Competition in East Asia." *Comparative Education Review* 42(4): 513–28.

Zeng, Zhen, and Yu Xie. 2014. "The Effects of Grandparents on Children's Schooling: Evidence from Rural China." *Demography* 51(2): 599–617.

Zhang, Junsen, Yaohui Zhao, Albert Park, and Xiaoqing Song. 2005. "Economic Returns to Schooling in Urban China, 1988 to 2001." *Journal of Comparative Economics* 33(4): 730–52.

Zhang, Yuching, Geldolph A. Kohnstamm, Ping Chung Cheung, and Sing Lau. 2001. "A New Look at the Old 'Little Emperor': Developmental Changes in the Personality of Only Children in China." *Social Behavior and Personality* 29(7): 725–31.

Zheng, Ruoling. 2007. "The Impact of the National College Entrance Exam on Social Mobility: A Case Study of Xiamen University" (Gaokao Dui Shehui Liudong de Yingxiang: Yi Xiamen Daxue Wei Gean). *Educational Research* 3: 46–50.

Zheng, Sarah, and Zhang Pinghui. 2018. "Chinese Students Say US Visa Restrictions Won't Affect Their Plans." *South China Morning Post*, May 30. https://www.scmp.com/news/china /diplomacy-defence/article/2148531/chinese-students-say-us-visa-restrictions-wont-affect.

Zhou, Hao. 2005. *GaoSan*. Guangdong: Guangdong 21st Century Media.

Zhou, Min, and Jennifer Lee. 2017. "Hyper-selectivity and the Remaking of Culture: Understanding the Asian American Achievement Paradox." *Asian American Journal of Psychology* 8(1): 7–15.

INDEX

ACT exam, 32, 233n41

admission rates, 17, 220n18, 221n28

adoration, 78–83

advisors, 1, 104, 156–57, 207

Aiya, 71

allowances, 129–30, 132, 155–61, 217n12

Amazon, 14, 129

Andrew, 115

AP courses, 42, 84

athletics, 4, 28, 39, 58, 80–84, 91, 147, 193–95, 222nn20–21, 227n18

Beijing Daily, 24

Bell Curve, The (Herrnstein and Murray), 224n18

Blau, Peter M., 218n31, 229n20

Bob, 71

body shaming, 144–46

Boston College, 65, 95, 115, 164, *215*

Bourdieu, Pierre, 6, 203, 218n25, 218n30, 223n2, 223n6, 225n6

Bowei, 136

Brandeis University, 46–47

Bryn Mawr College, 33, 155, *214*, 226n13

Byun, Soo-yong, 222n51

Calarco, Jessica McCrory, 228n14

Cambridge University, 1, 8, 18, 22, 45–48, 65–66, 166, 179, 189, *214*, 219n37

Canada, 44, 52–54

Cao, Mrs., 166–68

Cao, Tony: accomplishments of, *215*; Capital and, 36, 57, 89–90, 104, 110, 167, 169, *215*; COVID-19 pandemic and, 187–88; gaokao and, 169; grooming of, 138, 142–43, 146; interaction styles and, 201; as loner, 226n11; parents and, 138, 142–43, 146, 166–69, 179; peer treatment and, 71, 89–90, 94, 97; racial issues and, 190, 227n24; SAT exam and, 36, 71, 90, 167–68; status and, 41–42, 57, 61–62, 66; teachers and, 104, 110–11, 127

Capital (school): campus of, 22–23; enrollment of, 225n3; ethnographic data from, 12; formation of, 11; gaokao and, 21, 24, 26, 28, 49, 58, 68, 102, 121, 124, 169, 211; grooming by, 20–37, 132–33, 144, 146, 148, 154, 156, 230n16; hiring agents and, 35, 222n57; Lili Zhu and, 28, 61, 68, 75, 144, *214*; merit and, 198; military and, 20; parents and, 132–33, 144, 146, 148, 154, 156, 159–60, 164, 167–74; participant data from, *214–15*; peer treatment and, 68, 71, 75, 78–79, 84–86, 89–90, 95, 198, 225n3; reputation of, 21, 221n39; research methodology and, 207–13; school schedules of, *31*; Selena Su and, 33, 103–4, 154, *214*, 230n16; Shiying Liu and, 71, 101, 121, 169, *214*; Shuhua Tien and, 58, 61, 105, *214*; status and, 39, 41–43, 49–53, 56–61, 64–66, 223n4; teachers and, 99–110, 114, 118, 121, 123–24, 228n15; Tony Cao and, 36, 57, 89–90, 104, 110, 167, 169, *215*

Carnegie Mellon University, 8, 46–48

celebrity treatment, 70, 80–81, 96, 227n21

Central (school), 15, 29; accomplishments of, 20; enrollment of, 225n3; grooming by, 129, 131; merit and, 198; peer treatment and, 82; reputation of, 222n57; research methodology and, 207, *214*; SAT exam and, 226n13; zero-tolerance policy and, 35

and, 18–19, 187, 192–98, 219n36, 221n37;
Trump and, 9; Wall Street, 14, 201, 229n20,
232n17
University of British Columbia, 52
University of California, Los Angeles
(UCLA), 83–84, 147, 236n6
University of Pennsylvania, 53, 64, 103–4,
125, 134, 208, 214, 230n16
U.S. News rankings, 18, 34, 163–66, 167, 224n12

visas, 3, 9, 181, 187, 217nn16–17
volunteer work, 36–37, 190

Wall Street, 14, 201, 229n20, 232n17
Wanru, 68, 76–77, 82, 87, 144–46, 227n20,
233n45
Weber, Mex, 218n31
WeChat, 11, 146, 181, 209
Wenbin Liu, 180–81, 189, 215
Wesleyan University, 79
Where China Rules the World, 2
William, 35–36, 85
winter camps, 28, 122, 172–73, 214
working class, 6, 18, 198, 203, 235n1
Wu, Brandon: accents and, 213; accomplishments of, 215; college applications of,
147–49; COVID-19 pandemic and, 188;
extracurricular activities and, 226n14,
227n20, 233n45; follow-up interviews
and, 210; kindness of, 236n8; as low
performer, 83–84, 147–49; no credit for,
83–84; parents and, 35–36, 147–49, 156; peer
treatment and, 70, 83–84; status and, 230n11
Wu, Jianmin: accomplishments of, 215; gaokao
and, 123; as loser, 55, 122, 201; parents and,
177–78, 181–82, 231nn12–13, 232n16; peer
treatment and, 235n2; Pinnacle and, 55,
122–24, 215; status and, 55–56, 58; teachers
and, 122–24
Wu, Joe: accomplishments of, 215; extracurricular activities and, 233n45; internship
of, 188; Pinnacle and, 57, 215; status and,
57, 65; volunteer work of, 37
Wu, Mrs., 73, 75, 120, 123, 177, 178, 181–82

Wu, Xijun, 232n12; accomplishments of, 214,
233n45; kindness of, 236n8; peer treatment
and, 80–81, 96–97, 226nn10–12; Pinnacle
and, 80, 96, 109, 214, 226n10; racial
issues and, 191; as studyholic, 224n20;
teachers and, 109–10

Xiaolong, 38, 56–57, 62–63, 92, 201, 209–10
Xu, Mrs., 51, 228n6
Xue, Huating: accomplishments of, 214;
biological sibling of, 230n8; blaming of
mother by, 139–41, 144–45, 151; COVID-19
pandemic and, 162; gaokao and, 124, 140,
162, 209; methodology and, 209; no need
of parental assistance by, 154; Pinnacle
and, 124, 139; sibling terms and, 230n8;
Tsinghua and, 162
Xue, Mrs., 140–41

Yale University, 22, 65–66, 79, 81, 151, 163,
189, 191, 214
Yang, Mr., 102–3
Ye, Mr., 109, 172

zero-tolerance policy, 35
Zhang, Haocheng, 215
Zhang, Mrs., 84–85
Zhou, Kefeng, 215
Zhou, Tracy: accomplishments of, 214,
221n35; assistance on demand and, 111–12;
grooming of, 142–44, 148; Hong Kong and,
126, 232n17; interaction styles and, 127, 201;
parents and, 35, 142–44, 148, 183, 230n15;
relationship with, 210, 212; status and, 42,
50, 64–65; as studyholic, 42, 50, 71, 111, 118,
227n19; teachers and, 111–12, 115, 118, 126–27
Zhu, Lili: accomplishments of, 214; Capital
and, 28, 61, 68, 75, 144, 214; COVID-19
pandemic and, 188; gaokao and, 28, 68, 76,
87, 136, 210, 228n5, 236n3; grooming of,
135–36, 144; methodology and, 210; parents
and, 135–36, 144, 183; peer treatment and,
68–70, 75–76, 82, 87, 93–94, 224n22; as
studyholic, 61–62, 69, 75–76

A NOTE ON THE TYPE

This book has been composed in Arno, an Old-style serif typeface in the
classic Venetian tradition, designed by Robert Slimbach at Adobe.